# MY VOICE

# MY VOICE

## ANGIE MARTINEZ

A CELEBRA BOOK

*The events in this memoir are real, as I lived and experienced them. I did my best to describe all of the details and conversations as I remember them.*

CELEBRA
Published by New American Library,
an imprint of Penguin Random House LLC
375 Hudson Street, New York, New York 10014

This book is an original publication of New American Library.

First Printing, May 2016

Copyright © Media Noche Productions, Inc., 2016
Foreword copyright © J. Cole, 2016

All photos courtesy of the author except insert 2, page 7, photo 1
copyright © American Broadcasting Companies, Inc./Lou Rocco.

Celebra and the Celebra colophon are trademarks of Penguin Random House LLC.

For more information about Penguin Random House, visit penguin.com.

LIBRARY OF CONGRESS CATALOGING-IN-PUBLICATION DATA:
Names: Martinez, Angie, 1971– author.
Title: My Voice/Angie Martinez.
Description: New York: Celebra, 2016.
Identifiers: LCCN 2016000680 (print) | LCCN 2016004167 (ebook) |
ISBN 9781101990339 (hardback) | ISBN 9781101990353 (ebook)
Subjects: LCSH: Martinez, Angie. | Radio broadcasters—United
States—Biography. | BISAC: BIOGRAPHY & AUTOBIOGRAPHY/Entertainment &
Performing Arts. | BIOGRAPHY & AUTOBIOGRAPHY/
Personal Memoirs. | MUSIC/ Genres & Styles/Rap & Hip Hop.
Classification: LCC PN1991.4.M3585 A3 2016 (print) | LCC PN1991.4.M3585 (ebook)
| DDC 791.4402/8092—dc23
LC record available at http://lccn.loc.gov/2016000680

Printed in the United States of America
10  9  8  7  6  5  4

Designed by Kristin del Rosario

PUBLISHER'S NOTE
Penguin is committed to publishing works of quality and integrity. In that spirit, we are proud to offer this book to our readers; however the story, the experiences and the words are the author's alone.

I was once afraid of people saying,
"Who does she think she is?"
Now I have the courage to stand and say,
"This is who I am."

—OPRAH WINFREY

# CONTENTS

# FOREWORD

## by J. Cole

There was a time when hip-hop was brave. It was young and didn't know any better. The rappers were bold and courageous. They won no awards.

The people who documented this culture were fearless too. They were first and foremost fans, grateful to have something to love. And they themselves had something to say, happy to have a platform to say it on. They too won nothing.

Hip-hop today is afraid. It's older now and knows too much. It knows too much about business. It knows too much about charts and first-week sales. It cares so much about the awards.

The people who document hip-hop today are cowards too. Jaded by now. Entitled. So afraid of losing their jobs. Slow to see the waves coming. Quick to ride them when they do. Nothing to say that isn't being said already.

Angie Martinez is cut from the original cloth. This is the cloth they used before they realized that the new stuff was cheaper and more cost efficient. This cloth is more honest, more curious, more genuine. This cloth is much more thankful to even have the opportunity and less afraid to lose it.

I treasure this cloth because I know that there's much to learn from the way in which it was woven. If we study the products of the past, we may be able to improve the state of things now. That's why I be having so many questions for Angie.

Like. Where did you start?

# MY VOICE

# WHERE HIP-HOP LIVES

Wednesday, June 18, 2014
@the studios of WQHT 97.1
395 Hudson Street, NYC

*T*his is overwhelming. Like my-head-is-gonna-fucking-EXPLODE *overwhelming.*

It's my last day at Hot 97. This station—*Where Hip Hop Lives*—is where I've built my career for more than two decades. For my entire adult life, Hot 97 has been my home, the place where I grew up, and where so many of the people who have walked these halls with me have become like family. And to top it all off, I'm leaving without any warning. No hints, no rumors, no leaks.

*Nobody* in the whole building knows. Yet.

From the instant I get off the elevator and walk into the main reception area that separates our station, WQHT, on one side from our new sister station, WBLS, on the other, I'm smacked by the reality that today I'll be leaving the place that I've been day in, day out for twenty years. This is the place that shaped me from the eighteen-year-old who had no clue who I was, what I wanted to do with my life, or even what I was capable of.

I grew up in this building, and I didn't grow up here alone. These are the people who were raised with me and many who I raised myself. We spent holidays and birthdays together, shared each other's biggest milestones, and saw each other through some of the best and worst times of our lives.

As you can imagine, walking away from this family was not a decision that came easily. It was scary. It felt like the right move in my soul, a necessary step to push myself forward, but that didn't stop it from being terrifying and overwhelmingly sad.

Then the official e-mail went out to the whole Hot 97 staff: *Today Angie Martinez has resigned and will no longer . . .*

I knew everyone would be caught off guard and sad to see me go, but I never imagined to what extent. I didn't expect how hard the announcement was going to hit. The first clue came when I made it back to the programming office and saw that my show producer, Drewski, was inconsolable.

Gesturing to the hallway, I got him to follow me out so that we could have a moment alone. In all the years I've known Drewski he had never been the type to be rattled easily. He didn't even cry at funerals. But now he couldn't get a word out. Was he mad at me? Worried about his future?

All I could do was to try to reassure him. "You know I'll always have your back, Drewski," I began. "Change is good. It brings forward motion . . . for everyone. This could be good for all of us."

But after ten minutes of talking quietly in the hall, I headed back to the studio. And just as I turned the corner, I was stopped in my tracks.

There stood almost every single one of my coworkers lined up in the hallways, most of them crying. I froze.

*Oh my God. What's happening here?*

Somehow I'd fooled myself into thinking that I'd planned for whatever reaction was to come—going over all the different scenarios and carefully timing the news. I'd waited until I'd shared the news with the staff before posting on social media:

Today I resigned from HOT97. I am grateful to the Emmis family for my time with the company and the immeasurable way that it has shaped my life. We made history together and I will cherish those memories and my friendships forever . . . It was one of the toughest decisions I've ever had to make but ultimately it is time to move on . . .

I thought I was ready for everything, but in no way was I prepared for this outpouring of emotion. It knocked the wind out of me.

I began to flash back on my whole career and my relationship with every single person standing there in the hallway. And it seemed they were having that same experience with me. Everyone kept hugging me, wanting to share the moments that meant the most to them on and off the air. And this is twenty years of stuff!

It was too much for one person to absorb. I'm not someone who loves to be fussed over. And here I was in the middle of an Angie Parade. I was honored, I was humbled, and I was starting to freak the fuck out—especially when I realized it was almost three o' clock.

*Holy shit! Now I have to do my radio show and sit there for four hours telling the whole city that today will be my last day.*

Tomorrow the news would be everywhere that I was leaving to go to Power 105.1—the competition. That would set off another round of shock and even criticism. But dealing with that could wait. For now I just needed to be in this moment.

Man, how did I get there? Walking down the hall to do my last show, I thought about how many times I'd walked into this very studio to do countless interviews with my friends and some of the biggest names in hip-hop music. We broke news and new artists within the culture, and I built a relationship with my listeners that transcended not only hip-hop, but the radio. Together with my audience I witnessed and experienced so much over the years. We grew up together. And it was these longtime listeners who called me the Voice of New York, a name that would later stick.

So I guess the answer to the question of how I got here is that from the start I loved this shit, and even when I didn't love something, that never kept me from having a healthy enough work ethic to get past the discomfort. Some of my success was a product of good timing; a lot of it was the result of having great relationships with others who were living the same dream as I was.

Some of the most pivotal times in hip-hop happened in the mid-90s, and I was coming into my own at the same time. Initially what seemed like just a really cool job turned into more. Eventually I started to realize I was having a real connection with my listeners. That was never more real to me than my twenty-fifth birthday party at the Palladium, the hottest club in New York at the time. It felt like the whole city showed up. The place was packed to capacity, and everybody and anybody in hip-hop was in the building.

Wu-Tang was there. Fat Joe, Mobb Deep, Black Moon, and Jay Z all performed.

And there was nobody in the game hotter than Biggie, so when he walked in, everybody went nuts. We'd gotten to know each other pretty well from the many times he'd been on my show. He popped bottles and celebrated with me all night. Then he pulled me to the side and said, "Ang, I was gonna perform a few joints, but you know me and Fay . . ." He nodded over to his wife and Bad Boy labelmate, Faith, who had just taken to the stage to sing "Happy Birthday" to me. He then confided in me that the two of them were not in a good place, so at that point he didn't want to go anywhere near the stage. He didn't want the drama, he said.

It's ironic that Biggie wanted to avoid drama, because he soon found himself in the middle of one of the biggest feuds in music history.

How it had become a full-out beef between him and Tupac, I didn't fully understand. What I do know is that within a couple months after my birthday party, hip-hop entered a really dark place.

The Tupac-Biggie beef took center stage and escalated quickly. And I found myself in the middle of it when Pac called and invited me to LA to get his side of the story.

*Wait. What??? Pac is on the phone?!*

The conversation that would follow and the subsequent interview at his home in Los Angeles would be one of the biggest turning points in my career, and some of the lessons I took away from it have stayed with me to this day.

The interview was never aired in its entirety. It was explosive. That decision has often been questioned, but ultimately I'm the one who would have had to live with the consequences of what the interview could have done.

And that's just one of the memories that I'm having on my last day of work at Hot 97, almost eighteen years later.

Before these thoughts have time to play out, I'm turning around to see the studio filling up with all my fellow deejays who have come to hang with me for my last show at Hot 97.

It was a celebration, and all the rules went out the window. Nobody was worried about the ratings that day. I just cracked the mic and spoke from the heart. My announcement was trending worldwide. People were calling it the end of an era.

Artists started calling the show in a frenzy. Ludacris and Tyrese called together from the set of *Furious 7* to find out what was going on. Wale sent a long text about how much my presence on the air meant to him. Rihanna surprised me with flowers. Taraji P. Henson, a friend whose career has exploded with the massive success of Fox's *Empire*, popped up at the station to give me the much-needed gift of a pair of sunglasses, saying, "Girl, don't be in all these pictures with your eyes red and puffy." I promptly put them on.

Jay Z sent a text: *Snoop makes a decision and doesn't even consult Dre?* Jay and I used to call ourselves the Snoop and Dre of the radio. Many of my most classic interviews were done sitting across from him at almost every stage of his career. Sensing what I was feeling, he sent a second text: *Your future is ahead of you. Imagine the notion of the past 15 years of your life being a blip in your story.*

That boy has always been good with words, and the notion resonated with me because looking back was never my thing. I'm not somebody who obsesses over anniversaries or who lives in the past. I like to live in today and the future. That's the essence of radio. Every day on the air you have to deliver a new show and break new ground. Every single day. And I'm like that in my life—I show up and do today, deliver today, and move forward.

But I have to say that although looking back has never been my thing, what I learned that last day was that there are times in life that not only is it okay to reflect but you'd be a fool not to. There are too many lessons, too much history, too many amazing milestones worth remembering and cherishing. That simple realization is what made me want to share, not just for myself but for the people who helped me to find my voice.

Not everyone will one day crack a mic on the radio or make a name for themselves in media or entertainment, but now more than ever we should all care about cultivating authentic voices. Wherever they are— aspiring rappers, singers, painters, authors, journalists, activists . . . whatever. Every great and lasting art form starts down in the deep, hard bedrock of truth and self-expression.

The power of voice. That's where hip-hop was born and where it always lives. And that's where my story—our story—begins.

# PART ONE

# FINDING THE MIC

## 1971 TO 1997

# CHAPTER ONE

# BEAT STREET

*I said a hip hop / The hippie the hippie / To the hip hip hop and ya don't stop the rock / To the bang-bang boogie / Say up jump the boogie to the rhythm of the boogie, the beat . . .*

The seeds were planted for my obsession with hip-hop as soon as I heard those opening lines of the Sugarhill Gang's "Rapper's Delight." Whenever I hear that song, I'm instantly taken back to a night in September 1979, when I was eight years old and used to stay uptown at my grandmother's apartment in Washington Heights. Even though I was supposed to be asleep, I snuck out of bed and peeked into the living room, where my aunts Melanie and Cindy, my mom's younger sisters, were hosting one of their house parties. "Rapper's Delight" was blasting off the record player, and I was completely mesmerized. I didn't know what I was hearing, but the beat and the rhyming lyrics were infectious.

*Nothing could be greater than this!*

I looked around at my aunts' friends dancing and laughing and partying like whatever problems they had in the world didn't exist, and "Rapper's Delight" became the coolest thing I'd ever heard in my whole eight years on this planet. I was hypnotized. Like something inside me had been changed and now I was ready to hear and feel more of what I'd felt that night.

Where I come from, there were a lot of us kids having a similar experience. In fact, if you look at the history of hip-hop, it sprang from the same neighborhoods in the same time period as I did—from its roots in the house parties of the early 1970s, not unlike the ones my aunts would throw at my grandmother's apartment on Dyckman Street.

It was there—and at the nearby homes of other family members in the Bronx—where I was first exposed to the same melting pot of musical and cultural influences that also helped shape hip-hop. And on both sides of my family tree, which was mostly Puerto Rican but also Dominican and Cuban, there was always some kind of music playing, something great cooking, and we definitely had colorful characters and strong voices.

My mother, Shirley Maldonado, who raised me as a single mom, was no exception. At seventeen, she had gotten pregnant and then had me when she was eighteen. She was married one year before she walked in on my father, Julio (aka Nat) in the shower with another woman—or something like that. Despite everything, or perhaps because of everything, my mother always had dreams of getting out of a dysfunctional situation and doing better for herself—having more, learning more, going further. She just wanted more.

Petite, dark-haired, and fair-skinned, my mother always looked younger than other moms, yet her drive and independence made her seem more mature than most. Even though she and I ended up moving a lot in my early years, what I remember most was growing up with the knowledge that I was loved.

And that love was always on display whenever we spent time uptown, visiting my grandmother Livia and her husband, Tommy—whom she married after a rough relationship with her first husband, my grandfather Victor. My grandma Livia is a tiny little woman who has a natural warmth. She's been through a lot and has seen a lot and she's worked hard her whole life. Still she's one of the funniest people I know. I get such a kick out of her! Her husband, Tommy, is a stand-up guy with a great smile and a short buzz cut left over from his service in the Marines. Tommy is a real Puerto Rican, strong and stern—but the kind of stern that kids actually like. In fact, he's the man I know as my grandfather, probably the only steady male figure I've ever had in my life. If I ever decide I want to be married, Tommy would be the one to walk me down the aisle.

The other members of the household in those years included Aunt Melanie, Aunt Cindy, and Uncle Steven, my mom's three younger siblings. They were all close in age, so there were a lot of sibling fights, usually over clothes or something stupid like that, but they escalated quickly and definitely kept the household lively. Cindy, born after my mother, was the middle child, who was very close to my mom, feisty and petite at four eleven. And Melanie, the youngest, liked to party and hit the clubs in the eighties. She was over five foot eight—which was unusually tall for the whole family. Steven, the only boy in the family, was rambunctious as a kid and later struggled with mental health issues. Even so, he was really close with my grandmother, and she always did her best to protect him.

Our family's roots uptown had been planted all the way back in the 1940s when my mother's grandfather Miguel, Livia's father, came from Cuba to 172nd and St. Nicholas. We all called him Uelo, short for *Abuelo* ("grandpa" in Spanish). Uelo, who I just adored, had suffered the loss of his wife—my great-grandmother, who was from the Dominican Republic—after a tragic car accident that took her life before I was born.

I never met her, but my great-grandmother's death haunts me to this day. For good reason.

Uelo, always obsessed with taking photos, used to photograph everything and actually took pictures of the car wreck that killed my great-grandmother. The images of that car crash have stayed with me my whole life. To this day I'm never fully comfortable sitting in the passenger seat of a car.

Uelo was a larger-than-life figure, and I loved going to visit him. A fair-skinned Cuban, not tall but hefty—he liked to eat—Uelo wore thick reading glasses and long-sleeved flannel shirts and would keep a little disposable camera tucked in his shirt pocket so he could take pictures wherever he went. Uelo was known on the block. He'd walk into the Dominican restaurant and they'd say: *"El Viejo Miguel, arroz blanco, habichuela y un bistec?"* Yes, they knew his order before he told them. He was that type of guy.

Uelo also taught me something about the reality of the neighborhood. Despite the fact that he was known on the block, he admitted that he had to be careful because he was also getting robbed . . . regularly!

"I don't mind if it's with a gun, but it's the knives that scare me." He explained his robbery preference.

As a kid this was terrifying shit. Plus, it made me really angry. He was an old man! What kind of animal would rob an old man?! Especially my Uelo! Oh my God, it makes me mad remembering it today. Probably more mad than he ever was about it.

Uelo lived so long that when he did finally pass away at the age of 105, I couldn't believe he was really gone. That was more than eight years ago and I still miss him.

My mother and I lived with Uelo briefly, in between apartments of our own in Washington Heights and the Bronx. Between our stays with Uelo and those with my grandmother Livia and her husband, Tommy,

I felt lucky to get to know the older members of our family and to hear their stories.

As a kid I didn't know the details of Livia's divorce from my biological grandfather Victor. But as time went on I heard of his struggles with alcohol and gambling addiction and how drinking sometimes made him mean and often verbally abusive. His kids had different perspectives, but I think my mother, being the eldest, saw the most and the worst of it. What I've come to learn is that children of alcoholics have different MOs for coping. They either remove themselves or they learn how to lie or even turn to alcohol in some cases. Some cope better than others, but what I *do* know is that my family to this day has remnants of his addiction.

We all have family histories that are not perfect. Or at least I like to think that one of the reasons I'm sympathetic to people's flaws and struggles is because I really believe everybody's bullshit is often not even about you—it's about all the bits and pieces of where and what you come from.

· · ·

As best I can remember, my father, Julio (or Nat, as most of the family called him) Martinez, would have qualified as tall, dark, and handsome. The time I got to spend with him was at my grandmother Petra's apartment on 193rd in Washington Heights. My father would hoist me up onto his shoulders as soon as I arrived.

I only remember him as fun, throwing me up in the air like that and making me laugh like crazy. I didn't get to see my dad a lot, so like with most kids, the parent that you see the least, you're the most excited when you do see them. I'm sure that had to get on my mother's nerves.

What got on *my* nerves whenever I visited my dad was that there always seemed to be different women around who were always over-the-top nice to me. But I never fell for it. Even as a child, I had a good sense of when people were full of shit.

Aside from that, I loved everything about visiting my grandmother Petra—who adored and pampered me to no end. As the super of the building where they lived, she had this whole big basement floor, so there was plenty of room for both my father and my uncle Raymond to live there with her. My grandma Petra was old-school Puerto Rican and, in my memory, looked a lot like Celia Cruz. She had the same nails, that same complexion. She was a good woman with a big heart. She rented one of the rooms in the basement to this guy she referred to as the "Blind Man," which I know sounds rude, but she'd feed him and take care of him like he was a member of the family. She and the Blind Man would drink Schaefer beers together in front of the TV and watch telenovelas till someone fell asleep.

One of my earliest memories of being at my grandma Petra's took place when I was really little and had come down with a severe case of scarlet fever. My temperature was dangerously high, and I could tell how worried everyone was. Grandma immediately proceeded to give me baths in holy water because it was her thinking that the Santos would cure me. And I have to give it to her, because after that the fever broke. I can still see all the little statues of her Santos and the rosary beads on the side of her dresser. She believed.

In hindsight I realize there was a lot of dysfunction in that house. I rarely remember my grandmother without a can of beer in her hand, and I have too many memories of gunshots outside when I stayed there. One night the gunshots seemed louder than normal and the reaction on my grandma's face was different, too. In less than a minute, I turned to see my dad and my uncle as they busted into the apartment, out of breath, before disappearing into my father's room.

My dad was always in the streets, hanging out with his friends on the corner all day, and I'd be right out there with him whenever I could. At around the age of eight, I watched my father get into a fistfight with a guy who pulled a switchblade out of his back pocket. My father ran. The next thing I know, I'm chasing the guy who's chasing my dad down the block with a knife—because I'm trying to run after my father. And then my dad's girl of the moment starts chasing after me. We were like a parade of dysfunction running down 187th street.

Nothing terrible happened. I wound up running out of breath and getting pulled into a building lobby by the stupid girlfriend. We waited there until my dad's friends eventually found us. I saw a lot of shit there I shouldn't have seen at that age. Like when I picked up a handgun that was left sitting on the top of the television. I'm holding it in my hand in awe of its weight and my grandmother comes in freaking the fuck out, screaming in Spanish at my father. My Spanish wasn't the best, so I didn't really understand what she was saying, but I knew it wasn't good.

None of it was good.

The crazy thing is that as clear as most of these memories are, I only have one recollection of actually seeing my parents together, ever. My mom picked me up from my grandmother's house one afternoon and my father was there. They seemed to be pretty cordial when he asked if we could get ice cream together before she took me home. To my surprise, my mother agreed. *Wait?! What?! All three of us together?? And there's going to be ice cream?!* I was overjoyed and bolted to the other room to grab my things. You would've thought we were going to Disney World. I was putting my shoes on, excited and eager, when the house phone rang and everything stopped. I heard my father scream and I ran to the living room to find him on his knees, shouting into the phone, "Nooooooo! Please God no! Where is he? Where the fuck is he?!" They had murdered his best friend, Dom, a few blocks away. I just remember him screaming, "They killed Dom! They killed Dom!" My mom rushed me out of there. I remember realizing there would be no ice cream and also that I probably wouldn't see my dad again for a while.

My grandma Petra passed away not too long after. I was ten years old, and I never saw my father again.

I don't know what happened. After the funeral, it was like that whole side of the family just disappeared out of my life. Gone. Years later my mother told me that my father struggled with heroin, and relatives had called her and said, "You know, Nat's in bad shape. He's in a center trying to beat it and detox." They wanted my mother to bring me to go see my father, with the hope that maybe seeing me could help him. My mother said she thought about it but ultimately she didn't want to subject me to that, so she decided no. He disappeared after that.

As a kid I'm not sure I realized what was even happening for quite some time. But months would eventually turn into years. I never saw him again.

As an adult I don't have bad feelings toward my father. I feel like he was somebody who was struggling with his own issues and being a parent didn't really work. So, past a certain time, he no longer was.

From then on it was just my mom, and she always made sure I felt loved. Even so, there was some negative fallout. In relationships to this day I don't easily let others in. I believe in having four close friends, not twenty. Some people say I'm guarded, but I say I'm careful. And maybe that's not always a bad thing. In my business it's actually protected me from a lot of bullshit. So, at the end of the day, the way I was raised— complications and all—made me stronger and smarter about the people I do choose to let in.

• • •

Our move to Brooklyn when I was eight could not have come any sooner for my mother, the ever-evolving Shirley, who was steadily moving up the career ladder after getting her start as a secretary at PolyGram Records and then transitioning from the label to a job at the radio station WYNY, all while doing whatever she could to find the right child care to keep me out of trouble.

No easy task—I was a crazy kid.

I broke my leg in seven places after jumping out of a tree at six years old. Then, a year later, I fell in the park and slit my arm open and needed eight stitches. And right before our move to Brooklyn, when we lived uptown on 207th Street, I was arguing with my cousin and banging on the French doors and my hand went through the glass. When I pulled my hand out, it ripped my wrist open. My mother—who happened to be in the other room playing her acoustic guitar, her latest interest— heard the screams and thought, *Oh God, what now?*

That was until I come walking into her room and my wrist is wide-open. She calmly walks me to the bathtub, wraps my arm in towels, and one of the guys from the neighborhood rushes me to the hospital. The doctors said they could see my veins and I would need stiches inside and out. I still have a nasty scar on my wrist from that one. So yeah, all of this before the age of eight. It's a wonder my poor mother didn't have a heart attack.

Her solution was to keep a closer eye on me as she explored new avenues for growth and learning for herself. For example, she took me with her to various self-awareness meetings and Buddhist meditation groups where they would chant, *"Nam Myoho Renge Kyo,"* attempting to awaken their deepest enlightenment. I remember sitting in there, in the back with a few other kids who'd been dragged along, too, all of us looking at each other like—*What are these crazy people talking about?*

Even though at the time I might have thought they were weirdos, I appreciate that my mother exposed me to different ways of thinking and believing. She also gave me a set of values that included the importance of splurging—when it mattered. We might have eaten ramen noodles or mac and cheese out of the box all week, but once in a while she'd find a way to take me to a really nice restaurant. We mostly shopped for bargains, but I also remember, now and then, her buying me a pair of expensive sneakers. Those instances were memorable because they were reminders that those experiences didn't have to be out of reach. Lots of people I knew back then never even left the block where they grew up, mainly because they never could imagine themselves leaving and getting to travel the world beyond it.

In fact, it was while my mom was trying to evolve and remove herself from some of her childhood dysfunction that she decided to move away from our family uptown all the way to a one-bedroom apartment of our own in Brooklyn. And not just Brooklyn, but the end of Brooklyn, the farthest possible part of the city from Washington Heights—the third-to-last stop on the F train—Neptune Avenue, then known as the Van Sicklen stop. The train ride to get to our new neighborhood of Beach Haven took, like, two hours—an hour on the A train to Jay Street–Borough Hall and then another hour on the F train toward Coney Island. Despite the long subway ride, we would still manage to go back and visit family almost every weekend.

Brooklyn seemed cool. The proximity of Beach Haven to Coney Island was a plus. There was grass outside our building, which was a big deal, and it was directly across the street from this big tennis bubble that looked like some old monument, where people would play tennis indoors. I didn't know anybody who played tennis uptown.

Best of all, there were lots of kids in the neighborhood. Shortly after we moved in, my mother and I were in the hallway of the building when we got to talking with another mom and her daughter who was about my age—a pretty Jamaican girl who was tall and thin and who turned out to be Nikki, my future best friend. It all came from her mom and mine talking about how we were both eight years old and both going to PS 216. The moms decided that since the school was about a dozen blocks away, it would be nice if we could walk there and back together. And not only did we do that, but we did it every day for the next four years, sharing almost every experience.

Every morning we'd stop to get a bagel and two quarter waters for a dollar. That was our daily routine. All we needed was a dollar. Either she had the dollar or I had the dollar, or we scrounged change together to make a dollar. Nikki and I backed each other up, no matter what. She was the most reliable, honest, trustworthy friend any kid could have.

Nikki lived in 5H, on the fifth floor, with her mother and her two sisters and brother; I lived in 1H, so we'd constantly be running up and down the stairs to go to each other's apartment. It didn't take long for her family to become my family and my family to become hers. Now, Nikki's family is Jamaican, so I'd be the little Puerto Rican girl at full-on Jamaican parties with their family, eating oxtail and rice and peas. That's how I grew up from then until high school—being raised in part by a Jamaican family. If they were going on a family trip, the first question would be, "Is Angie coming?" And my family embraced Nikki just the same, and so she was raised eating rice and beans and *platanos*. For our mothers, both single working moms, having that extra support system had to have been helpful.

On top of that, since both of our mothers worked full-time, after school on most days Nikki and I hung out at the neighbor's house, a West Indian woman from Trinidad named Ann Marie who had two daughters of her own. She did have a lot of rules though.

*Rules? Oooh, not my favorite. Never a fan of too many rules.*

Ann Marie had a rule that if you wanted to drink orange juice, you better not pour it straight out of the container. You better fill the cup halfway with water and mix the juice into the water. "How dare you drink orange juice just by itself?" I guess this was her way to make the orange juice last longer. She also had one of those living rooms that you weren't allowed to go in and one of those plastic-covered couches that you weren't allowed to sit on. She was a really good lady, only she was tough and very stern in her rules.

It was at Ann Marie's house that I first heard Kurtis Blow's "Basketball." I remember getting such a kick out of it and thinking it was so funny that he would be "playing basketball without a basketball." I needed to learn the lyrics immediately, so I got out a notebook and listened to it on repeat until I could write down every single word and memorize it. This became my thing. I had to know every word of it. And I had to know it better than everybody on the block.

While there were only a few kids on my block as interested in hip-hop as I was, it didn't stop me from venturing out to find it. At night I would sneak out to make the ten-block walk from Beach Haven to the Coney Island amusement park—where I'd go just to hang out next to the Music Express ride because the music was so dope. Biz Markie, Audio Two, and—of course my favorite—Eric B. & Rakim. When I could convince Nikki to go, too, that was even better. She only went once or twice. The walk home—dark, deserted, and under the elevated train tracks—was not for her. Not the safest for two girls walking alone late at night, much less for one. But in the end that didn't deter me. I went alone when I had to. There were a lot of kids like me there just to hear the music.

If you were a kid who came from nothing, and you listened to the radio or read entertainment magazines or whatever, you didn't relate to any of that. None of it. So hip-hop became a reflection of real life. And over time, even if you didn't come from the hood—or maybe your circumstances were a little better or a little worse—you could still relate because what you heard was honest.

In the early eighties, I can remember Grandmaster Flash and Melle Mel, not only with the "The Message" that talked about the jungle of ghetto life but also "White Lines," which was the first of its kind to reference the coming crack epidemic. As a sixth grader, I was too young to really understand all of the themes, but the references felt familiar. It felt like I was getting the real story of what was going on in the city around me, the unedited version. And I loved it.

• • •

My growing love of hip-hop didn't prevent me from trying my hand at musical theater. I use the term "musical theater" loosely.

I was in sixth grade at PS 216 with Mr. Devinoff, who had sort of an old-school *Brady Bunch* look and was known for putting on the best school plays. And for some reason I thought it was a good idea to audition for one of the leads in *Oliver!* That is, until I heard Mr. Devinoff say it was my turn to get up in front of the whole class and sing. Oh my God, all of sudden I was terrified. I'd never sung in public before, and as soon as I walked to the front of the stage and opened my mouth, I completely froze.

No sound came out at all. I couldn't move. The only thing my body agreed to do was cry, so I did. Like a weird ugly cry. Inside my head I was screaming at myself: *This was the stupidest idea you've ever had! You're clearly not built for this. You're terrible!*

"It's okay. You're just a little nervous," Mr. Devinoff encouraged. "You've got to shake it off." He didn't let me off the hook. He didn't let me cry and then not do it.

Like a deer in the headlights, I just stared back at my teacher. I still couldn't move.

"Okay, I just want you to calm down. Take a deep breath." After I did, he insisted I sing the part that I had chosen to audition for.

And that second time, I kind of killed it. So much so that I wound up getting the part of the Artful Dodger!

I remember that moment, and I remember it mattered, like—*Oh! I see. I just have to get past the nervous energy.*

That audition left a lasting lesson. It proved to me that if something happens to throw you off, you can't curl up in it. You have to get past it. What sealed that message for me was the next day, when Mr. Devinoff pulled me aside during class.

"I went home last night and I was sitting with my wife," he began.

That was weird to me. I'd never thought about my teachers as full people outside of the classroom. *Mr. Devinoff has a wife?*

"I was showing my wife the video of the auditions," he continued. "She thought you were so great after you pushed through being scared. She thought it was the greatest."

How cool was it that I had a teacher who had the insight to know how much that would mean to me? I loved every minute of rehearsing and performing in that show, especially playing the Artful Dodger, who was coolest part of all anyway. And it was not lost on me that I could have missed out had I let my nerves get the best of me.

In the years to come, there would be plenty of times when I'd have to summon that same lesson to get past being scared. You just can't pay attention to it. You have to know that's only what's happening to you in the moment. You have to choose not to let your fear keep you from whatever your intention is.

You really can get past it.

The lesson was well timed for me, too, because the following school year I was headed to junior high and all of a sudden Nikki and I would be attending different schools. This was the first time since the third grade that we were to be separated. Nikki was going to the junior high school closer to where we lived, but I had tested into Brooklyn's Mark Twain Intermediate School for the Gifted and Talented. I happened to be really good at math. Go figure. There were kids who got into the school for gym or dance or other fun and creative talents, but not me. I spent my days doing math.

At the end of the school day, I couldn't wait to get out of there and go home and hang with Nikki and my other friends. And it wasn't just me. As soon as the bell rang we'd all fly down the halls and thunder down the stairs to get to the exit doors. One day as we were all rushing to go home, I'm on the stairs and this girl behind me is pushing her way out.

I turned around aggressively and shouted, "Yo! Watch who the fuck you're pushing!"

She quickly responded, "I'll push whoever the fuck I want."

That was all it took. She said something nasty, and I said something nasty, and there we were, fighting on the stairs, pulling each other's hair, dragging each other around. Mind you, the stairs were really steep, so we could've easily killed each other. Luckily, we didn't. I learned a quick lesson that afternoon—to watch how I talked to people if I wanted to avoid this type of conflict.

Other than that, school was uneventful. But what was happening outside of school was beyond eventful. Hip-hop was on fire! That next summer of 1984, I was thirteen and spent a lot of time at my grandmother Livia's. The movie *Beat Street* was out, and it changed my life. I saw that movie so many times, I could recite it line for line in its entirety. Still can. "*Your moves are wack . . . All your moves are wack . . . Your moves ain't worth the bit, punk . . .*" I'd never seen a movie with kids who looked like me and my friends and that told a story about how your obsession for hip-hop, dance, and art could actually take you places.

At this point, in my grandmother's neighborhood uptown, and most inner-city neighborhoods, you could find pieces of linoleum or cardboard on almost every corner, where you'd see people breakdancing with big boom boxes blasting beside them. I'd listen to the radio every weekend to hear Kool DJ Red Alert on KISS FM and Mr. Magic on WBLS, and would tape their shows religiously. I had tons of tapes. Out on the fire escape, I'd sit for hours with my cassette player, listening to songs like UTFO's "Roxanne, Roxanne"—rewinding and playing it over and over to learn all the words: *Yo Kangol, I don't think that you're dense / But you went about the matter with no experience.* Then a rapper took on that name Roxanne Shanté and answered that record with one of her own called "Roxanne's Revenge." I memorized that in one sitting: *Well, my name is Roxanne, and don't ya know / I just cold rock a party, and I do this show* . . . I was obsessed. I listened to my tape player religiously—until the damn thing wore out.

For the next couple of years, whenever I was uptown in Washington Heights at my grandmother's apartment—like in the summers or on weekends—I'd hang out at a park with kids I knew in the neighborhood. We'd stay out late at night, smoking weed and listening to music, watching the breakdancing. We'd sneak into the train yard and write on the trains with big fat Magic Markers and spray paint. Yes, I was a B-girl and into all things hip-hop, graffiti included.

One night in the park, as we sat there smoking weed, one of the girls said, "Yo! Have any of you guys smoked coke before?" A few of the kids said that they had tried some in a blunt, a woolie. The girl shook her head, like that was nothing. Then she reached into her pocket, saying, "Well, you need to try this. It's way better!" She was so convincing. She was like a fucking salesperson. I believed her. And before I knew it, she was passing around a glass pipe and insisting everybody try it. To me it didn't look like a big deal. For as long as I can remember, I'd seen my aunts and uncles smoke weed out of glass pipes or bongs or some other smoke-shop paraphernalia. So as it got passed around, I didn't think twice about giving it a hit.

And then *holy shiiiiiit*! She was *right*. This was unbelievable! And it hit us so fast. Before I had even passed it on, I felt like I was on another planet. And just as fast as it hit, it was over. For the next hour we all sat in a circle like in a congregation, talking about how amazing it was and trying to figure out when we could try it again—maybe we would for New Year's Eve. We were all planning to put money in and couldn't wait.

It wasn't until a few weeks later, after watching the news with my mom and hearing a report about the crack explosion, that I realized, *Holy shit! I smoked crack. This is horrible. How in the hell did my dumb ass let this happen???!!*

The news had stated that after one try, you could become addicted. The thought terrified me. *Was I now a crackhead because I tried it one time?* It scared the shit outta me so bad that I would never try it again— or anything, for that matter.

Later I saw firsthand with friends and family members what crack did to people. Whenever crackheads would stop by places like the hair salon and try to sell a broken VCR or half a pack of Newports, I'd cringe at how people would laugh at them and be mean. I felt sympathy for their desperation. Maybe they were just like me once . . . a regular kid who some knucklehead convinced to try something new. The only difference was that I was lucky enough to have dodged that bullet—getting the message just in the nick of time to stay away from something so lethal.

For some reason—I can't even put my finger on why—but for the grace of God, I've been protected when needed and have been able to wiggle my way past any type of real danger.

There was a minute there when I was persuaded to sell weed for someone at school. My career as a drug dealer resulted in the sale of exactly one nickel bag. It was not hard, just an easy exchange in the staircase. But I went no further than that. It wasn't like I got caught. The feds weren't exactly after me. It was just one of those moments when you listen to that little voice in your head that says, *Maybe I'm going a little too far left.* And you get your ass back on track and go right.

My mother gets the credit for encouraging that voice in my head, the sensibility that, yeah, you can play with fire, but once your skin starts shriveling up, maybe you want to pull the fuck out. *Retreat! Retreat!* I'm good for that; I'm curious, and I like to explore and be open-minded. But ultimately I know when I've gone too far.

. . .

By the time I got to high school—Brooklyn's John Dewey High—I was pretty much a hip-hop encyclopedia. I knew every artist, every song title, even all the lyrics. I was like a human Shazam app who could name that tune just by hearing a few beats of the intro's drum track.

At age sixteen I used to hold court on the stoop in front of my building, me standing up and everyone else seated on the steps around me. We played this jukebox game. The way it worked was that everyone would take turns just shouting out a topic at me and then I'd answer by singing or rapping lyrics that went with that subject or theme. Somebody would say something like, "The jungle!" and not missing a beat I'd go right into Grandmaster Flash's "The Message": *It's like a jungle sometimes / It makes me wonder how I keep from goin' under . . .*

Or somebody else would say, "The flu!" and I'd launch into "Hard Times" by Run-D.M.C.: *Hard times are spreading just like the flu . . .*

This could go on for hours. I was like a one-girl freak show in the neighborhood. Even I was surprised sometimes by how I could remember every lyric and call it up so easily. Music would just stick to me, as a part of who I was and how I took in the world.

Once high school started, Nikki and I were reunited and back to attending school together. She thought it was cool that I was the hip-hop head that I was—the way I'd hold my own at the lunchroom table with the guys as we debated rappers and who was doper than whom. But aside from a few songs she liked, Nikki was nowhere near as obsessed as me. I did convince her to learn all the words to "Ego Trippin'" by Ultramagnetic MCs, which she never forgot, and by the way, are not the easiest lyrics: *Using frequencies and data I am approximate / Leaving revolutions turning, emerging chemistry* . . .

I loved when Nikki would get on board because it wasn't that often, although she was a definite yes when my aunt Melanie offered to take us to a club—the Roseland Ballroom. In those days, a fifteen-year-old like us could get a fake ID on 42nd Street around the corner from Times Square. I'll never forget the feeling of walking into a club the first time, me and Nikki trying to act all sophisticated and, of course, Aunt Melanie just being in her element. Everything about it was exciting—the dark room, the beat hitting hard, the lights pulsing, and there in the center of it all, dressed in black leather pants, was KISS FM's Chuck Leonard hosting the show that night. Though I didn't have any inkling of what my future career would be, I remember thinking how cool this guy looked and how dope it would be to talk on the mic and introduce the acts onstage.

And in the middle of my excitement, all of a sudden, *Pop! Pop! Pop!* . . . There's a shoot-out in the club. Everybody in the club scattered, running in all directions in a panic. It was instantaneous. But weirdly, the music didn't stop. Biz Markie's "Make the Music with Your Mouth, Biz" kept on rocking in the background: *I get the crowd jumpin', get the girls' hearts pumpin' / All the party people say, "Isn't he somethin'?"* So as freaked out as we were, while we flew to the back and ducked under the tables, I was still very aware that my joint was on!

Hip-hop was growing, spreading out across the country, and that song put it into context: *Rock from New York City all the way down South / Sayin' rhymes and makin' music with my mouth* . . .

Nikki wasn't as gung ho to come back anytime soon, but we both got a lot of mileage telling that story at school. Well, I know I did.

Since John Dewey High School was across the street from Marlboro Projects, a lot of kids who lived nearby but didn't even go to our school would wind up hanging out with us. We'd play handball outside for hours, listening to music and talking shit. I wasn't the only girl in the crowd who was more tomboy than girlie; that was part of the hip-hop—or just the New York—culture. But tomboy or not, the fashion was real at the time, too. We were into Mickey Mouse and Coca-Cola clothing, those Benetton rugby shirts, and the bamboo earrings that had your name on the inside. I had 'em all. And no one could say shit to me when I convinced my mom to get me the red leather goose with the fur! I wore that jacket every day.

I loved going to school, but going to class was not exactly my thing. Needless to say, this was not a great recipe for staying completely out of trouble. More and more, I'd cut class and be at the handball courts all day or in the lunchroom playing spades. Then there were the hooky parties in Bushwick and Marlboro Projects. That was pretty much my high school experience summed up until, eventually, the shit hit the fan.

Being smart, I developed a system for not getting caught by painting the picture the way that I wanted. I had the key to the mailbox, so I could take out the pink absence slips from school before my mom saw them. I think she got hip to that at some point and started taking the mailbox key to work. That didn't stop me. Nikki and I figured out a way, with tweezers, to fish out the pink slips through the quarter-inch slots in the face of the mailbox. We were like surgeons with the tweezers.

Then I started making and printing out my own report cards, tricking my poor mother for quite some time. I'd give myself an occasional B or C so it didn't seem suspicious. But according to my report cards, I was a pretty good student. Eventually, my aunt Cindy, who had moved to Florida in those years, was home on a visit and decided to throw in her two cents: "This doesn't look like a real report card—anybody could print this out."

*Why is she so goddamn nosy? I got a perfectly good operation going here!*

It may have raised an eyebrow for my mother, but she let it go. However, not too long after that, she got a call from Mrs. Webber, the guidance counselor.

Mrs. Webber, a mousy brown-haired lady with glasses, was onto me and had been trying for months to track me down in school. She would see me in the hallway and call my name. "Angela!!!!" I would literally run the other way and act like I didn't hear her. There I was, racing through the lunchroom, and my friends were saying, "Yo, Ang, what's up?" and I'd be yelling back, "I can't stop! Mrs. Webber is chasing me!"

After finally having enough, Mrs. Webber did what any respectable guidance counselor would do and, unbeknownst to me on that particular day, called my mother at work to tell her that I had missed more days than I had actually attended that semester and that I was going to be expelled. My mom hung up, immediately left work, and headed for the train to Brooklyn.

At that particular hour, in the middle of the school day—no surprise—I'd cut out of school and was at home with friends, drinking a forty-ounce bottle of Olde English, smoking, and watching *Beat Street* on the VCR. So there we were, chillin' without a care in the world, until I heard jangling keys out in the hallway and the sound of the lock unlocking. Everybody stared at the door like—*Holy shit!*

And in burst Shirley—and she was PISSED.

"Mom!" I said, in shock. What else was I gonna say?

"Angela! Get everybody out of the house."

"But, Mom—"

"Do not say another word. Everybody out!"

The next thing I knew, I was on a plane to Florida to live with Aunt Cindy.

. . .

Florida was total culture shock, like living in a foreign country—especially when it came to music. And I was all about the music. So there I was listening to Run-D.M.C., Salt-N-Pepa, KRS-One, and Public Enemy while the kids at Coconut Creek High School in Margate, Florida—about a half hour outside of Miami—were into these Jam Pony Express mixtapes, 2 Live Crew, and Miami bass. Used to drive me crazy. How could they think any of that was good? Years later, I developed respect for why they liked it and I get it. But culturally and musically, it was so different. And I was just lost.

Before long I started to adjust, after meeting other kids from New York whose families had relocated as well. And in that group I met Derek, who was cute and from Brentwood, Long Island, so that cushioned the blow. His family was Puerto Rican, too, and his parents even reminded me of my relatives, welcoming and warm. Whenever I hung out with Derek at his house, we'd do fun things like go fishing in their backyard.

Being part of a family atmosphere mattered to me at a time when I was feeling homesick. Of course, Aunt Cindy and her husband did all they could to be supportive, but they were focused on getting a new business off the ground. And I also knew it was only temporary, as the plan was for my mom to move down to Florida, too, that is, once she'd saved up enough and possibly found work ahead of time.

But even as I adapted socially, I liked school less and less. Soon I was doing the same shit as before—lying, missing school, hiding report cards. Everything came to a head about six months after my arrival in Florida, when, at last, the intrepid Shirley Maldonado landed a great job as music director at Power 96 in Miami.

We didn't see each other much those first couple of days after Mom arrived because she was busy getting situated at work. And then came the moment of truth when, without advance warning, she walked into Cindy's house to get me just as I was in the bathroom fixing my hair.

All of a sudden the bathroom door flings open, scaring the shit outta me.

"Ma!" I scream.

Steely-eyed, she asks, "Did you get your report card?"

Without time to think, I say, "No, not yet."

She knew I was lying and proceeded to smack the holy shit out of me. *What in the fuck?!*

My mother had never hit me. She wasn't punching me or hitting me with a stick, but she was definitely hitting me. And it freaked me the fuck out. You know that saying "smack some sense into you"? Well, I'm here to tell you . . . it can happen!

Everything just stopped for me as if the smoke cleared and something changed inside me. And I just knew I couldn't do it anymore; it was not going to be tolerated. I really had my "Who do you think you are?" moment. My mother said so much without words, and I heard her loud and clear:

*She is the boss of me. She's not playing with me.*

And I got my shit together big-time. Not only did I get back to school, but I also went to night school and summer school, and somehow I graduated on time. So when people argue that you should never hit your kids, mostly I agree, but I do think that sometimes your kid being a little scared of you is okay and even necessary.

There were other lessons that came out of the hard work that was required for me to make up for lost time. One of those was the realization that it's true what they say—if you put your mind to something and you work your ass off, whatever it is, you can make it happen. That was a pivotal discovery in my life and something that would be of considerable help in my career later on.

The other eye-opener was that even if I didn't love all the required courses in school, I actually did love learning. In fact, whether I was conscious of it yet or not, one of the things that I loved about hip-hop was what you could learn from listening to the wordplay and unraveling the layers of code and figuring out the storytelling in the rhymes.

This was right around the time that Rakim became one of the greatest MCs I've ever heard. That has never changed. But back when I was seventeen, on albums like *Paid in Full* and *Follow the Leader*, I started to listen with new ears. Rakim spoke to me in a way that I felt he was saying some shit I needed to know—like he had answers to deep questions—and I felt a different kind of connection.

After that my relationship with hip-hop changed. Listening to Rakim, I cared more. He sounded so strong, and he made me want to learn about what he knew. Hip-hop wasn't just fun music anymore. It felt to me like it mattered.

# CHAPTER TWO

# HI, IT'S ANGIE MARTINEZ

The first person to open a door for me was my mother, who was able to get me an internship at Power 96 in Miami, where she was settling in as music director. The station played mostly freestyle and dance music; it was an eye-opening experience of things I could learn, things I could do. *How does this all work*? I was open and eager to find out.

While I was getting my act together and finishing up high school, my first job at the station was doing research, cold-calling people at home and quickly introducing myself. "Hi. My name is Angie Martinez, and I'm calling from Power 96 . . ." before getting to the question, "Can I ask you what kind of music you listen to?" And if they happened to listen to the type of music that Power played, or something close to it, I would do a music survey and play them little clips of songs off of a recorder. They'd tell me if they liked it, didn't like it, or were tired of it. That was good old-fashioned music research.

Besides the cold-calling, I would listen to music on the adult urban contemporary station and handwrite a log of the different songs. I'd sit and listen for hours to tapes of recorded music from the station, and as I wrote down the title of the song and the artist on the log, I'd expand my knowledge of music outside of hip-hop. In the late eighties there were groups like Cameo and Surface in this category of adult black radio. It was interesting to learn how music reached different audiences. All of that was new to me.

My job responsibilities also included answering the phones and helping the deejays with whatever they needed. How cool was that? Like hitting the big time. Of course, looking back I can see that the station was a small operation—very *WKRP in Cincinnati*. We were housed in a short-story office building with a drive-through KFC next door. We had one control room and downstairs they had two tiny Power 96 vans. And just like on the TV show, the jocks were all larger-than-life, over-the-top characters with names like "Tony the Tiger" and "Bo the Party Animal."

The first time I met the late Bo Griffin, I was starstruck. A big, beautiful super-chocolate brown-skinned woman with an even bigger personality, she dressed to the hilt every day, wearing super-tight leopard-print dresses, lots of jewelry, red lipstick, and always some sort of fur, all in keeping with her party-animal image. As a popular on-air jock, Bo was something of a celebrity, and she drove a white Porsche around town. When she walked into a place, it was like, "Oh, there's Bo!" I was slightly infatuated with her.

Bo Griffin wasn't my mentor per se, but by watching her, I learned a lot about leadership and team-building. She used her presence in a way that brought you in as she looked you in the eye when she spoke to you and called you by name. It wasn't like, "Hey you, intern girl, go do this," but rather, "Good morning, Angie! Would you do me a favor?" As the center of attention in any room, she had that rare ability to make every-body feel important—which is how she definitely made me feel.

In fact, I don't know how it happened, but one day I looked up and Bo was standing there, holding the keys to her white Porsche, and she proceeded to ask me to go get it and pull it up to the station for her. I almost passed out.

*Me? Drive your car for you?!?!?!*

Seventeen years old, driving Bo the Party Animal's white Porsche, for those two blocks with the window rolled down, you couldn't tell me shit! The fact that she trusted me enough to do this "favor" for her—that was crazy to me. And then there was that first taste of the good life and that flash of seeing myself one day behind the wheel of my own dream car. Yeah, I might have stretched out those two blocks to six, hoping someone I knew would see me. After that first time, Bo would ask me to go get the car for her on a regular basis. She may not have intended to plant seeds of possibilities in my imagination, but that's what happened.

And thanks to the internship at Power 96, I got to know Miami better—which, contrary to my first assumption, had a hot music scene that included hip-hop. It turned out that Margarita—one of my cowork-ers who was around the same age as me and answered the phones at the front desk—had the same love for hip-hop that I did. She was a Miami native whose family was Colombian. Together we found out there were a couple of underground hip-hop clubs on the beach as well as a hip-hop night at Cameo, a well-known club. We went religiously. We'd go in sneakers and dance all night! And I don't mean like two-step dancing; I mean like we watched Big Daddy Kane videos all week and couldn't wait to get to the club to run through all of the moves we saw his danc-ers Scoob and Scrap do!

Man, I still remember the day we heard A Tribe Called Quest for the first time. "I Left My Wallet in El Segundo" was our shiiiit! Sonically, it was nothing like anything I'd ever heard before—even if I wasn't sure what the lyrics were about: *I left my wallet in El Segundo / I gotta get, I got-got ta get it* . . . But it didn't matter because it was just infectious. I played it over and over on repeat. And I for sure noticed Q-Tip while reading about Tribe in *The Source*! He was *cute*. Strong, broad-shouldered, cool. And his voice was *ill*. I was a fan.

That was an exciting time in hip-hop . . . the Black Medallion, Native Tongues movement was *everything*. It was just a creative, fertile period with De La Soul, Jungle Brothers, Tribe, the whole thing. And it was all happening in New York. We still heard it in Miami, but we were getting stuff later, and I spent a lot of time wondering what I was missing back in New York. I missed home!

Then came BIG NEWS. After work one day my mother announced, "Well, I was offered a program director position at CD 101.9." CD was a jazz station in New York and this was a great opportunity for her. But still she had to ask, "How do you feel about moving back to New York?"

How did I feel? "Yes! Please, for the love of God, take me back!" I was so ready.

She made me a deal that she would try to help find me another internship at a radio station because she saw how much I loved it, but that I would have to go to school and get a job, too.

"Okay, okay, okay!" I agreed. My wish had come true. I couldn't wait to get back to my city.

• • •

It had been only ten years earlier that I'd first heard "Rapper's Delight" at my aunts' uptown house party. But here I was, age eighteen, seeing how much had changed and how quickly hip-hop was moving from house parties and the streets into the clubs and the nighttime social scene.

I'd barely had time to go check it all out when my mom finds out that Hot 97, a freestyle dance station at the time, is looking for interns.

"The program director's name is Joel Salkowitz," she says. "See if you can apply."

Compared to Power 96 in Miami, the station—then on Thirty-Eighth Street in the Garment District—was a big step up. Nothing fancy. But when I went in to apply for the internship, I got really excited as I looked around at the New York version of a radio station.

Joel Salkowitz—a white guy with thick glasses, dark hair, beard, and mustache, which he tugged at a lot—glanced down at my application, asked me a couple of questions, and then said I could start working a few days a week and then we'd see how it went. Just like that I got the job!

I started at the bottom. I did everything, whatever they needed me to do—running to get coffee, office work, errands, and the same kind of market research as before, only this was New York, so cold-calling people at home and asking them to name their favorite songs, I'd get hung up on all the time. But I did it. Whatever anyone asked, I was *on* it. Pretty soon everyone knew if they needed something, they could ask me. "We'll get Angie to get it. She'll do it." I was that kid at the station.

Looking back, it's strange that I still wasn't sure what I wanted my future to be. But then again, at eighteen years old, neither did any of my friends. I did like being in that environment. I liked the idea of radio and the fact that everything was live and it was happening now. You could come up with an idea and execute it the same day, just get on the radio and do it. All that energy was exciting to be around.

Before long I'd found my way into every department as I tried to learn as much as I could about all the moving pieces that made a radio station go. Then I wound up getting hired part-time to work on their street team. It was not glamorous. For something like three dollars an hour, I'd drive the van, hang up posters at events like sales appearances and whatever other outside errands needed to be done. Every day I would come to work looking like a member of TLC. My uniform of choice was oversized tees and baggy pants and kicks. Nobody else at the station dressed like that. That was just me . . . I was a hip-hop kid working at a dance station.

. . .

The lessons of hard work were starting to pay off. But I had a lot more to learn about time management and setting priorities. I had kept my agreement with my mother that if she helped me get an internship, I'd go to college. But after enrolling in a full load of classes at Borough of Manhattan Community College, I was failing. Between school and the radio station, I clearly cared more about my job than about my classes. For a while I did enough to avoid getting kicked out of community college. And then my mother started paying less attention, so I started dropping classes. And eventually I stopped going altogether. There was no way I could keep taking on more and more at the station while trying to pretend I was going to college.

I was doing too damn much. If I would see my younger self right now, my advice would be: "You need to sit your ass down for five minutes. Focus. Set some goals."

Did I have any goals that I was working so hard to achieve? Not really. Maybe I had an instinct that I was somehow going to run into my goal and find what it was that I was supposed to do. But for the time being my attitude was just that I was happy to be there and I was eager to do whatever was asked of me so that I could learn everything. My motivation came in the form of wanting to go above and beyond because, why not? I had all of that young, dumb energy to give. Never underestimate the value of that passion.

Too often I see interns starting at entry level, trying to move up from there with minimal enthusiasm. I have to wonder—where's your fucking energy? You may not know what you want to do, but so many opportunities are in front of you that you can't waste a moment. You will not be young forever. So when you are, when you don't have big responsibilities yet, and you have an opportunity, you should do it till your knuckles bleed. You should keep going hard until somebody peels you up off the floor and is like, "Go take a nap." Why wouldn't you?

While I was in that zone of hyper-energy—working in the office, getting coffee, being on the street team, driving vans—I had to drive one of the radio personalities, Deborah Rath, all the way to Great Adventure for an event she was hosting. Tall and thin and blond, Deborah was known for playing dance music and did lots of events like this. The drill was that after driving her in the Hot 97 van more than sixty miles to Great Adventure, I was supposed to drive back to Manhattan and then down to some dead-end, rat-infested parking lot in Midtown. When I parked there, I would stomp my feet so the rats wouldn't come running my way.

As usual on that particular day, after driving back from Great Adventure, I was supposed to park the van in that nasty lot. Well, I had been going nonstop, from school to work and back to work again. I was on no sleep. And the next morning I was supposed to pick up the van and show up at another event. So instead of putting the van in the lot for a few hours, I thought, *I'll keep it, go home, and get a bit of sleep.* It was against the rules for a street team member to do that, but I was exhausted. It was the only thing that made sense. I had to.

At that point I lived on the Upper West Side with my mom. I was still living at home, not even a full adult yet. What a relief when I drive the van home, go inside, and go to sleep. *Ah . . .* But as soon as I wake up and go outside to get going, what a shock: There's an ominous piece of paper on the windshield of the van!

*Holy shit, I got a ticket.*

Obviously, when the station received notice of the parking ticket, they'd know that I'd kept the van. But for some dumb-ass reason, I just didn't tell them, and I waited until they got the ticket in the mail. Maybe I was hoping it would never come.

Cut to a few weeks later:

"Angie, did you take the van home? You know that's against the rules." I'm standing in the marketing director's office and he's giving a speech that's going on and on. *Blah, blah, blah.* Then he says, "You know we have fired people for that."

*Shiiiit!* Two thoughts cross my mind. Number one—*I don't want to get fired.* But number two, *I understand what he's saying and I know this is the rule, but let's just talk about common sense here.* I wasn't confident enough to verbalize it at that time, but from common sense I knew that what I did wasn't wrong. Well, *I* knew that. But even so, I was written up and sent home.

It felt like the end of the world.

A few days later I was back at the station for a meeting with the general manager, Judy Ellis, where it would be determined whether or not I was going to get fired. Judy was this little five-foot dynamo. She was tiny, yes, but she could be in a room full of six-foot men and dominate. She demanded your attention, your respect. She was fierce. She was smart. She was a big part of what Hot 97 would become.

At the meeting, I'm sitting there in front of the powers that be—the marketing director, the promotions director, and the general manager. They're going back and forth about how this is not acceptable; it's against the rules; we've fired other people for this; what are we supposed to do; we're gonna have to let her go.

I'm just sitting there as they talk among each other for what felt like ten, fifteen minutes. And as they continue to talk about me like I'm not even there, I start to get irritated.

"Can I say something?" I finally interrupt.

"Yeah, sure, go ahead," Judy said.

"First of all, I've been working here now a pretty long time and I do whatever anybody asks at any time, and I don't want any credit for that. But I do think that the least I deserve is that if something goes wrong, somebody would ask me what happened." I paused, took a breath, and then continued. "I think I've earned enough respect for you to ask me. You're talking about what I did. You're talking about me. Nobody has said to me, 'Hey, how come you took the van home?' Nobody's asked me. You guys are all talking, everybody's writing notes and making decisions, and not once has anybody asked me, 'Why did you take the van home?'"

*Oh shit . . . did I just raise my voice a little right there?*

They were all quiet for a second, and then Judy offers, "Okay, tell me what happened."

"Well, I had two events that I did back-to-back. Then I took Deborah to Great Adventure. By the time we came back, I only had a four-hour turnaround before I had to do another event," I explained. "I didn't want to be late for it. And I didn't want to show up to a sales event half asleep. My thinking was I could just take a quick nap. And I know it was against the rules, but I just tried to make the best decision I could in that moment."

"All right, give us a minute. We'll talk to you later, okay?" Judy said. Her face remained stern as she and the others stayed put and I left her office.

Later, Judy called me back in. It was just the two of us. "First of all," she said, "don't take the van home."

"Okay."

"I'm not gonna fire you."

My face must have regained its color. But was there something else? Judy smiled and went on. "Second of all, can I just say something?"

"What?"

"Can I just say how proud I am of you? You were absolutely right. Not only did we assume that you were just out with the van and did whatever you wanted, but we never asked you your side of the story."

Judy had just acknowledged me for doing something that turned out to be a pivotal moment for me—when I first saw the importance of finding my voice and using it to stand up for myself. Getting that ticket could have been the end of my career right there. I could have been fired and then I would have been asking myself—*What's next? Okay, let me go work at the sneaker store or something.* Instead I learned the big lesson that sometimes situations will come up when you will have to fight for yourself—even if you're humble and happy to be there—when you have to rise up and speak on your own behalf. Otherwise you'll be finished before you even start.

That was not the last time in my career when it could have been all over before it started. But, without a doubt, Judy Ellis was a champion who saw something in me, I guess. In fact, not only did Judy decide not to fire me, but shortly after that she also went on to hire me to be her assistant. Later she told me I was actually a shitty assistant—even though she didn't let on at the time. Nor was she overly critical whenever I gave her the tapes I'd record of me doing air checks. Some of the people around the office had been encouraging me to give it a shot.

"Hi, it's Angie Martinez, on your Hot 97." They were terrible. But she was always kind about it and would listen.

"You know, they're not that bad," Judy said every time. "You're really not that bad." Even just "Not that bad" was encouraging. Especially since

I had given my tapes to both the program and music director at the time and their reaction or lack thereof was not so encouraging. So for Judy to say, "You're not that bad"—to me that was encouraging.

Judy was the first person to believe that I could be on the air. She was supersmart, so when she believed I could, I started to believe I could.

So my next step would be to learn to run the boards. Board operators were always in demand because the pay was low but the job required training to run them. Yet I knew by now that running the boards was going to be my way inside the studio, so I asked some of the board ops if they would start teaching me. I had done only one or two sessions when my program director, Joel, came up to me one day and stood there, tugging on his mustache, and then explained, "Hey, I need someone to run the public service show on Sunday at four a.m. Are you cleared? Are you ready to run a board?"

"Yes!" I blurted out. I was not.

Like, not even close. I'd done two training sessions at the most. But I was so excited to have the opportunity that I jumped out the window with a bald-faced lie. "Yes, Joel. I'm ready! I can do it."

Running the board involved knowing how to start the reel, stop it at a certain time, and play the commercials. I had done those couple of training sessions, but I was all over the place. Seriously, I had no idea what the hell I was doing, but this opportunity was too important to let that stop me.

I showed up that Sunday morning at four a.m. as Curtis Elder was getting off his shift. In his glasses and comfortable sweaters, Curtis always reminded me of a wise, older soul. A seasoned board op, he had been there since ten p.m. the previous night but was nice enough to help me set up for my shift. I'm sure it didn't take more than a minute for him to see that I had no clue what I was doing.

As I took everything in, I was overwhelmed. The boards with all those buttons and switches—everything looked so big and complicated, like I was about to operate an airplane.

*Holy shit, I'm totally going to fuck this up.*

Curtis could clearly tell that I was nervous, that I wasn't ready. He calmly asked, "Well, do you know how to link up the reel?"

"Kind of." So, without confessing that I'm clueless, I'm trying to set up the reel-to-reel machine, inserting two reels of tape onto spindles cued up at just the right spots. It's falling off the thing, and the tape is not latching on properly. Nothing is happening right.

Curtis felt so bad for me that he wound up staying with me the whole shift. He walked me through the entire show and gave me a crash course in how to run a board properly. By the next time I came on to run the boards, I was more comfortable. And from then I started doing it all the time.

But that first night, literally, we could have had dead air for four hours. The public service show wouldn't have aired. And they would have never given me a chance to do that again. Man, people like Curtis are rare! He didn't get paid for those hours, and he never ratted me out. That type of kindness will get me watery eyed every time. He saved me that night. Once again it could have been over before it began.

. . .

By the early 1990s, when I was nineteen or twenty years old, at the same time that I was starting to think maybe I'd found my direction in radio, Hot 97 had started to question its musical direction. The question was answered when the station brought in a new program director, Steve Smith, and everyone at the top had this epiphany that New York was the market, if anywhere, where a full-time hip-hop radio station could thrive. I don't know what led them to that, or at what business meeting it was said that we could build the radio station around hip-hop.

Steve Smith—a tall white guy with a big head of curly blond hair—was not what you'd expect as the person to lead that charge. But who was? The concept didn't even exist, as far as I knew. So when the whisperings of it started, the thought of it was like a lightning strike.

*Wait! What?! How amazing would that be? A radio station that played hip-hop all day!!!!?*

We had never heard of such a thing. Anywhere. Hip-hop was strictly for weekends, and if you did hear it during the week, it was for sure after ten p.m.

But sure enough, pretty quickly they started bringing in some possible deejays to interview. There were a few I knew from MTV and other places, but no one seemed official. Just before Steve started, in the spring of 1992, they brought in Funkmaster Flex, who was already a name in a couple of clubs where I liked to go. Club 2000 was popping at the time and he was killing it there. With his dark skin and great smile, Flex had charisma and was the real deal. So when he came into the station for a meeting and brought his hip-hop credentials with him, I started to believe.

*Wow! They might be serious here.*

The first thing I remember thinking about Flex was, "He's good. He's a real hip-hop deejay!" And when they announced that they were hiring him, I knew this was starting to get real. This was the first step in creating the first ever hip-hop station, and I couldn't believe how lucky I was to be in the middle of it all.

Though by no means did it happen overnight, slowly but surely it became apparent that the decision to bring Flex to Hot 97 had been the right move at the right time. People were tuning in. People were talking about Hot and believing that Steve Smith was onto something. But there was also tremendous pushback. While Steve battled for a transition into full-time hip-hop, there were still major remnants of what Hot once was . . . and people fighting to keep it what it once was. Many who had been at the station for longer periods were wholeheartedly against the transition.

Freddie Colon, a heavyset Nuyorican who'd been in radio for years and was a nighttime on-air personality at the time, made no apologies for saying, "This is the worst thing this company has ever done. Hip-hop is a fad. And they're going to brand their radio station next to it?! What happens when the fad is over?" I was young and I respected him so much as a jock. So although I knew his perspective on this was wrong, I kept my opinion to myself. And what I have learned over the years is that this type of change—*unprecedented change*—is always accompanied by doubt.

Freddie's feelings were mirrored by much of the regime in those days. And I got it. They had put time and sweat into the dance station that Hot 97 was. I'm sure it was hard to let it go, especially knowing that it would mean they would eventually have to say goodbye.

Hip-hop wasn't an easy bet. That's part of what makes it real. So even as we started to see that it was more than a fad and Flex was proving that now that he was on the air regularly, there was still an atmosphere of not knowing what was going to happen next. As I'd gotten pretty good at running the boards and had been assigned to Flex's show, I lived that history. And there I was every night—standing next to Flex— running the boards, *excited* as shit! There was one show I'll never forget, when Flex played "Top Billin'"—*I am from Bed, Do-or-Die / The Audio Two, The two's Audio / I got a brother and his name's Gizmo . . .* You would've thought I was getting a royalty check. It was like we had arrived at a kind of Promised Land and I couldn't keep myself from jumping around the studio, singing every single word! *Milk is chillin', Giz is chillin' / What more can I say? Top billin' . . .*

You have to understand that before this the programming had been freestyle and dance music all day and night on Hot 97. Up until Flex started to move the needle, we had zero hip-hop credibility. If you wanted hip-hop, it was public service radio or WBLS and KISS FM on Friday and Saturday nights. But here we were, changing the game. Not only was I feeling it, but so were a lot of hip-hop fans. And the competition started to notice.

KISS FM reacted by adding a few hip-hop songs to their playlist (*only* the bigger hits and *only* at nighttime), and they were still playing scared. For every one hip-hop song they would add, we added five. This was happening and it was happening fast. And Flex was our leader! Even so, he was a far cry from the Flex that fans would come to know. Surprising though it may be—given how legendary a "Flex rant" would later become—in those early days at Hot, he hated talking on the mic!

Talk on-air? Nope! He just wanted to play records. Steve Smith had to force Flex to talk. I'd hear Steve make the point to Flex all the time: "You have to talk to the listeners. They need to know who you are." In fact, Steve put Flex on a *You must talk at these times* schedule.

Flex *hated* that. He was so weirded out and nervous about it that he would just open the mic and talk to whoever was in the room with him. And lucky me, running his boards, standing there every night . . . it became the norm to get thrown a "What's poppin', Ang?" or a "Right, Ang??" Flex would just start talking to me, and that's how I first started to get comfortable on the air and to feel confident just being myself. This phase didn't last long for Flex, because once he started getting a taste for talking on-air and seeing the reaction he would get in the streets, he got comfortable on the mic—quick!

There were no two ways about it. Flex was on fire! He had the Tunnel rockin' every Sunday night. It was the Mecca of hip-hop clubs, the go-to spot for fans, artists, hip-hop label execs, drug dealers, aspiring artists—everyone wanted to be at the Tunnel! And it was Flex's. By design. He was a student of the game, so he understood the business. He understood how to market himself and he was aggressive about it.

He made the whole team these Nuthin But Flavor Funkmaster Flex black leather jackets with his logo all over them, and we wore them everywhere proudly.

Hip-hop was now exploding in New York. Loud Records had come up with the street team and had the streets plastered with signs; Bad Boy was forming and Puff was flooding the streets with his Windbreaker Bad Boy jackets and the B.I.G. Mack cassettes with Craig Mack's "Flava in Ya Ear" on one side and The Notorious B.I.G.'s "Unbelievable" on the other.

Flex was on the air from ten p.m. to two a.m. At almost twenty-three years old, I lived at the station. I was there almost every night. Salaam Remi, a gifted up-and-coming producer—who would later produce everyone from The Fugees to Amy Winehouse—was there all the time, too. Salaam wore many hats at that point: He helped Flex with his records and monitored the other stations. Flex used to call Salaam "The Overseer." Whenever Flex was mixing, Salaam and I would sit in the studio all night, doing what we had to do while cracking jokes and talking hip-hop. We quickly became friends. We had a similar sense of humor and sometimes entertained ourselves with pranks and other dumb shit.

There were a couple of nights when, as usual, people were calling in to the request line with the standard, "Hi. I'm Jane from Brooklyn!" "I'm Tito from the Bronx." "This is Oscar representing Harlem!" As they waited to get on the air, instead of putting them through, we'd click all the lines at the same time and create a listener party line without them even knowing. They would all think they were calling Hot 97 and say, "Hello?" "Hello?"

"I'm calling Hot 97 . . ."

"Me too . . ."

"What do you mean, me too? I'm calling you."

"Nah, son, I'm calling you."

They'd wind up arguing or hitting on each other or sometimes just talking shit, but it was always hilarious. Salaam and I would just sit there and crack up. Yep, it was dumb, but we did have fun.

One night when I was working in the back office before running the boards for Flex, someone mentioned that A Tribe Called Quest was coming up to the station. "Oh, I love them," I said. "I love Q-Tip!" I wasn't trying to fan out or anything, but I was excited that they were coming and I made sure that when they made their rounds at the office, I got a quick pic. I remember them being so cool and regular and everything I'd hope they would be.

After Tribe made the rounds and took about a hundred flicks, they made their way to the on-air studio to interview with Bugsy, who was on the air before Flex. DJ Fred Buggs was a radio pro and had been in the game for years at New York's WBLS, which was an adult urban station. He was a strong interviewer and, of course, I had to tune in. I was still working with the street team at the time, so I was in the station's prize closet packing up tees while I listened on a little portable radio. They talked about the new music they were working on and plans for the group; the interview was good and pretty standard. That is, until all of a sudden, out of nowhere, Bugsy says to Q-Tip—on the air!!!—"You know that girl Angie in the back? I think she has a crush on you."

*Oh MY GOD!!!! Whaaat? Whyyyyyyyy would he do that?! Come on, Buggggs!*

I knew he meant no harm and was just trying to be funny on the radio, but I was absolutely mortified!

First of all, it was embarrassing. I wanted to crawl under a desk somewhere and die, and I most certainly did not want to go anywhere near the studio.

Then I heard Tip, in his very Tip voice, say on-air, "Wait, who is that? The girl with the long brown hair, right?" I froze.

*Wait—he knows who I am? Wait—no! Not the point. Again, the point is—why would Bugsy do that?!*

Now I would have to hide every time Q-Tip came to the station. The moment the interview ended and I was certain that the group was long out of the building, I ran into the studio and begged Bugsy to never, ever, *ever* do that again. He laughed and agreed. And that was that, at least for the moment, as far as Tip and Tribe were concerned.

. . .

After four or five years at Hot 97, I was happy being behind the scenes and running the boards. Every now and then I'd get to talk to Flex on the air and a few times they even let me do a whole shift—Sundays at four a.m., or if they had a scheduling emergency, here and there at other times. Terrible little time slots, but I was happy *whenever* they'd let me be on-air. I still worked in the office as well, doing whatever anyone needed done.

And that's where I was, in the office one evening around six p.m., after business hours were over and most of the staff had gone home, when IT happened—that is, when Steve Smith stuck his head out of his office and gestured for me to come see him.

At first this was no big deal. But I immediately knew something was going on when I saw Judy Ellis sitting there, too.

So after I ask what it is, they both stare at me for a moment, and then Steve says, "Okay, well, this is happening—we are going full-steam hip-hop. And if you're ever going to really learn how to be on the air, you need to be on every day. Judy thinks you could be good, and I think you could be good. But the only way we're going to know for sure is if we put you on regularly. So we want to offer you the overnight slot."

Shock. Confusion. Disbelief. *MY OWN SHIFT?!* I almost passed out dead on the floor right then. This was just unbelievable!

All I could say was "YES!" Then, catching my breath, I had to ask, "Can I still work with Flex??"

Judy and Steve looked at each other and then at me. "Yes," they said in unison.

This was amazing!

# CHAPTER THREE

# OH MY GOD

There is truly no such thing as overnight success. Over the years I would see that again and again with icons I interviewed who once seemed to come from nowhere yet suddenly made it to the top. Every single one has a story of struggle and crazy hard work that came before. And most have a story about a time when an opportunity was given to them and they had to prove themselves.

That's not exactly how I saw it in those early months of doing overnights at the station. But still, it was wild to be twenty-three years old and getting my own show—even if it was at a time when most people were asleep! My schedule was to first run Flex's boards from ten p.m. to two a.m. and then do my own show from two a.m. to six a.m. every day. In hindsight, I realize how insane that was because Flex would leave at two a.m. and it was just me there. Every now and then Salaam would stay late to keep me company, but for the most part, overnights were just me alone—in a dark, empty station, in that dark, empty building on

Thirty-Eighth Street in the Garment District, where even the neighborhood was dark and empty.

To keep myself from getting too creeped out, I would stay busy by talking to my listeners all night on the request lines, and on Thursdays I'd also keep a separate radio on in the studio so I could listen to *The Stretch Armstrong and Bobbito Show* on WKCR 89.9—the public radio station housed at Columbia University. It was one of the few authentic hip-hop shows in the market and they always sounded like they were having a good time. So having it on in the background made me feel like there were people in the room hanging out with me—or at least a little less alone. Unfortunately, Stretch and Bobbito were only on once a week. Plus, the request lines would get light once three or four a.m. rolled around. So during the segments of programmed music, the challenge was to keep myself from falling asleep, especially between the witching hours of four and six a.m. Every now and then I flat-out failed and would wake up in a full panic to dead air! Maybe it was more than a few times. Fortunately, I never got caught.

As I learned in those first months of being on the air and adjusting to the schedule, overnights were a different way of life. You sleep when everyone else is up; and when you're up, everyone else is sleeping. This is not a small thing. To this day, when I go through a toll late at night, I look at the person in the booth and feel a certain compassion for them. That life can be dark (literally) and sometimes lonely.

Then again, I tried to take it in stride and enjoy the fruits of my labor—like the fact that I had finally moved out of my mother's apartment and was now living on my own for the first time. My mother never minded me staying with her, of course. But as I was so independent in other ways, this was the next obvious step in my growth, to go along with the fact that I was moving up in the world at my job.

By moving up in the world, I mean that all I could afford was a dumpy little apartment in Astoria, Queens. It was right next to the train station, and I could hear the trains running past my window all day and night. On an up note, I had easy access to and from work. That's all that really mattered, and the twenty-four-hour McDonald's right across the street came in handy on those late nights and early mornings.

On one of those early mornings, in the middle of my show I got a call on the station's hotline. *Yes!* At four thirty a.m., the hotline ringing meant it was at least someone I knew. Someone else was actually awake and calling!

So I answered. "Hello?"

"Hey, is this Angie?"

The voice sounded familiar, but I couldn't really place it. "Yeah, who's this?"

"It's Tip."

"Who???"

"It's me, Q-Tip. Is this Angie?"

Flashing back to what Bugsy had done on the air when Tip was at the station last, I was mortified all over again. In an effort to play it cool, all I could think to say was, "Yeah. Who you calling for?" Maybe I had overshot.

Tip only laughed. "I'm calling for you. Who the hell else is up there at this time of night?"

I laughed and immediately lightened up. Tip told me that Tribe was doing all these promo shows and he was always up late so he would often catch me on the air on his way home. From there our conversation was effortless.

I can't really explain how this happens, but there are certain people I've met in my life that, from the moment when we first meet, I immediately feel connected to them. It doesn't happen often. But when it does, I pay attention. The connection doesn't have to be a romantic one. In fact, it usually is not. I felt it when I met Shawn "Pecas" Costner—who later became my manager and one of my closest friends. Twenty years later we are godparents to each other's children. I've felt that immediate connection when first meeting a few of my close girlfriends, and I felt it that night talking on the phone with Tip. It's that type of familiarity that you can't really attribute to anything but connection.

A Tribe Called Quest was touring at the time, in the wake of their *Midnight Marauders* album—which had included the single "Oh My God" that I loved. While the tour was ongoing, in those times after the show or the after-party, I'd often get an in-studio call in the middle of the night. Tip and I began to talk pretty regularly about music, family, TV shows, just regular shit. What was weird was that as much as I had been a fan for years, our conversations felt comfortable.

I liked him, but I tried not to make too much of the attention, like— *Oh, he only calls 'cause he knows I'm sitting in this studio till six a.m. He's probably just bored and no one else is up.*

But I was wrong. In fact, when Tip eventually came back to town, we went on our first "date." He picked me up from work. I was in sneakers and sweats and didn't even mind because he made me feel comfortable just being me. We ate Chinese and then shopped for vinyl at a downtown record store. He put me on to a lot of new music. When I got home, I had to ask myself—*Was this even a date?* It wasn't exactly romantic, but we did have fun.

· · ·

Hot 97 was redefining its mission and transitioning from dance to a twenty-four-hour hip-hop station, and they needed someone who fully represented the culture. I was on overnights for just about a year when they started trying me in different time slots. I did some weekend shifts and even did a midday slot for a month or so. And then, when the opportunity opened up—holy shit, I got it! I was the new nighttime jock!

That's when I felt the difference. The six-to-ten-p.m. slot was prime time. This was a big deal. Everyone was so happy for me and offered to help in any way. The only downside was I would no longer be able to work with Flex because, as Steve explained, I'd need to give my full attention to this new opportunity—and that I did!

I immediately started brainstorming what the show would sound like. To give it something different, I wanted to come up with a feature where I could play new music. I had an idea for a segment where I would play two new songs and then listeners could call in to vote on which song was better. Salaam and I stayed on the phone all night trying to come up with a name for it, tossing around a bunch of stupid ones, until finally we hit on "Battle of the Beats."

It felt right.

Salaam offered, "Yo, I'm gonna do a promo for you. I got an idea."

The timing was ideal. He had just worked with the Fugees on the "Nappy Heads" remix, so he had a sense before the rest of the world of how dope Lauryn Hill was. He asked her to sing the intro for me. Lauryn was on the come up and was happy to get on anything she could at the time, so she sang, *"It's the baaattle of the beats,"* and she killed it! I could not *wait* to play it on the air!

Battle of the Beats took off. We broke so many new records on the air, the word of mouth was over-the-top—all in the days before social media. There was nothing more interactive than radio at the time, where you could call up and hear something happen live and experience it all together. Radio was the 1995 version of Twitter. Listeners were engaged and passionate about it. And so was the station.

Hot 97 also became one of the few places to find hip-hop artists. There were *The Source* and *Vibe* magazines, and you could catch *Yo! MTV Raps* once a week. But for people who wanted it all day, every day—it was Hot 97. And as hip-hop culture and its audience grew, so did our ratings. We turned around to see that Hot 97 had become New York's number one station in the ratings.

This was all happening at a time when hip-hop was not only flourishing but when the music industry at large was exploding. Everybody— major labels and homegrown independent labels alike—started to add to or expand their hip-hop rosters.

Battle of the Beats gave a nightly platform to new voices and new work from the more established artists. Needless to say, promoters hoping to break their latest records started to seek me out more and more, hoping to get their releases in a battle. One night that I'll never forget was when I put on the first single release from a little-known Brooklyn rapper by the name of Jay Z. The song was "In My Lifetime." It eclipsed whatever the other record was that it was up against. I was floored by how many calls this virtually unknown artist got.

This was rare because part of the reason more established artists often won the battles was because once you've already adopted an artist, their next release sounds familiar and you feel it even more. Not so in this battle. We were looking at numbers we'd never seen from an unknown. *Who the fuck is Jay Z?*

The answer came a couple of weeks later when Jay Z and Damon Dash—Jay's manager and business partner on their newly formed Roc-A-Fella label—showed up at the station to thank me in person for playing the record. They pulled up in front of the building in a white buggy-eyed Benz that had their Roc-A-Fella logo on the hood.

*What in the hell is that?*

Nowadays in New York, it's pretty common to see trucks and vans plastered with artists' logos all over town. But at the time it wasn't the norm and this was the first time I'd ever seen it done on a Mercedes-Benz.

When I went to meet them, Dame handed me a bottle of champagne and asked if I wanted to see Jay's video.

"Fuck it, yeah! Let's see it . . ."

Dame Dash and Jay Z played the video on a screen rigged out of the back of the trunk as I watched from the street with my backpack in one hand and the bottle of Cristal in the other. I was impressed, not just by the music or the video. Their whole presentation was like nothing I'd ever seen. It was clear these guys were different.

It also became clear as time went on that Jay was genuinely interested in getting my feedback on his work. As his career started to take off and I'd have him on the show regularly, we clicked as friends. We soon developed a routine that whenever he finished up an album he would come by and play it for me. He'd come pick me up at the station, and I'd run down to the car and listen to the whole thing. He trusted my opinion. He knew that I was a hip-hop head, that I listened to the lyrics and cared. I think he appreciated that.

Jay also seemed to appreciate that I was honest. I'd tell him, "I don't love this." Or, "That is genius." Or, "I hate the third verse on this song." There are some artists who don't love hearing anything besides praise. But Jay seemed to value my opinion. And I was thrilled to give it, because from the start I saw Jay's greatness. I really did.

I was fortunate to be in New York, to watch artists like Jay and so many others who were coming into their own at the time. Almost every night I had somebody notable in the building as a guest. One night it was Wu-Tang, next it was Mobb Deep, and another show it was the Lost Boyz or Nas.

One of the ways record labels and producers would try to break out new artists at the time was to have them record promos for my show.

DJ Premier was working with a new artist Jeru the Damaja, so they recorded a really cool promo for my "Hot 5 at 9" countdown feature, with an original beat by Premier. It was really good! One night when Biggie was driving around listening to my show, he heard the promo and fell in love with the beat. He immediately called Premier to find out what it was. Premier explained that Jeru recorded it specifically for my show and he would have to ask me if I was okay with him using it. I got a call from Premier, and he asked my permission. Technically, he didn't need to, but I guess it was a sign of respect. As much as I appreciated the gesture, I said, "Are you crazy? Of course, give it to B.I.G." So Biggie took the beat and made "Ten Crack Commandments." To this day, it makes me happy to hear that song and feel extra connected to it.

The show just seemed to take on a life of its own. There was no competition in town. There were no expectations. So there were no rules about how long you could talk or what format to follow. We were just freestyling. A guest would come and I'd do whatever I wanted—we'd talk for twenty minutes or play cuts if we felt like it. We learned and set the rules as we went. Nothing was calculated. Nobody had ever trained me how to conduct interviews. I didn't have a clue about interviewing dos and don'ts. I just loved the music and had genuine interest in the artists. And it happened to work. Ratings were through the roof.

My show became the place for anyone in hip-hop to stop by and chill and talk shit. Black Moon, Queen Latifah, Redman, Puffy with a young Mary J. Blige, Craig Mack, Keith Murray. If you were a rapper and you had a song out, you stopped by the show. For hip-hop fans, it was the first time you could hear your favorite artists on the radio and learn about them and hear what they sounded like, as themselves, in conversation. There were really no mainstream outlets for that. The artists liked hanging out here and we encouraged it. Artists like Biggie would come up all the time, maybe bring up some food, chill out, smoke Newports, and then we'd go to a club after the interview. This was not uncommon.

"Where Hip Hop Lives," was the motto that Steve Smith decided to claim for Hot 97. It *was* that. And we ran with it all the way.

. . .

After a period Q-Tip and I had gotten pretty close, but it didn't really seem to be going anywhere. Neither one of us had the time. My schedule was definitely keeping me busy. Since I got off the air at ten at night, that was when I'd go chill with Flex for a while when he went on the air or maybe go out to eat and then hit the clubs! On top of that routine, I started getting booked to host parties around the city. And getting paid for it. The first few times I thought it was a fluke. But no, the offers kept coming.

*Five hundred bucks to show up somewhere for fifteen minutes or a half hour? And I'm twenty-four years old? YES!* Sometimes this would happen multiple times in a night.

So I was going to parties where I liked being anyway, and making extra cash. Not bad. For all intents and purposes, I was living a charmed life, going out on the town nightly at a time when the New York club scene was poppin' like never before. As just a fan, it was crazy. You'd go up in the club and see all your favorite artists, live and in person. When you went to the Tunnel on a Sunday, you would see Busta Rhymes, Redman, Wu-Tang, everybody. And then the next day I'd get on the radio and talk about where I'd been and who'd been seen at the club the night before.

This was back in the day when if something happened in the club, people wouldn't know because it wasn't on Twitter. It wasn't on Instagram. There was no social media. Actually, we were the social media. We were *Where Hip Hop Lives.* So if you wanted to know what went down you'd have to wait to hear it on the radio the next day—who was there and what happened. And everyone wanted to know.

My career was on the rise, the station was killin' it, and not long after Tip and I slowed down, I started dating Girard, who was cute in a way that reminded me of my high school boyfriend Derek. He was brown-skinned, heavily into hip hop, clothes, and was always up on the new trends, which probably went along with his job in marketing at Loud Records. Between work and staying over a lot at G.'s apartment on East Twenty-First Street in Manhattan, I barely ever had time to go home to my shitty apartment in Astoria—which, unbeknownst to me, had become infested with mice.

*Yes—mice! Horrifying!*

Funny thing about that was one of my neighbors used to always mention the rodent problem in the building. All that time, because I'd never seen anything, I just thought she was crazy. How could I see anything if I was never there?

Those mice must have been chillin' in my apartment for months before I noticed. That is, until the day I walked in by myself and saw a big mouse run across the living room. Oh my God! I froze. I then proceeded to backward walk right the hell outta there. I called Nikki, who came right over and helped me lay down some glue traps. That night I stayed at Nikki's. When we went back the next day, not only did we catch that fucker, but we caught about fifteen of his friends, too.

*Oh, helllllll nooooooo!*

We were outta there!!! We grabbed my valuables and threw a bunch of my clothes in some Hefty bags and I never went back. It was time to step it up anyway. I was starting to make a little more money, my career was thriving, and it felt like I'd begun to carve a real niche for myself on radio.

· · ·

n January 1996 the station decided to go all out and throw me a twenty-fifth birthday party at the Palladium on East Fourteenth Street, one of the most iconic hip-hop clubs. Before heading out to the party, I had to take an extra-deep breath as I checked my white leather outfit one last time in the mirror.

All day long I had been stressed about the turnout. More than once I had said to Salaam, "I hope people come." A lot of artists were invited, and it was important that they showed. But the real question was whether our listeners would come out in the middle of winter to get into the club—especially after we made such a big deal promoting it.

Even today I never count on turnout for big events because in my mind everybody's got their own stuff to do. Whatever it is, I never think anybody's gonna come.

On my way to the Palladium, I get a call from Salaam. "Yo, fam," he says, "there is a line of fucking people wrapped around the block! And there are helicopters flying over!"

"Are you serious?"

"Yeah. It's crazy! This is the longest line at the Palladium I've ever seen!"

As soon as I get there, I see the line is all the way around the block, down Fourteenth Street, back to, like, Third Avenue. In winter! And up above there are helicopters circling outside!

Whenever I'd go to the Palladium there would be a line, sure, but this—*unbelievable*!

That was the night when Biggie thought it would be better not to get onstage because he and Faith weren't in the best place, and I understood why. But, man, if he had, the place would have gone bananas. Still, it was a night to remember.

G. was there, and wasn't all the way thrilled when Jay Z and Dame Dash gave me another bottle of Cristal, which we popped open right there on the side of the stage. I tried to include him in the moment, but by the look on his face, I could tell he was uncomfortable. This was a tension that I would become all too familiar with in this relationship and ones to come. But otherwise the night was spectacular. The celebration was less about me and more about a coming of age for the station; for me it was more about the love, my relationship with hip-hop, my relationship with the artists, and my relationship with the city. That night was the first time I felt they were all in a position to give it back to me, for me to see a real reflection of our connection.

It was overwhelming. My life was changing. That night was a definite turning point. I left feeling that my show was starting to really matter.

# CHAPTER FOUR

# CALIFORNIA LOVE

t was winter 1996 and the whole city was upside down. Tupac and Biggie had been going at it and Pac was always in the news, at the center of what people were now starting to call an East Coast–West Coast beef. The previous year, I'd been at the Source Awards at Madison Square Garden when Suge Knight went off on his infamous public rant against Puffy and Bad Boy Records. The reason Tupac wasn't at the Source Awards that night was that he was in jail after being sentenced for sexual abuse, just three months after he was shot five times at Quad Recording Studios. Suge had posted Tupac's bail of $1.4 million and Pac immediately signed with Death Row Records. While no one was held responsible for the shooting, Pac seemed to be holding Bad Boy responsible for the attempt on his life, fueling this beef. From there everything progressed quickly.

In December, my friend and coworker Monie Love, a pioneer for women in hip-hop, made a cameo in the Dogg Pound video "New York,

New York." In the video, Snoop Dogg and his West Coast crew were shown crushing buildings in New York City, Godzilla style. The video was shot in Brooklyn, Biggie's hometown. The Dogg Pound said the video was misunderstood, that it was intended to be a tribute to New York. But personally I questioned why they would choose to shoot something that could be taken the wrong way at such a sensitive time. And in fact, it was taken the wrong way. Gunshots were fired on the set. Nobody was injured or ever arrested. But the event heightened the East Coast–West Coast beef even further. Poor Monie. She only went there to support Snoop, but people gave her so much shit for it, calling her a traitor and questioning her allegiance. She's such a sweet girl, and I felt bad that she got so beaten up for it, but it was a hostile time. We were all so young and so invested and it seemed so real.

I didn't know what to make of it all, but I knew it felt dark and I knew it felt scary. So imagine how I felt when I got a call from a record exec at Interscope saying that Tupac wanted me to appear in his "I Ain't Mad at Cha" video. *Oh, hell no! I don't want to be any part of this.* I relayed that message to the record exec, who called again a couple days later and said, "I spoke to Pac and he wants to talk to you himself." So before I know it, the hotline is blinking and Tupac is on the other line.

I really had no idea what to expect. I didn't know if Pac was this bad guy people were making him out to be. I didn't know if he was trying to set me up. I had an image of this crazy, aggressive guy. He was a troublemaker. I had that notion of who he was in my mind, but I would do my best to suspend judgment.

I was surprised at how polite he sounded on the phone. *This is definitely not what I anticipated.* Not that I expected him to be screaming "Thug Life!" on the phone, but he was nice, humble even.

All I knew was that he was involved in this thing and now he was on the phone wanting to talk to me. *What do I say to this man in the middle of this war that's going on?* I'd never met Pac and I didn't know what to think . . . other than maybe he was someone to avoid.

"I can't be in your video," I explained, clarifying from the start of the conversation. "I can't show up to work tomorrow if I'm in your video. I've got to walk around in these streets. I can't stand next to that right now." And that's when Pac started explaining himself. He said that when he was in jail he felt like everybody, especially in New York, was shitting on him and making up stories. He explained that it wasn't a coastal thing; it was a media thing.

"You were one of the only people that reported what was happening without a negative spin on it. You didn't put any extra dirt on my name. I appreciated that," he said. "You know, this East Coast–West Coast thing is really not that. It's not a whole coast. How could I be mad at a whole coast?"

"Yeah, but nobody's heard you say that," I said. "It's the first I'm hearing it. Why don't you come up to the show and we'll do an interview?"

"I would love to, but I'm shooting this movie right now in LA. I can't leave. But if you want to come here, I'll send you a ticket for a flight," he offered. "Forget about the video; don't even worry about it. You're not comfortable. I understand. I'll send you a ticket. Come out here. We'll do the interview out here."

"Okay," I said.

"Aight, I'm going to have somebody call you to set it up."

I knew that I had to go. I just knew. With everybody going so crazy, it was getting bad. I honestly thought I could help. If I could get Pac on tape saying that the war was *not* between all of the East Coast versus all of the West Coast but rather between a specific group of rappers, that could be helpful. That could be the beginning of making peace.

Could I do that? I was twenty-five years old and had so much to learn. But I had to try. That's all I knew.

I was excited. I was nervous; I was all of that. Tupac was flying me to LA for what could be the most important interview in the entire country. This was hands down the biggest opportunity of my career.

After work I headed to my boyfriend G.'s apartment. I couldn't wait to tell him the news, but his reaction completely threw me off.

All he had to say was, "What're you going to go see that nigga for? You're gonna be out there with a bunch of dudes. How do you think that looks?"

There were no words to express how this type of mentality from men irritated me. How could I not feel resentful of that reaction? I'm not sure how I responded, but I know what I was thinking:

*That means all you do is see me as a girl going to hang out with a bunch of dudes. That's not how I see myself. I'm not some chick that's going to go running up there in, like, a tube top and short shorts, trying to fuck Tupac. That's not what this is. If that's what you think, you don't respect me, you don't respect what I'm trying to do, and you don't understand my intention, my goal. The fact that you would even jump to that is offensive to me.*

I may not have been able to articulate it that clearly, but I knew he had offended me. And I knew that it didn't matter. I was going.

Looking back, I have to say that G. wasn't a bad guy in all this. He was twenty-three at the time, young and way more image conscious than me. And because he was in the business—where guys often worry too much about what other guys might say about their girl—that was where his mind went. All shit that had nothing to do with me but, sorry to say, was something that I'd confront a lot.

Now, back at the station when I announced that Pac was going to fly me out to Los Angeles, there was another concern. Some of my colleagues were adamant, saying, "What? You can't go out there. It's not safe." After what happened at the Dogg Pound video, nobody was ignoring how dangerous the East Coast–West Coast issue had become. Then Ed Lover—a host of the *Morning Show with Ed* at Hot, who three years earlier had come over with Dr. Dre after they'd made a name for themselves on *Yo! MTV Raps*—had a suggestion about a friend of his from LA, Big Spesh. Ed advised, "You should take him with you because he knows LA. He knows what's safe."

We made a plan for Big Spesh—short for "specialist"—to fly out separately and be around to make sure I was okay.

I'd barely traveled and had never been to Los Angeles. I had no luggage, so I borrowed a suitcase from a friend. Having never had to pack for a trip like this, my solution was to throw my regular work clothes into the borrowed bag and be done with it. These days that would not work. Radio has changed so much from then to now, and media in general, especially for women. Now when I go places, especially with social media, there's always this pressure of how you look. Of course, I care about looking nice, but it's annoying to have to be overly concerned about hair, makeup, and wardrobe when that's not really what I'm here for. Although I can't front; looking back, it would have been nice to wear something better than the Nautica T-shirt I'd chosen to throw on.

The magnitude of what was happening didn't quite hit me until I boarded the airplane. I'd never flown first class before, and now I'm sitting in this big seat in the front of the plane in my squishy Windbreaker sweats, reading through a stack of hip-hop magazines. Preparing for the interview, I was just trying to wrap my brain around everything that had happened up to that point. According to the articles, Pac had accused Biggie and Bad Boy Records CEO Sean "Puffy" Combs of being somehow involved in an incident where Pac was robbed and shot five times in the lobby of Quad Recording Studios in NYC in November 1994. That I knew. I also knew that Suge Knight had gotten shot at a party in

Atlanta and there was speculation that Puffy was involved. I knew people were taking sides. In his first release postprison, Pac had delivered a video for his new single "California Love" featuring Dr. Dre and it was dope, so well-done and over-the-top. As a New Yorker, I couldn't help but feel a little salty, watching Pac throw up westside "W's" with his fingers, in an aggressive, big-budget, national way.

When I first heard the song and for months after, it irritated the hell out of me, because I took it as a dis to my city. *California knows how to party* . . . Please understand that today, as a grown-up, I realize how nuts that sounds. But in the moment it felt very real.

The truth is "California Love" wasn't a dis record at all. But there was no confusion four months later when Pac released the real dis song "Hit 'Em Up." *First off, fuck your bitch and the clique you claim / Westside when we ride come equipped with game* . . .

Like I said—shit was crazy.

Before I know it, I'm landing at LAX and being greeted by Tupac's assistant, Mindy, a cute, thin, blond-haired girl. Not exactly what I expected. Later I learned that Pac actually had a lot of women around him that handled his day-to-day. That surprised me. Mindy was sweet, organized, and super-efficient, and let me know as soon as I landed that he was busy just then on the set of a movie he was shooting.

"He said for me to take you to the hotel, for you to get settled, and then I'll come back and pick you up tomorrow," Mindy explained as soon as I buckled my seat belt. "He's trying to knock out everything and move things around so he can block out the day for you tomorrow and have a lot of time. He's really excited to talk to you. He keeps asking, 'Did Angie get in? Is she here?'"

As I'm hearing her say this, again I'm reminded of the magnitude of this interview.

Blue skies, bright sunshine, palm trees everywhere. We pulled up to the Hotel Nikko on La Cienega Boulevard, and it looked imposing—beautiful, huge, all very impressive. I felt way out of my element.

And just then I can't help but hear "California Love" in my head . . . That irritating song started to get the better of me and became the sound track in my head the entire time I was out there . . . *California knows how to party / In the citaaay . . . city of Compton . . .*

Now I had the night to see the city. Ed Lover's friend Big Spesh came to get me and took me to the hood where his family lived, to a fried-chicken spot in Crenshaw. He was older, respectful, protective, just a nice guy. I got to see regular LA, not Beverly Hills. I definitely felt more comfortable there, more at ease. Later that night he dropped me off at the hotel and planned to come with me to the interview the next day.

And so the following day at the appointed hour Spesh and I are picked up by Mindy and driven to a glamorous high-rise doorman building. As Pac's home was in Malibu, Mindy explains, this apartment was where he stayed while he was working. Mindy walks me into the living room and all of the Outlawz and Pac's entourage are there hanging out. Big Spesh moves to the background as I take a seat alone on a brown leather couch.

"Sit tight. I'll be right back. He's almost ready," Mindy says.

She disappears as Spesh fades farther into the back of the living room somewhere.

There is a picture of Janet Jackson and Pac from *Poetic Justice* on the table behind the couch and lots of photos all over the place. A big neon sign is lit up on the wall in the dining room: *Thug Mansion*. And there I am in my Nautica T-shirt holding my little microphone—me and the Outlawz in the living room. Minutes pass. They give me a head nod or two and a "Whassup," but there isn't very much conversation happening. It's a little awkward and quiet sitting there.

Then in walks Pac and the room immediately lights up. He's laughing, giving his friends pounds and hugs. He comes over and gives me a big hug. "You made it!" he says. "How was your flight?" Immediately, everyone in the room feels more at ease with him there. "So, you good? You hungry? I had my peoples go to this spot and get you some pizza." He shows me the box and it says NY PIZZA. "I wanted to make you feel comfortable," he says. "I want you to feel at home. I know people be saying bad shit about me. I'm a good guy."

I laugh and nod, making sure I'm ready to go when he is, checking the batteries on my handheld recorder with a microphone attached to it. I didn't have a video camera, sound equipment, or anything fancy. It was just this tiny little recorder with a microphone and my list of notes from the plane.

Pac isn't in a hurry, though. Soon we're eating pizza. Somebody lights a blunt, and now the room is starting to feel comfortable. Pac's smoking Newports, people are passing the blunt, and there is a lot of smoke in the room. He plops down on the couch next to me and says, "All right, you ready to do this?"

I fumbled with the tape, hit record, and so it began.

ANGIE: I'm sitting with Tupac in his crib right now . . . If we get anything positive out of this then it's more than worth it. First thing I think we need to talk about is the East Coast–West Coast thing . . . That's really what's on people's minds in New York right now in terms of you. A lot of people feel like you kinda flipped on them.

TUPAC: I dunno why people could feel like I'm flippin' on 'em. 'Cause I'm trying to give it up to where I'm from . . .

ANGIE: But aren't you from New York?

TUPAC: That's where I was born, but that's not where I learned how to make money . . . When I came out to the West Coast, this is where I got laced. This is where I learned. This is where I became a man . . .

Right from the start I could see that he was far more articulate and calculated than I was. And at this point, way more seasoned than me. I could have asked him anything. He already knew what he wanted to say. He answered my questions, but he also was very clear about what he wanted to get out of this. He had some shit to say, and he was using me as the vehicle to do that.

**ANGIE:** So are you saying that you do not have a beef with New York?

**TUPAC:** Nah . . . I have a beef with anybody in my way, anybody that'll come against me that feel like they could criticize me because they bought my album. That feel like just because they read an interview that they know who I am—I have a beef with them interfering with me getting my money. I got a beef with Wendy Williams saying I got raped in jail because that disrespected me, my family, and what I represent. I got a beef with New York rappers just saying whatever they wanna say about where I'm from . . .

He went off, continuing his laundry list, which finally came around to the main beef. And because I still didn't fully understand, I asked exactly how his relationship with Biggie had gotten so bad and what exactly Biggie had done.

**TUPAC:** He acted like he didn't know what happened when I got shot. He didn't know what happened. I was tripping out. I was buggin'. I must've been fuckin' on drugs when I got operated on. This nigga only got shot once. He was acting like a movie when he came upstairs. That type of shit? It's going down . . . Puffy's the one that really . . . snapped me back to my senses. When this punk muthafucka said "Thug Life you gon' be a thug, you gotta be a thug forever you can't go in and out of it." Okay, now when a cream puff nigga like that tell me that, it's time to ride. 'Cause I had legitimately just walked away from the shit. I was gonna take my shots and move on. I already knew what happened. Only thing that pissed me off is when niggas tried to make me seem like I was buggin' or bullshitting like I just shot myself. Nobody knew what happened. That's what really made just me trip the fuck out. And then Mobb Deep doing shows and they introducing people onstage like this the nigga that shot 'Pac.

**ANGIE:** Where was that?

**TUPAC:** In Queens! It get real deep and everybody involved know it get deep. This is basically what it is—fear is stronger than love.

His point was that New York was an innocent bystander. And there was no question where the battle lines had been drawn for him.

**TUPAC:** Niggas that represent New York, some of these rappers—there's a lot of cool niggas out there . . . But as far as Bad Boy, Puffy is the head of Bad Boy. He's a cream puff. He's being extorted. So the niggas that's extorting him don't pump no fear in my heart. They pump fear in his heart. I rode against the niggas extorting him. They tried to kill me. Biggie and them watched it and acted like they didn't know what happened. So now I'm gonna end his business. I'm gonna end it so the extorting niggas don't get no money. Biggie don't get no money. Puffy don't get no money. I get all the money, and they be out the rap game. That's what poppin'.

**ANGIE:** And how do you intend to do that?

**TUPAC:** I'm doing it. Them niggas ain't doin' no tours. They ain't livin' good. They sleepin' with extra security. They got guns out. They was out here panicky like a muthafucka . . .

**ANGIE:** This whole thing that's going on—

**TUPAC:** Is a military move.

**ANGIE:** This whole thing is your beef with Biggie and Puffy.

**TUPAC:** No doubt.

**ANGIE:** So it has nothing to do with you disrespecting New York—

Every time Pac came close to giving me something concrete that I could use to defuse the East Coast–West Coast beef, he'd back off and say something even more inflammatory instead.

**ANGIE:** But what I think needs to be clarified is this beef, this whole thing—

**TUPAC:** There is no beef! When Biggie get attacked, he run to New York and say, "They after us! They after us!" We ain't after y'all. We after Biggie! Y'all just need to mind y'all business! Every time somebody say something in rap, New York is not the only muthafucker that can answer. In hip-hop there's so many battles that nobody trip off but mines everybody's involved in. Why you can't respect a soldier for being a soldier for the uniform that he's wearing! Don't get mad at me 'cause y'all niggas is not—they punks! If Biggie was fighting, you would never have thought I was attacking New York. Only reason it look like I'm attacking New York is 'cause I'm stompin' this nigga. I'm smackin' him up against the wall and he's not answering. So I'm bangin' him up against New York walls and it's like he ain't doing nothing.

**ANGIE:** So what's gonna come outta this?

**TUPAC:** I want my respect. It's not gonna be over till I drop my Nagasaki. They did they shit. They bombed Pearl Harbor. They shot me five times, okay. But until I get my Nagasaki, we can't have peace.

I could tell by his aggression that I wasn't going to get what I was looking for in this moment. I would have to come back to it. My job was not to judge but to still ask hard questions and not be intimidated. At one point I tried another way to subtly challenge Pac, this time about Faith Evans and his claim that there had been a relationship between him and her, something that she denied. I asked why he would drag her into this.

**TUPAC:** Why? 'Cause that was her husband. And I'm his enemy. And she gave me some pussy. I was supposed to dis her. Any real bitch would be on my side like damn, that's a player for real. But you acting like suckas like, Why'd you dis her? She was married to this nigga and she slid me some pussy 'cause she was caught up in my image. For real though. Let's be real though. So what did I do? I did what—I didn't wanna fuck her 'cause I wanted to be with Faith! Fuck Faith!

**ANGIE:** Did you make her believe that?

**TUPAC:** She knew exactly what was goin'—c'mon. C'mon, Angie! You wouldn't even come to my video! She was married to the nigga and she was fuckin' me! C'mon, you smart!

I just looked back at him, not saying a word. He kept going.

**TUPAC:** . . . I don't lie on my dick. It brings me nothing. This right here made me look bad to females to fuck Faith and tell everybody. It made me look bad.

**ANGIE:** It did.

**TUPAC:** I would not get more pussy like that. Everybody know that. But I'm not doing it for the bitches. I'm not doing it for the girls. I could care less. I'm destroying a nigga right here. And believe me, every time he touch her, every time he thinks about getting back together with her, every time he think of his wedding anniversary, he's thinking of me fucking his wife. And that's as gangster as you can get. Yup. And if you don't understand, don't matter to me. Niggas understand.

Pac was very animated and dramatic about everything. It was overwhelming. I was in no way on his level, to be able to challenge him the way I wish I could have. He was a performer—the way he delivered, the way he spoke, he was poetic. He'd be tearing somebody apart and screaming, like he was out of control. But he was very much in control. And even at some points charming and attentive. There were a couple of moments when he'd be yelling and be really aggressive, and then he would stop and ask, "Are you okay?"

"Yeah, I'm okay."

"You know, none of this is towards you. If I raise my voice, if I'm screaming, it's just how I feel. I want to make sure you're okay and you're comfortable. I just get hype. Matter of fact, I'ma get you a gun. You can sit it by you if you get nervous."

I laughed. "We all right." Is it weird that I thought it was a charming gesture? Probably.

But in getting more comfortable, I still knew Pac was talking circles around me. I was trying with everything I had for Tupac to say some things that would make the East Coast–West Coast situation simmer down. Ultimately, that's what I was there for, and so when he mentioned how crazy the idea of having beef with a whole city was, I encouraged him to speak to that.

**ANGIE:** This is what I'm trying to get at . . . No one in New York has heard you say that.

**TUPAC:** Well, why don't you tell them how I flew you out here? This wasn't no publicity stunt. Why don't you tell them how I called you personally and I wanted to get this shit settled and I flew you out here to show you that there was no problem? And tell 'em how you not in a hotel room. You in my home. So what beef?

**ANGIE:** And I have and I've let them know that this was you that wanted to speak to New York. So I'm giving you that opportunity to let people understand what's really happening...

The whole time all the Outlawz were sitting there. I could tell that they all looked up to him. Everybody in the room was somewhat as in awe of him as I was. Fatal from the Outlawz was especially nice to me that day, as I recall. He recently passed away in a car accident and I was really sad to hear that. Every time I'd run into him, even years later, it would always bring us to that moment of sitting in that room.

Looking back, I feel that the weight of history wasn't just felt by me, but that something inside Tupac had given him a sense of urgency. It's true that he had been vocal in the media at the time. But he clearly seemed to think it was important to go on the record and cover not just what I'd come for but other thoughts he had, including his hope to inspire other artists coming up, other voices. At moments I even felt that Pac was just talking to me directly about why it was important to be authentic and not feel like you had to overexplain yourself. He said he was tired of talking down to people and that if you respected your audience and put them on your level, they'd get it.

I couldn't have agreed more, and I carried that with me over the years.

After more than two hours, I reluctantly began to wrap up the interview. I honestly felt like I could have talked to this guy forever. Pac echoed my feelings right about then, saying, "All right, we just talking shit at this point," and so I stopped the tape.

We took a bunch of pictures. Pac sincerely thanked me for coming and told me that if I ever needed anything to let him know.

An hour later, after Mindy dropped me off at the hotel, I still couldn't get "California Love" out of my head. My mental track was punctuated by two hours of Pac saying crazy shit about Puff, crazy shit about Big. I had gotten word from a couple people that Biggie wasn't so happy that I went to do that interview in the first place. His reaction bothered me to an extent but not enough to feel like I did the wrong thing. I understood if he felt like that, but there was nothing I could do. I still had to do it. It was the other side of the story.

Many times in the future, I would have to wrestle with instances when I chose not to take sides and with feeling the weight of knowing you have friends and important relationships on both sides. But ultimately, you also have a job to do. There would be many times when I'd have to talk to people who'd say crazy things about people I cared about. No matter what the situation, I could only do what I believed in and that was to try to give everybody a fair platform.

At the hotel, I was getting calls from people at the station: "How did it go? How did it go? How did it go?" I couldn't even talk to anybody yet. I had to just be in my own zone for a little bit. Again, I desperately wanted to help the situation. People were too invested in this East Coast–West Coast beef. How much further could it go, what with people getting shot? And I just did not want to go home without Pac's statement that, "This is not an East Coast–West Coast thing." Which he did say a few times. But then he went on to say other crazy shit. So the big challenge, as I tried to get to sleep, was how I would help the situation as opposed to inflaming it.

*What am I supposed to do with all this?* The responsibility was weighing on me.

. . .

People were literally waiting for me at the station when I showed up the next day after taking a flight from LA early in the morning. No answers had come to me yet about how to edit the interview. And I didn't know who to ask. Why? Because I didn't really trust anybody. Everybody was so opinionated about it and so biased; this had to be one of those times when I decided for myself.

Being open to input can be a good thing. But sometimes too many opinions are not a good thing. Sometimes if I start asking people for their opinions, it confuses me. I'm a person who likes to get quiet. And then, once I've kind of figured it out, I may pick people's brains about how to do it. Nobody else is going to have to deal with the repercussions but me. I think I've always been like that.

That was the space I was in when I ran into Ed Lover and a couple of other deejays who were all there at a time when they normally wouldn't be there, all waiting to hear something. It was intense. I shrugged them all off and went to sit in the editing room by myself and started listening to the interview. I transferred the cassette to a reel-to-reel tape so that I could begin editing. I had a little razor blade and was cutting the tape and piecing it together with the unused strips falling on the floor. That was the technology of the day. I used to get little slices on my fingers whenever I needed to hurry up and edit, often causing me to go home with Band-Aids on my fingertips.

The sections that were the most direct were the ones that I focused on.

**TUPAC:** I really do feel like fuck it, then. What more can I do? I'm not sucking y'all dick. I'm not mad at you. I don't got no beef with you. I'm beefin' with the nigga you proclaim to be the king of your set. I'm attacking him. I'm tearin' him down. As long as y'all stay on one side of the block, I promise you, I will only destroy this side of the block . . . All I wanna do is get my paper and all I wanna see if niggas out there get their paper . . . Biggie is a fake player. See, I wanna deal with some real niggas. That's all I'm saying. My beef is just with them. Soon as they gone? We gonna try to make New York—man, everything we got you can have. Like we cousins. Y'all wanna borrow some sugar? What y'all want? Man, everything. How do you expect me to sit down at the table with niggas that tried to kill me?

Ed Lover came into the editing room and was standing over my shoulder, listening. Apparently, he heard enough that at some point he decided to mention something to Puff about what he had heard. Puff then called Steve Smith and told him, "If this airs, it's going to make the situation worse. I'm going to have a real problem with the station."

So he got to my program director and got in his head. Now, mind you, I'm sitting in the studio by myself, with the little razor blade, listening to the interview over and over again, trying to decide what to play.

Before I could even figure that out, Steve Smith calls me out of the editing room and says, "Well, I don't know if we should be playing this. And Puff doesn't think—"

"Puff? What does he have to do with any of this?"

"Well, he just thinks that more people could get hurt," he says.

It irritated me that, all of a sudden, a decision had come from somebody who was deeply involved in this situation and didn't work for the station. *I don't work for him.* It bothered me that everybody was so eager to please Puff before I even had a chance to evaluate the right thing to do. I knew Puff had a lot on the line, but I felt like he was trying to bully the station.

"Well, you're not telling me I can't play it, right?"

"I just want us to be very careful," Steve said. He paused, as if he were about to put his foot down.

"Hold that thought," I said, backing out of the room. Before he could tell me something I didn't want to hear, I got out of there quickly, like a ninja. I tend to do that before somebody's about to say something I'm not interested in hearing.

*I see where this is going. I'm not going to let it go there. I'll be back.* I'm actually brilliant at extracting myself from conversations I don't want to have. It's a gift.

I went back into the editing room and continued as if I were still making the decision about what we were going to do. Ultimately, a lot of what Pac said scared me. My intention, truly, was to help. But what he gave me was so aggressive and at points angry, it verged on explosive. Everything main topic was so sensitive, and some of it was so inflammatory that I could see where it would make a bad situation worse. That was never my intent.

Now, granted, airing it in full would have been the biggest interview in the country. At the time, before all the online content and commentary, pre–social media, radio was the one place where you could experience what it was like to be there in the moment, hearing everything as it was unfolding. It was a really big deal. But the material could also accelerate this crazy war that I had suddenly found myself on the front lines of. The magnitude of this position and the responsibility hit me hard.

So with what I did eventually air I chose to stick by Pac with cuts that reflected his truth but that were also positive. I stuck to clips of him defending himself against the rape allegations and talking in general about wanting to inspire people. And yes, I took the best of what he had said about there not being an East Coast–West Coast beef and his clarification that it was about one person dealing with another person. My

L to R:  1. My mom at eighteen. She's pregnant with me in this photo.  2. Me and my father at the beach.
3. This is the only photo I have of me with both of my parents. (My aunt Melanie is next to my mom.)
4. Me and my mom uptown leaving Uelo's apartment.  5. Me and my mom.

L to R: 1. My early attempts at breakdancing. It wasn't as easy as it looked! 2. I was always hurting myself and breaking bones. 3. With my best friend, Nikki, on my birthday. Who let me wear these pigtails? 4. Nikki and me hanging out at Coney Island, Brooklyn. 5. Lunch room chronicles: headphones in place with no intention of going to class.

L to R: 1. With Uelo, who came to visit while I was living in Florida with my aunt Cindy. 2. Looking at family pictures with Uelo in our apartment on 71st Street. 3. Uelo at his 100th birthday. His last name was Roca, so I got him this hat with his name on it. 4. With my grandparents, my mom and my aunt Zunia.

L to R: 1. The Hot 97 van I drove around for years to events, with Big Dennis. 2. Freddie Colon, legendary New York radio personality. 3. In Astoria, Queens, across the street from my first apartment. 4. The day I met A Tribe Called Quest for the first time in the studio, along with Deneen and Eduardo, who worked in the office with me. 5. Me and Mary J. Blige back in the day. 6&7. Some of my first interviews were with artists like Channel Live and the Lost Boyz.

L to R: 1. "Ladies Night" with DJ Coco Chanel, DJ Jazzy Joyce, MC Lite, and Rosario Dawson. 2. One of those days in the studio. 3. New Year's Eve at Extremes Nightclub in the Bronx. I was hosting. Nikki was holding me down. 4. At a party in New York with Q-Tip and Lauryn Hill. 5. The Notorious B.I.G. 6. The video shoot for "Heartbeat" with KRS-One and Redman. 7. The pre–Puerto Rican Day Parade festival on 116th Street, East Harlem.

L to R: 1. Interviewing Monica in the studio. 2. With Flex at a Hot 97 event in the Hamptons. 3. One of my first photo shoots. 4. Jay Z, Puffy, and Monie Love hanging out in the Hamptons. 5. Me and Q-Tip at Summer Jam, 1994. 6. Big Pun and Lance "Un" Rivera. Un was responsible for putting me on "Ladies Night."

Hot 97's
"Butter Pecan"
Angie Martinez
invites you to come
celebrate
at her
Big Birthday Bash
Friday January 19th
Special VIP Reception
in the Balcony 9-11pm
FUNKMASTER FLEX
on the 1&2s
Special Surprise
Performances
PALLADIUM
126 East 14th Street 473-7171

This invite
admits one

L to R: 1. Backstage at Summer Jam interviewing Puffy for The Box. 2. Me and Snoop. 3. Onstage at the Palladium. 4. With Salaam. 5. Ol' Dirty Bastard and Fat Joe.

The fire at Tip's house in February 1998, with Q-Tip, Ali, and Lite. These are hard to look at even today.

decision was to use the brief on-air cuts to put some good in the world—to leave his message in but take out the super-inflammatory stuff, even if it was about eighty-five percent of the interview. In the end I played the pieces that really captured the best part of Tupac.

I struggled with the fine line between my journalistic duty to keep his meaning intact and not contributing to a dangerous situation as a human being who deeply cared about the culture.

Everything had happened so fast—the phone call, the trip to LA, the interview, and the drama over what to air. Even so, all these years later, the details have remained incredibly vivid. I even kept a few mementos. Sadly, over the years, I rarely kept any. That's actually one of the few regrets that I have in looking back. But I did save some from that day. I kept the plane tickets to LA and back and Pac's box of Newports with four cigarettes left in it. Back then I smoked cigarettes occasionally. And I was smoking Newports with Pac, so I held on to the box. I just knew that it was such an unusual moment and one that would stay with me forever.

I'd come to a turning point. Before that interview, my job was just fun. I finally realized, *Oh! This does matter! It can matter. It is mattering.*

# CHAPTER FIVE

# UNBELIEVABLE

Bryant Park was buzzing on September 4, 1996, for the after-party following the MTV Music Video Awards that had been held earlier at Radio City Music Hall. As I pushed my way into the thick of it, I couldn't help but feel good that hip-hop was well represented that night. Everybody was there.

Snoop and Dre were in town. And so was Pac, as he and Dre had been nominated for Best Rap Video for "California Love"—although they lost to Coolio for "Gangsta's Paradise." The biggest names of the night were The Smashing Pumpkins and Alanis Morissette, each winning multiple awards in the rock and pop categories. As much as I loved Alanis's *Jagged Little Pill* album, when it came to the show, I was most excited about the hip-hop awards and performances. Nas and the Fugees killed it with a medley of "Fu-Gee-La," "Ready or Not," and "If I Ruled the World." Definitely not a bad showing for the culture. Not everybody was happy though. At the after-party, Suge Knight and Pac complained plenty that Death Row was not given its due awards-wise or on the show.

In fact, Tupac, flanked by the Outlawz and Suge—all carrying signs that read "Death Row East"—talked to an entertainment reporter about how they were expanding to include East Coast artists. Aside from what was going on with Biggie, Pac called out Nas and apparently now had a beef with him, too. Shit was still crazy.

Walking into the party, I'd known there was a chance of running into Pac. And I had hoped I would. Snippets from my interview with him had aired over the last several weeks, and I honestly had no clue how he felt about it. All in all, my cuts had gone from a two-hour interview to about twelve minutes that wound up on-air. There had been no word from Pac so, naturally, I was somewhat worried he might be angry after he spent so much time and money to make the interview happen. That didn't change my feeling that I'd made the right choice not to fan the flames.

So there I was in the middle of the tented festivities at Bryant Park. The coastal war was still very much a thing, and you could feel high tension in the air—especially because Pac and Nas were both there. There was this moment when I thought, *Oh God, when these paths cross, this is going to be a problem.*

And all of sudden, like in slow motion, everybody realized that Nas and his crew were walking toward Pac and his, all with the same intensity. You could almost hear a gasp from everyone watching, with all of us probably thinking the same thing: *Oh God, this could be really bad right now.*

But Nas and Pac talked. It did feel a little aggressive, not because of them, necessarily, but the people around them. That is usually where most of the problems happen—with the crews. But somehow it seemed to be managed, and whatever Pac and Nas said to each other that night, it ended in peace.

At some point in the night, I found my way over to Pac. He had a cup in his hand and his shirt was half unbuttoned. He looked like a superstar. He just kind of looked at me and I was like, "Hi." I'm in some stupid little silver sweat suit. Like a shiny TLC sweat suit. And Pac was like, "Hey!"

"You know, I just wanted to come say hello," I said. "And I don't know if you heard the interview. I aired it. But I just want you to know I had to edit a bunch of stuff out, because I felt like it was the right thing to do. But I did my best to not misrepresent you."

"I understand, Angie. It's all good," he said. "We good." And he gave me a big hug.

As he did, the tension lifted off of me. I had been so worried and it turned out he was so okay and comfortable about everything.

Pac reassured me even more, adding, "It's cool. We cool, and I'm still happy you came."

We could have talked longer and I would have had more to say, but there was a crowd around us wanting their own moment with Pac, everyone waiting for his attention, so I excused myself. I said, "Thanks, Pac. I'm glad I went, too."

He winked at me, and I just kind of crawled away in relief. We were good.

That was the last time I ever saw him. It was the last time that most of the people at Bryant Park that night ever saw him.

• • •

On September 7, 1996, three days after the MTV Awards, we all got the news about what had happened that night in Vegas, after the heavyweight championship match between Mike Tyson and Bruce Seldon at the MGM Grand. Initially, the news was just that Tyson had knocked out Seldon in the first round, making it one of the shortest fights in boxing history. But then came word that Tupac—who had been at the match with Suge Knight—had been shot in a drive-by incident as the two of them cruised through town on their way to a club. Apparently, before leaving the MGM Grand, Pac had been in a fight in the lobby that had to be broken up by security. The cause was said to be gang related. Nobody knew if the shooting had come about in retaliation, but from what was known, a Cadillac had pulled up on the right side of the car Suge was driving and multiple shots had been fired.

The thing about Tupac is that he was always in the news and he had been shot so many times. I thought—as everybody did—"Oh, he was shot again. He'll be fine." Nobody thought that he could actually die.

But as the next couple of days went by and I heard reports from the news and other firsthand accounts from people I knew who were there to check on him, I started to lose my certainty that Pac was bulletproof. I heard that when they carried him in, half conscious, Pac told a medical worker, "I'm dying." He had been hospitalized since and was in critical care. He had to be sedated because he kept trying to get up out of the bed.

Telling myself he was going to pull through, I still felt a pit in my stomach, like a sense of dread. He was so good to me, so kind. And I just liked Pac. In the span of one trip to LA we had bonded in a real way. What could I do? How could I say something to cheer him on? There was no texting him or sending an e-mail to an assistant or anything like that. So I wrote him a letter. That's how old-school it was. I wrote a handwritten letter, got a stamp, and mailed it to the hospital:

> *Hey, I hope this letter finds you. I hope you are recovering and on your way back to doing what you were born to do. I just want you to know that people are praying for you . . .*

We were all waiting to find out how Pac was. By chance someone who worked at the station knew someone on staff at the hospital and had been giving me confidential updates, confirming what I was hearing—that he was in a coma. That was not good, but I'd remind myself that gunshot victims recovered from being in comas all the time. Then, on September 13, I called our connection at the hospital and asked, as usual, "Just checking in to see if you have any information on how Tupac is doing."

There was a pause. Then in a cautious voice she relayed the news that Pac had passed. He was twenty-five years old. Same age as me.

My first reactions were shock and disbelief. I put down the phone and sat back in my chair, convinced there had been a mistake.

*There's no way. There's no way he passed. No way. That's impossible. Why would somebody say that?*

Now, at this point, nothing had been announced. It wasn't on the news yet. So I picked up the phone again and called the hospital and somehow got through to an administrator who told me that, yes, it was confirmed that Tupac had just passed. Literally *just* passed. Moments ago.

In the middle of feeling so devastated and sad, I knew it was important to share the news with our listeners. I couldn't even begin to think about how, so I turned to Red Alert, who happened to be on-air, mixing. Red Alert was the original iconic deejay, who had not only been a pioneer of hip-hop, but I had grown up taping his show and mixtapes on KISS FM for years—the only place where a kid like me could hear hip-hop on the radio. Right before we went back on the air, I quietly and quickly gave Red Alert the news that Tupac had passed. He looked as stunned as I felt.

"What do we do? Do we say it on the radio?" I asked.

Red Alert took a deep breath and said, "Yeah, Angie. You have to tell people."

And I knew I did.

Nothing like this had happened before. I had no expertise in how to announce a tragedy. I didn't know how it went. I wasn't a trained news reporter or a journalist with experience in how to cover breaking news stories, horrible crises, wars. I was still that kid who liked hip-hop and somehow got a show on the radio. I don't know how you report on death. And I was so affected and emotional about it. Nobody had taught me a protocol for how to convey this kind of important news to our listeners. All I could do was trust my instincts and crack the mic.

We spoke from the heart. Red Alert began, "It's Hot 97, Red Alert and Angie—we have some bad news. Really sad, bad news."

And I continued. "I just got word from University Medical Center of Southern Nevada that Tupac has passed away."

Suddenly, it sank in. I was overcome by emotion that caught in my voice and in my chest. I had never experienced anything so real on-air. It was the realest it had ever gotten. And I just lost it. I just started crying. The mic was on. There was nothing I could do but just let it go, and all I could verbalize was, "It just is what it is . . . God. I'm sad, as I'm sure a lot of you are."

At some point we weren't even saying anything; the mic was just on for like a minute. And to this day people tell me that they had that moment with us, that they were there, listening. It was the first time I had felt that type of vulnerability on the radio. It's not like it was something planned. It was just what was happening. It was just how it felt. It was just sad. It was awful.

And then, of course, not that much longer after, MTV had gotten wind of it and reports started to show up on the news that Tupac was pronounced dead. The aftermath of that was so weird. Everything had changed. I think everyone in the culture started feeling crazy about how far everything had gotten and this man's life was taken now.

Over the past four months I had known that Biggie had been none too pleased about me going to talk to Pac. All of that changed when Tupac died. A short time later Biggie came up to the show to talk about how terrible it was that Pac had lost his life. No matter what they had been going through, he didn't wish that on anyone.

We all felt the loss and understood the weight of the moment, no question. But we couldn't yet appreciate what Pac's legacy was going to be, or really how much what had just happened would change the whole trajectory of hip-hop and how big of a part of hip-hop history this turning point would be.

For my part, as grief set in, I was too emotional to think that far ahead. How could someone with so much talent and so much potential be gone? The news took longer to travel in those days, but as people started reacting with memorials and fans connected all over the world, I was amazed at how much larger than life Pac already was.

For the longest time I'd be walking through the street and so many strangers would approach me to say that they were listening when the news broke. They'd say, "We were crying with you on the radio. My whole family had the radio on."

Over the years I've often wondered if Tupac had a kind of sixth sense that maybe his life was going to get cut short and so he had to just live more in less time. Clearly, his lyrics and images were full of death and dying. I do know as complex as he was, he knew things. In fact, during my interview with him there were two major lessons he taught me that have stuck with me ever since.

The first came up when I made the mistake of starting a question with, "Well, people say . . ."

And he stopped me. "Who are you talking about? What people? Because if you are just talking about niggas in the barbershop, you know they gonna talk shit no matter what you do. So don't talk to me about people and what people say."

Maybe I knew that, but because I was young and nobody had ever put it like that, in those terms, I listened. He was right. And in my career I needed to know that, yeah, there were always going to be people who want to talk shit. Because that's what they do. They sit in the barbershop—or wherever—and talk shit. And it helped cushion the blow later when there was talk that I needed to ignore. Pac telling me that was important at that point in my career. It saved me a lot of time that would have otherwise been wasted.

His other lesson was along those same lines but different. At one point I had asked him if he regretted a career move that had turned out to be kind of stupid. He waved me off and said he wasn't afraid of making a mistake. "My career ain't about that," Pac said. He told me that, yeah, he was gonna fuck up, but that was not ever going to be enough to erase everything else, all the years of work. It may have been obvious, but I hadn't heard it put that way, and I took it as gospel. So what if you make a mistake and fuck up? It can't erase or outweigh the other great things you've done, if you've been at your career and working hard. A mistake or a setback doesn't have to define you.

Both those lessons gave me courage that I carried from then on. He delivered his points as if he knew I'd value them. And he was right.

• • •

The hip-hop world had barely stopped reeling from the loss of Pac when we faced another devastating blow.

Biggie had been doing his best to keep positive and move forward after Pac passed. He took a trip to Los Angeles to promote his second album and to present at the Soul Train Music Awards. Lots of people thought it was too soon for him to go to LA, but I think it was his way of showing love to the West Coast and letting everyone know that things would be okay.

Aside from all the drama that had been going on with Pac, Biggie was busy making history of his own. He was already thought of by many as the greatest rapper alive, with just one album out. I remember when I first heard him rap on a cassette tape given to me by Salaam, it was like nothing I had ever heard. That tape became legend before he even put out his debut album. In my opinion nobody had ever put words together like B.I.G. That, combined with Puffy's marketing and branding genius, made Biggie's first album huge—not just in New York, but everywhere. People were expecting greatness with the second album, and he was ready to deliver.

After all of that sadness, Biggie was our future.

But on March 9, 1997, early on a Sunday morning, when I was asleep at my new apartment in Queens, I got a call that Biggie had been shot and killed. *My God. No.* I was shocked, overwhelmed, numb. And before any other thoughts could register, I knew where I needed to be. I just popped up and ran to the station.

It was supposed to be the calm after the storm. The sadness we'd felt as a culture after Pac died was supposed to be the worst of it. No one was prepared for more.

*I can't believe this happened. I can't believe this is still happening.* At this point, it was just too much to process.

I arrived at the station barely able to process how I would get on the radio and talk to my listeners about the death of our hometown hero. This was different. This is New York and I would be talking to the people who knew B.I.G. best. Not just his fans, but his family, his neighbors, our peers in the music industry who knew him well. It was way more intimate.

We had all gotten to know Biggie. He was a really likable guy, the type that would walk into a room and make everyone feel good. He made everybody laugh, quick and witty. We knew what block he was from.

We partied together. We rooted for him. And as famous as he'd become, he was still very much ours. He was accessible. When I hosted events at local clubs, it wasn't uncommon for him to show up. I'd be surprised every time and ask what he was doing there. His answer was always the same: "I came to show love."

As I'm getting my thoughts together, my boss asked me to talk to the local news channel, NY1. He wanted a representative from Hot 97 to explain the impact of Biggie's death on the hip-hop community. Most of what he said went right through me. I was in no condition or mind-set to do anything so formal, but I didn't have the energy to argue. I went downstairs to be interviewed in front of the building, and when the camera rolled, I just lost it. I was so spent. And it was just so fucking sad.

I spent the whole week on air letting people call in and talk about their BIG experiences. Plenty of artists called in and showed up to the station as well. Everyone was taking it really hard.

I remember pulling up to the funeral home on the Upper East Side and seeing hundreds of people behind the barricades, many holding signs and many crying. Fans and followers reacted to his death like they had lost a member of their family.

During the open-casket service, I kept looking over at different faces—Junior M.A.F.I.A., Lil' Cease, and everybody else I had enjoyed so many happy, fun relationships with. All of that was in contrast to this terrible moment of sorrow. Real, deep-down sorrow.

Biggie songs and lyrics kept coming to me that day. The thing about the Notorious B.I.G. was that you always knew it was him from the first word he spoke. Before he died he had only released one album, back in September 1994, and that was true of every song—from "Big Poppa" to my favorite, "Unbelievable." It was painful to recall that the first album was titled *Ready to Die*.

After the funeral service, there was going to be a big procession to accompany Biggie's hearse and drive through his neighborhood of Brooklyn. As we were all walking out, I saw Mary J. Blige, Lil' Kim, and a few others heading toward their car. One of them turned back to say, "Ang, come with us."

So I followed them, not sure where we were going. As we were walking, Kim was crying, like crying from her gut.

They both got in the car, but I waited outside. I didn't want to intrude on this moment. It was too real. And then I heard someone call, "Come in the car. Kim wants you to come in the car." I remember sitting in that car with Kim and a couple of her girlfriends, and Mary was sitting next to her. I didn't even know what to say or how to feel.

I had just watched the movie *Steel Magnolias* and loved that scene when the daughter dies and at the funeral one of them says to the mom, "I don't know how you're feeling on the inside, but you look amazing on the outside." And really, looking at Kim, she did look beautiful. If I had to show up to a funeral for somebody I loved, I would probably be in a scrunchie and something that didn't match. I mean, how do you pull yourself together at a time like that?

I could tell she was in pain, but she still looked good. So I just said *that*. I said, "Kim, I don't know how you feel inside, but you look beautiful."

And she stopped crying for a minute and looked at me, and she just laughed for a second like—*are you fucking kidding me?* Then Kim said, "That's the weirdest thing to say, but thank you."

Everything else about that funeral was a blur. That next day, in all the coverage about the send-off for Biggie, the newspaper featured a picture of Kim walking with Mary. You could see Kim's pain in that picture.

For all of us, I think in a way it was the end of innocence. We had learned hard lessons. Everyone was changed.

. . .

Fittingly, when the album Biggie had just finished before he died came out posthumously, it was called *Life After Death*. It went on to sell more than ten million copies, barely edging out Tupac's posthumous album of *Greatest Hits*, which sold a little under ten million, and Pac's *All Eyez on Me*, which is up at around nine million copies sold to date.

In the wake of their deaths, there was a sobering process that took hold across the industry and in the community. The whole battle between the two coasts faded in the rearview mirror of where hip-hop was headed next—to becoming really big business.

You could just feel it as we got into the later 1990s. Hip-hop was not being so niche anymore. It was definitely the time of the bigger money, the big multimillion-dollar production videos, and the crazy excesses that came along with going fast from nothing to everything. Biggie had warned everyone—"Mo Money, Mo Problems."

It was an interesting time coming up. Because I had found my voice and my lane in radio and would start to be given other opportunities, the next challenge for me would be to find a way of keeping my focus without getting caught up in all of the craziness. The lessons I'd learned so far from Biggie and Pac would eventually help me stay grounded. But not right away. I'd have to make a few mistakes first.

It may sound strange—coming from someone like me who doesn't look back at the past much—but I think of the lessons of this period all the time. Something that has kept them fresh comes from a discovery that a friend of mine made about three years ago. In an exhibit of Tupac memorabilia, one of the items preserved was a handwritten letter on notebook paper that Tupac wrote to me all those years ago. It hangs on my kitchen wall today:

*2 Angie Martinez*

> *4 being true when false behavior was fashionable*
> *4 never dirtying my name on the air*
> *4 being what iz so hard 2 find . . . . . .*
> *A real motherfuka*
> *I O U 1*
> *Collect whenever needed most*

*Sign: Tupac Shakur*

There was irony in that I never received this letter and that he never received mine.

PART TWO

# VOICE OF NEW YORK

## 1997 TO 2001

# CHAPTER SIX

# ALMOST FAMOUS

As the clouds and haze of that heavy period lifted, my relationship with my listeners was stronger than ever. Like any relationship, when you go through something together, it brings you closer. You begin to have shared memories and you get to know each other on another level. I often talk about that with aspiring radio personalities because I think it's the key to longevity. In developing a real relationship with your audience, you're giving them a chance to get to know you and trust who you are. Knowing that helped me immensely because the answer to how to handle any challenge on-air became—just be honest. Just be yourself.

The summer of 1997 was a memorable time. Our Summer Jam concert that Hot 97 put on each year was shaping up to be bigger than ever. Twenty thousand people would show up to MetLife Stadium to see who was going to dis who, who was going to kill it, and who was going to get booed. Legendary things happened at Summer Jam that everyone wanted to be there to witness. It always set the picture of what was happening in hip-hop, almost like a recap of everything that had happened in the year so far.

What I remember most from that year was a sense of wanting to come together to remember Biggie. As much as we were all trying to move forward, there wasn't an artist that hit the stage that didn't pay some sort of homage to Biggie. "Rest in Peace" shout-outs were the theme of the night.

As one of the deejays who got to welcome the crowd, this was the time every year that I got to come face-to-face with so many members of our core audience in one place. It was always overwhelming to see people I talked to every day on the radio looking back at me. They came from so many different backgrounds. Black, Latino, white, you name it. They were hard-core hip-hop heads. They'd come up and say they're teachers who listen and try to engage their students in hip-hop. Others would say that they'd just gotten out of jail and the highlight of their day was listening to my show. They'd tell me their favorite Battle of the Beats or why they loved a certain interview.

I really started to notice a difference in how people were responding to me. More and more people were showing up at the parties I was hosting, and stopping me in the street to say hi. Ever since I'd been at Hot 97, taking part in the Puerto Rican Day Parade had become my favorite public event. I had been going since I was a little kid and never missed it. My grandma Petra used to take me, and we'd sit on the sidelines waving our flags with pride. My most vivid memory was of being eight years old and seeing Erik Estrada pass by on a float. He played Ponch in the TV show *CHiPs*. The show was a big hit that year, and Estrada was the breakout star. And he was Puerto Rican! My grandma and I got so excited, you would have thought we'd just seen the pope! I was jumping up and down and all the girls around us were screaming. He looked right in our direction and smiled and waved. *Mannnnn*, I talked about it the whole way home. So, I loved this parade. I felt connected to it.

All of the years had been fun to be on the float with everybody from the station, and the crowd was always with me. But that summer of 1997, in particular, there was more attention than usual. People started to ask for pictures while we were setting up the float on one of the side streets. Of course, it was a big float that said Hot 97 all over it and we were blasting hip-hop before the parade even started, so it wasn't weird that people would walk over and hang around and take pictures with all of us. What I did not see coming was that when it was our turn to hit the parade route, at the instant our float turned onto Fifth Avenue, I heard a monstrous roar. People's flags went up and that roar of excitement came from the crowd and filled up my whole being. In the moment, you can't really explain to anyone what is happening to you, so you just go with it! You roar back! I waved my flag with all my might and did my best to make eye contact with as many people as I could.

I saw groups of young girls that looked like they could be my sisters screaming my name from behind the barricade. *"Angie!!!! We love you, Angie!!"*

Oh my God! This had never happened before. I felt so humbled and grateful that so many people who came from where I did felt such a connection to my success. It was theirs, too. I fought back tears for the next thirty-five blocks.

People were showing me love on a regular basis. And I know that may sound like no big deal to some, but I promise, it is a strange and amazing thing when you are not prepared for it. You want to give it back to everyone, but as one person it's challenging, and I've always felt almost guilty about it. I wanted to shout: *I'm a regular person. I'm not a celebrity.*

Through highs and lows, I was always okay with keeping fame at arm's length. I've always been fascinated by celebrity and how it affects people. And how most of the time it makes people act nuts! One thing I had going for me is that I'd been around radio for a long time, so I didn't let any of it go to my head. My mother being in radio helped, too, because she had prepared me for the fact that even the most popular of radio personalities can be replaced; so I never got too comfortable or gassed. I was still just so grateful to be there. And it was my goal to stay there.

So while my ego was intact, I wasn't completely in the clear; I did feel the pressure to step my game up. People around me were definitely cultivating the lifestyle that went along with that. Flex had jewelry and cars with big rims. I saw rappers who started with nothing rapidly become millionaires. The irony of starting to become sort of famous was that I was still not really making shit from the radio station. On the other hand, I was getting a paper bag full of cash every night from being in the clubs. So why wouldn't I think I should buy a BMW? Why wouldn't I think I should move into a luxury high-rise building? Why wouldn't I want to live that life? G. and I had broken up and I felt like I needed a new start anyway.

As Nikki liked to point out over the years, every time I had a breakup, my next step was to pick up and move. She's right. And I did.

I found the brand-new high-end building in Forest Hills, Queens, called the Pinnacle, with a valet, doormen, beautiful views, and a wrap-around terrace. It was crazy! I took the first apartment I could find in the building and paid my deposit in cash. I was livin' the life. Fancy restaurants, new clothes, partying in VIP. The only problem was that I had no idea how to balance a checkbook! And it wasn't even something I cared too much about.

My phone service would get shut off, and I'd just call and get it back on. My lights would get turned off, and I'd call the electric company, pay the money, and have them turned back on. I would run out of gas in my car on the road all the time. I had *no* order in my life and I'd never had money before, so once I got it, I spent it. And when late notices arrived, who had time for that? I was out of control, and then shit got crazy!

I came home late one night from hosting a party in the Bronx. I had been out of the house all day and I was exhausted, so I could not wait to get home. I valeted my car, and as I walked in the building, Hector, the doorman and an avid Hot 97 listener (as most of the guys in the building were), said, "Yo, Ang!"

"Hey, what up, Hector?"

"I think they locked you out of your crib," he said.

"Huh??? What're you talking about??"

"Yeah, the landlord came with the sheriff and put something on your door so you can't get in."

As fast as I could move, I flew into the elevator, rode it upstairs, and ran to my front door. Sure enough, as I stood there staring in shame, there was a padlock on the door and an oversized notice barring my entrance. I had been evicted! I was so EMBARRASSED. Everything I owned was inside the apartment. Standing there just looking at that notice, I was certain that everybody in the building probably knew by now. Mortified, I rode the elevator back down and had to walk back past the doorman again, this time with my head down. I could feel Hector judging me.

I drove to Brooklyn that night to sleep at Nikki's new place on Flatbush Avenue. And then a few days later, I found myself walking into the courthouse and entering that damn eviction office. I kept thinking about how half the people sitting in there were probably my listeners. Again I'm feeling the judgment! Hiding behind sunglasses, I felt that awkwardness of my public persona glaring back at me.

*My God. How did I let this happen?*

It took a couple of weeks, but eventually I paid all the fines, got my paperwork together, and got back into my place. And I vowed that this would never happen to me again.

* * *

While I was zooming through the whirlwind working nights, Flex and I saw each other less. He seemed to have backed up from me a little bit, and our relationship felt strained. I didn't really know why at first, but my label rep friends would tell me, "Yo, Flex says that if I bring my artist to your show first, he wouldn't support them." It was so weird being in that place with him. I loved Flex, and I respected him, but somehow we had become in competition with each other and I didn't even know it.

Maybe I should have. It very well could have been my fault. I was so consumed with my own ambition. In hindsight, that could have been an issue. But why wouldn't I be? Why wouldn't I try to book the hottest parties, the best guests, or get exclusives for the Battle of the Beats?

You see, in my mind, Flex was always just so far ahead of me that it never occurred to me I may have been stepping on his toes. And our relationship wasn't developed to the extent where he trusted me enough to know that my heart was good. I wasn't trying to be an asshole. I just didn't know any better. I confronted him about it a few times, but he just kinda brushed it off.

It was a weird time at Hot 97. Ed Lover and Dr. Dre had been doing mornings now for a couple years, and the station was focused on branding them. Wendy Williams was on in the afternoon. Wendy had come in after Hot 97 bought adult R&B station KISS FM in December 1994, and there was almost an air of resentment from her toward the station and all of us. So I was cordial, but I kept my distance. And then Flex was on after me. I mean, we were all poppin' in our own right. Ratings were like nothing anyone had ever seen, and there was really no outside competition. But because of that, I think we just started to compete with each other—which may have given me an incentive to say yes to opportunities I might not have otherwise.

I'm thinking of the night when I happened to be hosting a party at a club in Long Island and KRS-One was performing. Before he went onstage, I was on the mic, and afterward KRS says, "You know, you're really good on the mic. You've got a good presence. Your voice is strong. Have you ever rhymed before?"

I laughed and said, "You know, just for fun, whatever, here and there. But no, I'm not a rapper."

"You should come to the studio one night," KRS says. "You'd probably sound really good on a record."

*Whaaaaat?? Me???? This is KRS-One—arguably one of the best emcees to ever grab a mic. Is he out of his mind?! He must be.*

But there was no way in hell I would miss an opportunity to be in a studio and play rapper with one of the greats! So of course I went!

KRS told me he had a session with Showbiz at Chung King Studios in Midtown and that I should meet him there around ten o'clock. I showed up a little early, at nine forty-five, nervous and questioning my decision. No sooner had I entered the lobby than I heard that big iconic KRS voice. "Annnngieeee, you made it!!! Welcome! Welcome . . . Come in," he said as he walked toward me and then stopped. "You by yourself?" He was surprised.

"Yeah, I'm alone." If I was gonna play myself, I preferred to do it in front of the smallest amount of people possible. But I didn't say that.

Instead, I followed him into a dark room. It was loud. It smelled like weed and incense and the beat playing was a sample of Treacherous Three's "Feel the Heartbeat." It was all dope and everything I had always imagined a KRS session should look like. And then I spotted Redman!

Redman's *Muddy Waters* album had just been certified gold and there he was sitting in the corner, smoking a blunt without a care in the world.

"Annnng, what up?" he said from his position on the black leather couch, notebook in hand.

*This is too much! KRS-One ANND Redman are here?! Why am I here? This is fuckin nuts!*

KRS said, "You don't have to do anything. I'm gonna write a verse for you."

Redman just laughed at this. I don't think he knew why I was there either.

"Okay, but you sure? I—I've never done anything like this. I mean, I'll try it. If it sounds terrible—"

"Just try it," KRS encouraged. "Who cares? If it sounds good, I'm gonna keep it. I'm not gonna keep it if it's wack." So he wrote it down. I mean, he definitely wrote the verse. I went in the booth and I tried it.

*It's the butter pecan Rican speakin' deletin' other radio jocks that think they competin'...*

When I came out of the booth, Redman was sitting there, still smoking a blunt, and he said to me matter-of-factly, "Yo, you sound all right. I can't even front. You sound all right on that."

"I don't know. That shit sounds weird to me."

But KRS loved it! They wound up keeping it and putting the song out and calling it "Heartbeat." And for the most part people liked it.

Sure, some people felt weird about it, like, *What is she doing? What are you doing with her on there? She's not a rapper.* I wasn't, but this was KRS-One and Redman . . . What was I supposed to do? Say no? No way!

Then came the video. KRS told me to come up to the video shoot on the roof of a theater by the radio station. This is how green I was. There was no stylist. There was no hair. There was no makeup. I'm in a squishy nylon sweat suit and some sneakers, like—*Okay, I'm here for the video.* That was it. And they just threw me in.

I'd never done a video before, and then all of a sudden I'm just doing a video. I was so in awe of being there with them. I didn't know what the fuck I was doing there. Actually, that video never came out, but they wound up using a clip of it in KRS-One's "A Friend" video. The clip was cute, and we really did have fun shooting it—KRS, Redman, and me boppin' in unison on a rooftop. It was a B-girl's dream come true.

For a brief stint I thought that was the end of my ride as an artist and didn't think twice about it. But out of the blue one day I got a call from Lance "Un" Rivera. He was Biggie's former business partner and Lil' Kim was signed to his label, Undeas, at the time.

"I'm putting a bunch of girls on this song 'Ladies Night.' You sounded really good on that 'Heartbeat' joint," Un said, explaining that Kim was doing a "Not Tonight" remix with Left Eye, Da Brat, and Missy Elliott. And they wanted me on the song!

My new Ladies' Night show on Friday nights with DJ Jazzy Joyce and DJ Coco Chanel was taking off. So he thought it was a good fit.

"You should jump on this, do the intro."

It's so funny how once you rap on something people just assume now you're a rapper. And I'm expected to write a rhyme. I'd never written a rap. That last rhyme, KRS-One wrote for me. Now I'm expected to write a rap that would have to stand next to the biggest female rappers in the game. So I called Salaam, DJ Doo Wop, and a few people for advice. And

Doo Wop, God bless him, gave me some pointers. "Maybe change the words to this . . . and try this . . ."

I must have spent two days in my house with a pad and a pen, writing pages' worth of shit that was probably all terrible. I wrote about one hundred bars 'cause I didn't know what was good, what was wack. Finally, at the appointed hour, I went into the studio session at the Hit Factory and Un was waiting.

"Do you have something? You got a verse?"

"I don't know if I got a verse, but I got about two pages of rhymes," I told him. I actually didn't even know how to count bars or what the standard structure of a verse was.

Un gave me a look like "it's not that serious" and said, "Get your ass in the booth."

So I went in the booth and I just started doing all of it, everything that I'd written. We did it a bunch of times and Un picked the best eight bars.

> It's ladies night what, it must be Angie on the mic
> The Butter P honey got the sugar got the spice
> Roll the L's tight, keep the rhymes right
> Yo, I just made this motherfucker up last night
> And uhh . . . I'm the rookie on this all-star team
> Me and Kim is gettin' cream, like Thelma and Louise . . .

"This is the part," he confirmed, and then added, "I may have you come back in once I get all the other girls in place and do some ad-libs."

"Okay, cool, whatever you need," I said. "If you don't like it, you don't have to use it. It's okay. I understand."

"No, no, it's good. It's really good."

This was all so outside my realm of experience that I couldn't tell if it was really good or he was just saying so. In any event, not too much later I was called back to the studio to do some ad-libs. Left Eye was there when I arrived. TLC was one of my favorite girl groups of all time, and Left Eye was iconic. She had recently been all over the news for burning her man's house down. It was the biggest story at the time, being circulated all over the world, and there I was in the studio while she wrote: *I be the one to blame as the flames keep rising to the top and it don't stop.*

With all her success and everything she had been going through, Left Eye could have been standoffish. But she wasn't. She was sweet and giving. One of the first things she said was, "I really like your verse."

"You do? I was so worried."

"Yeah, it sounds really good."

When I went in the booth, Left Eye did everything she could to make me feel comfortable and confident, like I belonged there. Five years later, when she died too young, I remembered how helpful and encouraging she had been to me that day.

Thinking back, all of the women on the song were like a team, and everyone—Left Eye, Lil' Kim, Da Brat, Missy Elliott, and me—had good vibes toward each other. The next thing I knew we were flying off to West Palm Beach to shoot the video. This was back in the day when the big-budget music videos were everything. They had us scuba diving and riding Jet Skis. And so many other top female artists like Mary J., Queen Latifah, and SWV came out to do cameos and support the video. It was like living out a fantasy that I would have been embarrassed to even admit I'd ever had.

But still, I wasn't getting ready to quit my day job. At the same time, I was just riding the wave as the song's success built. People were coming up and quoting, "It must be Angie on the mic . . ." and telling me how they just loved the video. It wasn't just a New York thing. In fact, after the single was released in July of 1997, "Not Tonight (Ladies Night Remix)" took off and stayed in the Hot 100 for twenty-one weeks, peaking at number six! When Grammy nominations were announced, it would be nominated for Best Rap Song by a Duo or Group. Though it would later lose to Puffy and Faith's "I'll Be Missing You"—a tribute to Biggie—getting the Grammy nomination was a huge deal.

Even before that, just as nuts, we were asked to perform at the MTV Video Awards in September of '97.

*Perform? As in perform LIVE and in person on TV? I don't know how to fucking perform.*

At Radio City Music Hall on the night of the awards, June Ambrose styled us. But June had her hands full. Along with Kim and Missy and everybody else, she was also styling Puffy, who was performing "I'll Be Missing You." Clearly, I was at the bottom of June's priority list. So she gave no fucks about me. Like literally we're about to go onstage and I still had no shoes.

Not trying to be a diva or anything, I nicely said, "I don't have any shoes. Do you have anything?" And one of June's assistants came up with this terrible pair of clunky black shoes. I didn't have management. I didn't have a stylist. I just showed up with a ponytail like—*Okay, we're gonna perform at the MTV Awards.* It was a nightmare. More than anything, it was embarrassing to be unprepared.

Not that I saw being an artist as part of my destiny. At the time, I chalked all of it up as a blip—a really cool one but just a moment.

While that's how I was looking at it, record labels saw it differently. Not too long after the MTV Awards, I started to get calls. And not just calls but interest from multiple labels for me to do my own album!

This ride just kept getting crazier. A whole album? Salaam was the one who convinced me to at least take the meetings. "If you still want to say no, at least you'll know what you're turning down." He was right. Why the hell not hear what they had to say?

My attitude was—here I go again, into uncharted territory. I tried to do what had worked for me in the past by staying open and looking to learn all that I could.

That attitude freed me. And it helped me up my game in other areas, too.

# CHAPTER SEVEN

# READY OR NOT

At twenty-six years old, in that fall of 1997, I'd started to understand the importance of keeping my inner circle tight. For the most part, I'd always been a good judge of character, and my friends not only protected me as my popularity grew, but they kept me grounded. That became meaningful to me the more I found myself surrounded by people in the business—record promoters, club promoters, deejays, and aspiring artists. Not that they were bad people. It's just that when you let too many others into your life, especially people with agendas, it leaves room for error. And messiness.

See, the thing about success is that people want to stand next to it. They want a piece of it; they want access to it. People begin to see you as an opportunity, and if you are not careful you could wake up one day and realize that all of your friends are not really your friends. I've seen it happen to too many people and always refused to let it happen to me. My defining line became *I don't want to be around people who don't want the best for me. And I don't want to be with somebody who resents my drive.*

For all those reasons, I actively cherished friends closest to me like Nikki, and my girlfriends Tracey and Liane. Of course, I'd known Nikki for most of my life and at this point we were more like sisters than friends. Nikki, still tall and model thin, always more conservative than me, was moving up professionally in her career in the Financial District. We still didn't have the same interests, but she had my back and I always trusted her judgment. There were times when I'd bring a new friend around and Nikki would say simply, "Ehhhhh, I don't know about her," and that was enough for me because she was *always* right! When Nikki and I met Tracey and Liane, we all clicked right away. Tracey, also Puerto Rican and from Washington Heights, loved hip-hop as much as I did. She knew all the lyrics and would come to the clubs in sneakers because they were easier to dance in. She was my type of girl! As Tracey started to make her way up the business ladder in sales and marketing, she could be more conservative in attire—but her heart was always hip-hop. Now, Liane—who was to Tracey what Nikki was to me, best friends for many years—was much more conservative. Liane's family was from Spain, and she was way more girlie, almost prissy, always put together perfectly. She and Nikki always had great manners, while Tracey and I never really gave a fuck. Liane, who would go into PR and eventually become an executive, was very into fashion, style, and pop culture. Between the four of us, there was never a lack of fun or fun stuff to talk about. And most importantly, we trusted each other.

On the romantic side of things, in this period I had started seeing Q-Tip again, and this time it was more of a real relationship. He was still that guy who, the first time we met, made me feel like we'd known each other forever. Tip was someone I trusted as a friend, who made me comfortable, who gave me encouragement and acted as a sounding board for me. As the competitive atmosphere at the station began to intensify, especially in the wake of the MTV Awards and possibilities of getting an album deal, Tip was the first person to come to my defense if somebody said something bad about me.

Tip would invariably say, "They're fucking crazy." He had my back no matter what. Even sometimes when I might not have been in the right, he would defend me and take my side. You have to love that. Between Tip and the advice I'd gotten from Pac not to worry so much about what is said by people who are gonna talk shit anyway, I tried to keep a thick-skinned attitude.

And that's what I did at first as far as some comments I started to hear about Wendy Williams having a problem with me. But why? If I thought back to when she first arrived at the station, I couldn't remember any reason for it. During this time, when I was doing nights, Wendy Williams was on afternoons. So, obviously, I came on after her and the two of us would see each other in passing at the station. Wendy was a really big personality in her own right. Tall and intense, everything about her was a lot—a lot of hair, a lot of makeup, a lot of presence. She'd walk down the hall like she owned it. She'd done radio for way longer than me, and I always liked her on the air; she was offensive and outrageous but extremely entertaining. As much as I enjoyed her, I was smart enough to keep my distance.

Wendy would go about her business and I would go about mine. She would talk shit about the artists all day and then they would come to my show at night to tell their side of whatever the story was. It was like an unintentional game of good cop, bad cop, and for the station it was a win-win. But as much as she was killing the ratings and people were tuned in, I'm sure getting booed at events wasn't fun for her, and I'm sure the fact that I was booking all the guests was irritating, too.

Flex pulled me aside one day to say that Doug E. Fresh's promo calling me the "hottest chick on the radio" was Doug E.'s way of shitting on Wendy.

*Huh?? It was????*

I never looked at it that way because for a few years now I had been the *only* chick there. That type of personalized drop was the norm. But I did take notice and I tried to be a little more sensitive. Not that it would matter to Wendy.

People would repeat an unflattering comment Wendy had made in general and they'd add, "She's probably talking about you."

My reply was consistent: "Whatever. That's just Wendy. She talks shit about everybody."

But then it started to come more directly, with others telling me, "Yo, she don't like you. Clearly."

The sensible thing to do, I figured, was to talk to her, keep things cool, and clear the air. I hate weirdness with people. I planned to approach her at work after her show ended, before mine got started.

So when I arrived, as Wendy was going off the air, the first person I saw was my producer, Paddy Duke, who was getting my show ready. He was a small guy with a big Italian personality who was a fiercely loyal member of the Hot 97 team. Then I saw Wendy about to leave.

"Paddy, would you mind stepping outside for a minute?" I asked, and waited a beat as he left. Then I turned to Wendy.

She could see I had something to say, so she stood there, like—*well?*

"Wendy, people keep telling me you're taking jabs at me," I began. She stared back as if to say, *What are you talking about?*

"I'm not saying you are. I'm just saying that that's what the perception is," I went on. "I've been ignoring it, but I just wanted to make sure that we're good . . ."

"Well, you know, I'm just doing my job. I didn't really say anything, but okay, whatever, no problem." She was defensive and barely looked me in the eye and was clearly uncomfortable, so I let it go.

Then she did it again. I kept bringing it up to her but being nice about it. In essence, I'd say, "Look, I don't want us to have any problems. I know you're not saying my name, but you're saying shit that feels funny." I gave her examples, like her comment that, "You know these 'other' radio personalities are out here hanging out with the artists."

Wendy came from the school of "you can't be friends with the artists because then you can't talk shit about them." And I understood—that was her thing and she was great at it—but I never felt that way. To me, I respected the artists, I respected the culture, and I always wanted them to feel comfortable in my house. That's just who *I* was. I wasn't necessarily out here looking for friends, but I always wanted to treat people with respect. We had different radio philosophies. She was a radio person who wound up at a hip-hop station. I was a hip-hop kid who wound up doing radio. Two very different types of human beings. But ultimately she was great at being Wendy, and all I ever wanted to do was be great at being me.

Again I ask her if she has an issue with me.

Again she blows me off. "No, no, it's fine. I didn't even say anything . . . Whatever."

"No seriously, Wendy . . . we work together. We have to see each other every day. I'm looking you in your face and asking you to please stop making this uncomfortable."

She finally hears me. Or that's what she says: "I hear you. I'm sorry . . . I'll stop."

And she did. For a few weeks. Then the bitch did it again!

I was driving to work and had the radio on and I heard her say something about my relationship. No mistaking that when Wendy said, "I'm not the one dating a rapper up here. Ugh . . . if I was, maybe I would like that song."

Just catty dumb shit like that. It was so unnecessary and weird.

*And now I gotta walk into work and be cordial again?!*

Nope, I had to try a different approach. The time had come to go to management.

"Listen," I began, not mincing words. "I gotta see this woman every day and I'm uncomfortable. You gotta talk to her or we are going to have a problem."

For many other reasons, management had their own issues with Wendy. Steve Smith assured me, "I'll talk to her." And it worked!

For a few weeks. And then again . . . She said something catty about my relationship with Tip. *What the fuck?!*

So I go into the station that day and I'm like, "Wendy, do me a favor. Don't talk about me at all. Because now it's a problem." I start getting stern about it. "Seriously, don't do it. I gotta see you every day. I don't want a problem with you. I hear you. I see you. Stop!"

She actually looked me in the eye this time and said, "Okay, fine. I get it. No problem." She added, "Angie, I'm sorry. I will stop." Finally, she didn't deny it.

*All right, cool. Finally we got it out. It's gonna fucking stop.*

I couldn't wait to get it all behind me.

A couple of days later I'm at Margarita's house—my friend from Miami who was now living in Queens after landing a job at a record label—and we're hanging out and talking shit when I get a strange call.

One of the record reps is calling to ask, "Yo, have you seen Wendy's website?"

"I haven't."

"You should go check it out."

Wendy had launched a website. At this point websites weren't that big of a deal because not everybody was online yet and personal websites had just started—it was almost unheard of. So I go to her website and it says: "One of my coworkers is dating Q-Tip from A Tribe Called Quest. Oh well. I guess some women like men who like men."

Everybody was gay to Wendy. Every rapper you could think of in that era, I had heard Wendy Williams call them gay. Not one or two. Like *every* one of them. She was all about the gay rapper. That was her thing. And she was running with it.

*Are you fucking kidding me? We* just *had a conversation about this.*

I am on fire. And immediately I call to tell Tip.

"Whatever," he says. "She's crazy."

I wasn't even trying to hear him.

"Fuck that!" I insist. "I worked too hard and for too long to let this lady keep disrespecting me. I am going to deal with her tomorrow. This is going to stop."

I woke up the next morning as infuriated as the night before, and headed into work early to confront her. As I approached the station, I could feel my anger building. I couldn't focus on anything else and I couldn't shake it. The crazy thing is that normally I never confront anyone when I'm too emotional or angry. I try to be smarter than that. It's impossible to operate from a sensible place when you're that worked up. I knew it could lead to a bad situation, but at this point, she had pushed me into a corner.

As I got into the elevator, I began to regain some of my senses and talk myself off the ledge.

*You know what? You're being crazy. You're not in high school. It's just Wendy. This is her shtick and this is what she does. Don't bring yourself*

*down to her level. You're not gonna do anything to her. That would be*
*dumb. There has to be another way to work this out . . .*

I was almost calm when I stepped off the elevator and started making my way to the studio area. Then I saw Wendy. She was prancing to
the bathroom with her big weave bouncing all over the place like she
didn't have a care in the world. "Hey, Annngggie!"

And, man, there was something about the way she said my name
that made my fucking blood boil! It was so phony and condescending.
The whole time she was in the bathroom, I was right outside of the ladies'
room waiting, pacing.

Then Wendy comes out of the bathroom and I'm standing right
there. She stops. Quick.

"Didn't I tell you to leave me the fuck alone?"

"What are you talking about?"

"Wendy, I told you to leave me the FUCK ALONE."

She rolls her eyes. "Uggggggghhh."

And I lost my fucking mind. Before I knew it I was swinging at her.
It was a quick scuffle. It took only a few seconds for me to realize that
she wasn't really hitting me back—she was just trying to get me off of
her. I think she was just stunned. Nobody got hurt or anything like that.

And then Skeletor, her board op at the time, came running out of
the studio, shouting, "Girls, girls, what's going on? Angie, stttooooppp!"

By that point Wendy began yelling, "What is *wrong* with you?!" She
grabbed the mop that had been leaning against the wall outside of the
bathroom and just stood there with it like she wanted to have some sort of
sword fight or something. It was actually kind of funny, even in the moment.

I asked, "What are you going to do with that Wendy??"

She said nothing.

Calmly, I asked, "No, seriously, what are you going to do with that?"

She put it down and stormed back into the studio. I calmly walked back to the programming area, into my music director Tracy Cloherty's office. "I just want you to know before anyone else tells you that I just put my hands on Wendy."

Tracy bounced right up out of her chair. "What?!!" she said. "Sit down. Are you—are you crazy? Stay right here." And she went storming out to go to the studio. I must have lasted four seconds sitting there, thinking. I'd tried to handle it the nice, positive, right way multiple times. As I sat there recapping in my head, I start to get all fired up again.

*She put me in a fucking corner, man.*

So I storm out of Tracy's office and follow her to the studio. I bust in and she's already in conversation with Wendy. They both turn around and just look at me. They both have a glare in their eye, like—*Oh my God, what's she gonna do? Why is she here???*

Tracy says, "Angie, get out of here right now."

I pause and look at Wendy, who is visibly shaken, and she lets out an erratic "You're crazy!!!"

*Meeeee??? I'm the crazy one?*

I could tell by the seriousness on Tracy's face that we were done here. So I went back to her office and waited for her to come back. This was another time my career could have been over before I even hit afternoons. I could have been fired. By the way, I should have been fired. Instead I got suspended. And so did she.

• • •

The *Daily News* ran with the headline: Angie Martinez Pounces on Wendy Williams.

To this day, I don't know what Wendy really felt, if she was mad or embarrassed or just shocked. When she went on the radio the next day, she stated, "For the record, nobody hit anybody. Nobody punched anybody."

People had warned me there might be a lawsuit, but once she said that, I was relieved. *Oh, great. I don't ever have to worry about anything there.*

Then a divide happened. Wendy had always been an outsider at the station. She would bring ratings, but her personality was not that of a team player. And as an outsider, she'd caused resentment in the past, and people started feeling comfortable enough to voice it. Flex got on the radio and read the article, treating it as if it were funny. "'She pounced.' Ha!" He was laughing at Wendy on the air. This was a coworker still. He shouldn't have done that. But Flex was Flex. And he knew that people would eat this story up.

The truth is that if it wasn't me it was gonna be somebody else. She was disrespectful to so many people all the time. And this may sound crazy, but I actually believed that it was a good thing it was me because I wasn't someone who really wanted to hurt her. I was just trying to defend myself. I thought maybe I saved her from someone else feeling they needed to run up on her. Someone who actually could have hurt her. Yes! At the time I actually believed that it was for an all-around good cause. I for sure got a few thank-you notes.

My mother, who knew the world of radio as well as anyone, even if she didn't know the day-to-day dynamics at Hot, asked me the following night, "Well, what really happened?"

"Well, you know, I just kind of pushed her." I shrugged, trying to downplay what happened.

"Really?" she said. "'Cause the paper says you pounced on her."

My mother was concerned. I was embarrassed.

A few days later she came to me and said, "You know what one of my colleagues said?"

"What?"

"You know, the thing with Wendy," my mother began, and then paused, careful and thoughtful with her words as always as she continued. "As much as it's the wrong thing to do, to ever put a hand on someone, especially at work, it does set a precedent that you are not somebody that can be pushed around."

And my mother, by the way, is the queen of doing everything by the book. She never wants to offend anybody. She never wants to do anything illegal. You know, if she owes you $4.07, here is your four dollars and five, six, seven cents. She is by-the-book Shirley. So for her to understand and say, "In the big picture, down the road in your life and your career, at least people will know you are not somebody that will allow someone else to push them around."

That was her way of saying "I trust your judgment and I support you."

A few weeks passed, and when they brought me back from my suspension, that's when the conversation happened. I really should have been fired, but everybody there was already tired of Wendy because there were a lot of problems with her. She wasn't happy there either. And I think they were looking for a reason to get rid of her as it was.

"Listen, we know Wendy's a pain in the ass," Steve said. "We'd love to get rid of her. But the problem is, if we did that, you have to do Afternoon Drive."

I never wanted to do Afternoon Drive. I loved being on air at night. I loved the freedom. I loved the artists. I loved being able to go out after, and I didn't want to do Afternoon Drive. To me that was corny. I mean, I was on in the nights, when I could be edgy. Plus, I was young and still wanted to be in the streets.

Steve may have understood that I didn't want to do that. But he put it to me in no uncertain terms, saying, "Listen, if you don't do Afternoon Drive, I cannot let Wendy go. I don't have anyone else strong enough to take that slot. The only way I can let her go is if you take it."

After talking to Flex and Ed and a few others at the station, I agreed. I would take one for the team.

So now, not only am I moving to a time slot that I don't want, but the thing about Wendy Williams is that she is super talented and amazing at what she does. I don't do what she does. And I was scared as shit!

And soon the story was everywhere:

## DUELING DEEJAYS
### Friday, October 24, 1997

After getting into a shoving match with fellow Hot 97 deejay Wendy Williams, it must taste sweet to Angie Martinez to have taken over Williams's drive-time slot the last two weeks. Despite her high ratings, the trash-talking Williams has been gone from the station for three weeks, and management ain't saying whether it's permanent . . .

The *Daily News* headlines continued throughout October 1997, and Wendy's listeners were wondering if she was gone for good. And now that I was on afternoons but no official announcement had been made, Wendy's listeners became most unfriendly. I used to get threatening faxes—it wasn't texts or e-mails or tweets; it was faxes that said things like, "Bitch, get off the radio. I'll break your jaw." It was awful and it made me insecure. Worse, the newspaper reported that Wendy's fans had other plans, too:

## FANS' RALLYING CRY: WHERE'S WENDY?
### Friday, October 31, 1997

Fans of WQHT afternoon deejay Wendy Williams, who has been off the air for almost a month with no official explanation, are planning a protest rally at the station Monday to ask why. The rally is planned at Hot 97 studios at 395 Hudson St., 2–4 p.m. Station officials couldn't be reached yesterday for comment on Williams' status. She is aware of Monday's rally, but it isn't known if she will attend. Williams was reportedly involved in a heated argument at the station a month ago with sister deejay Angie Martinez.

They were planning a rally? A fucking rally!

How had my charmed radio life been turned upside down? I was somebody who loved what I did and tried to have a voice that mattered to my listeners, and had never had any aspirations or claims on anyone else's arena. All of a sudden everyone is putting the pressure on—saying, well, you're filling the shoes of Wendy. Can you get her numbers? Can you fill her spot? Can you deal with this type of heat on you? It was the first time people were nasty to me. Apparently, I had to develop a much thicker skin.

You just keep pushing. You can't quit. You just keep showing up every day. I sucked for a while because I was off balance. What I had been doing for so long at night didn't work in the afternoon. Not surprisingly, at first I couldn't deliver. But I couldn't let myself believe that would be forever. So I just had to keep going.

Bit by bit I began to get the difference. In the afternoon, you have to be a little quicker with it. Nighttime, I could be like, "Who's ordering chicken?" We could talk about that for eight minutes and it was entertaining. In the middle of the day, when people are at work, that's going to lose the audience. That challenge is that you have to develop a whole different timing. And I had to get beat the fuck up for a while. From what I heard later on, I almost didn't make it.

Blundering along, I think the part that hurt most was feeling so alone. Management started to wonder if they had made a mistake. And Flex was still telling labels that guests had to come to his show first. He was taking all the exclusives. I was drowning.

Finally, I called Flex and said, "I want to talk to you." Our relationship had become flimsy. We barely talked anymore—but really, I had no one else to turn to. I couldn't do this alone, and I needed him. It was a tough call for me to make, and for weeks he blew me off with one excuse or another.

At last he agreed that I'd come to meet him in his office and we'd go somewhere for lunch. We jumped into one of his muscle cars and headed out for something to eat.

On the way, I started in, explaining, "Look, you don't understand how hard it is for me out here. I'm trying to navigate my way through shit by myself. I don't know what to do a lot of the times." I couldn't believe how upset I allowed myself to be, pouring it all out. "Even this Wendy thing—I don't want to do afternoons. I'm taking it for the team. She had to go. You all agreed, and now I don't feel like I'm getting support from anybody. I don't even know what happened to us . . . Like you're talking shit—" And in the middle of what I'm saying, I start crying . . . bawling like a little girl, sniffling and trying to catch my breath.

Flex looked so shaken. And confused. You see, Flex is the type that thrives off competition and is motivated by a proverbial "enemy," so I think once I wasn't (in his mind) on his team anymore, he just put me in the "competition" box and treated me as such. But in that moment I think he realized that not only was I not his enemy but that I actually loved him and needed him.

And in that moment something changed.

Flex looked over and smiled his great smile. "It's all right, Ang. You know, you did the right thing," he said. "You're gonna be great. Don't worry."

From that day on Flex has probably been the most important person in my radio career. He has defended me when I didn't ask him to and was a bully for me during a lot of crazy times. I know I wouldn't be on the air without him. But I also don't think I would have survived some of those tough periods had we not had the one-two punch of Flex and Ang. We lit those fires when those fires needed to be lit. Once we established trust with each other, then it was like we were unstoppable.

That conversation was a defining moment maybe for the both of us. Flex and I became like the mother and father of the whole station. He could do the dirty work—playing the power politics and pushing his weight when it had to be done—and he left me a lane where I didn't have to. I didn't want to do dirty work. I didn't want to argue with people. I just wanted to be gracious and boost morale and hopefully motivate.

Flex came through time and again. He has been my friend, my confidant, my mentor, my guy. That's not to say he hasn't pissed me off over the years. But he pissed me off in the way a family member would piss you off. Like I'm gonna call you and tell you, "What the fuck did you do that for?" We disagreed plenty of times. But even when we did, there was not ever a doubt about his loyalty or our friendship.

That adjustment to the new time slot took some time. And eventually I found a rhythm; eventually I found my voice in the afternoons.

The lesson was a first for me—the fact that shit ain't always sweet. People are not always gonna like you. When I looked back at the past, I had to say to myself, of course you found your niche and got real comfortable and people liked you and you were grateful for it but you also somewhat took it for granted. That was back in once upon a time when you could just do what you love and it's all gonna be sweet. And now you've moved on and that's not the case anymore. There was no more Battle of the Beats, which I missed. Now I was doing the Hot Five at Four instead of the Hot Five at Nine. Now my interviews had to be a lot quicker. It was a tough adjustment. But you know, I found my way.

Wendy found hers as well. I watch her TV talk show sometimes and she has really mastered her lane. I find myself watching and laughing out loud. I don't have any ill feelings toward her. When I think about what happened, I understand that she was doing her and she didn't care who she offended. And I was fighting for myself. I was very protective of my personal relationships, and I felt violated in a place where I shouldn't ever have to feel violated. And so what do you do when you're in a corner? Sometimes you have to fight back.

As dramatic as the episode was, it was only a moment in time. I haven't seen her since.

# CHAPTER EIGHT

# THROUGH THE FIRE

Half asleep, early on the first Saturday of February 1998, I'm at Tip's town house in Englewood, New Jersey, and I hear him banging around and making noise like he's trying to wake me up on purpose.

We had been fighting a lot that week, and the night before I got so pissed off that I grabbed my pillow and went to sleep by myself in the other room. So as I hear him walking around and shaking the house, my blurry thoughts are—*Why is he being so loud??? Is he just trying to be a dick 'cause I slept in the guest room?* I was so sleepy. And so annoyed.

That's when he bursts into the room—"GET UP!!!!"

"What? Why??!"

"You don't smell the smoke? There's a fire in the house!"

I jump up. "What? Where?!"

"I think it's in the studio. Get dressed! We gotta get outta here."

While he runs downstairs to see what's happening and try to find the extinguisher, I bolt into his room to grab some shorts and slippers.

By the time I get back to the staircase, the flames are there, climbing up the sides and quickly building at the bottom.

"Tiiiiiiip!!" I scream. He comes running around to the bottom of the stairs trying to beat the flames with a blanket.

"Come on!!!!!" he calls to me from the bottom, where I can barely see him. "Just run down fast. I got you!"

I was terrified. I looked around and quickly assessed my options. *I can't do it. I'm just going to jump from the balcony.* I'm not sure why I thought the twenty-foot jump from the balcony was a better option than running through the flames, but that was my plan.

"C'mon!" he yelled.

"I can't do it, Tip. I'm scared . . . I'm just gonna—"

Before I could finish, Tip threw the blanket over his head and ran up the stairs to grab me. He covered me with the blanket, grabbed my hand, and said, "Keep your head down and don't stop." And together we ran down the stairs and out of the house.

Tip's road manager and friend Lite was with us, and the three of us stood there covered in soot and watched the house burn down. For what felt like hours, we watched it all burn, and I mean everything—clothes, photos, unreleased music, equipment, and probably the most painful to Tip, his entire beloved record collection . . . ruined. If you know anything about Q-Tip, you'd know these albums were not just a typical record collection. This was his life; this was what got him out of the hood. He spent countless days finding exclusives and rare vinyl and then hours each day listening to the nuances of these albums, trying to rework them. I mean, it was devastating; and we were numb.

Ali Shaheed Muhammad, his longtime friend and collaborator from Tribe, came over soon after, and I remember watching the two of them standing over the melted vinyl. It was brutal. We took a photo of the moment and tried to keep perspective. In the spirit of "These are only material things; let us be grateful to be alive," we posed and did our best B-boy stance. Years later, when I came across the photos, it was obvious we weren't fooling anyone. We did do the poses, but in our eyes there was nothing but sadness.

We tried to give ourselves a sense that life would go on and it was good to be alive, so we decided to leave the scene for pancakes. There we were, Lite, Q-Tip, Ali, and me, at the IHOP in Englewood, New Jersey—covered in soot and reeking of smoke and fire. It was such a sad day.

Tip and I made it out of the fire, but our relationship, already strained, had new challenges. He had just converted to Islam, and in finding his path he became exacting in his beliefs. Though I made an effort to read the Koran and get as familiar as I could with the religion, that was not my path. It wasn't as if the fire caused the breakup. But I think when you go through any kind of life-threatening ordeal, it forces you to take stock of your life and figure out what's important. We both saw that our lives were in different places, and as much as we loved each other, Tip couldn't compromise what he saw for his future and I couldn't compromise mine. Ultimately, it didn't work, but I adore him and we are still great friends to this day.

• • •

That year delivered huge hip-hop albums—including Big Pun's *Capital Punishment,* making him the first Latin rapper to ever go platinum. This was such a big deal because not only was he Latino, but this was real hip-hop and he was dope. Latinos were proud. Big Pun was signed to Fat Joe's newly formed Terror Squad, along with Cuban Link, Prospect, Armageddon, and Triple Seis. Some of my favorite memories of this era are of hanging out with Big Pun and Fat Joe up at Jimmy's in the Bronx. Fat Joe's then girlfriend (and future wife), Lorena, would become one of my closest friends. She is the definition of a rider, the type of friend you'd want to go to war with or commit a crime with because you know she'll have your back till the end.

I'd known Joe for a lot of years at this point and we also developed a friendship. Fat Joe, a big Puerto Rican with an even bigger presence, could tell a story like nobody else, always entertaining and extremely likable. There was a certain innate camaraderie I had with him—being authentically part of the culture, and also Latino and from New York. As Joe's career grew, he went from being a solo artist to the leader of the Terror Squad. Pun was another Puerto Rican from the Bronx and a notorious prankster with a quirky sense of humor, the kind of humor where you weren't sure if he was hilarious or if you should be offended.

There was this one time when Big Pun came to my show and brought weed cookies. "Have one," Pun said with a twinkle in his eye.

Though I smoked weed, I'd never eaten it before, so I didn't know what the difference was. I tried a cookie and it had no effect. "I don't feel anything!" I told him.

Ten minutes pass, still nothing. Fifteen minutes later, nothing. "Have more!" Pun said, because he was a fucking asshole. "Eat more!"

Whatever. I didn't really want to eat more, but he was relentless, so I ate a shitload of cookies. And when those things kicked in, Pun had already left, and I thought I was going to die. Actually die.

"Call 911! Take me to the hospital. I'm poisoned!" I screamed to my producer, Paddy Duke. As I was just learning, the thing about weed cookies is that it's not the same type of high as when you smoke. When you smoke, you chill. This was crazy aggressive and so nauseating that I started to throw up as my head spun, telling me one thing—*I'm going to die.*

"Paddy, I need you to call 911."

"I can't call 911." Paddy reminded me that I still had an hour left of my radio show to do. He said, "If we call 911, everyone is going to know that something happened to you. The bosses are going to ask what happened, and we're going to have to tell them that you were eating weed cookies on the air with Pun. We can't call an ambulance."

"Well, I'll take myself to the hospital then!"

I stormed out. I never made it to the emergency room but instead had to be driven home, where I then slept it off. Never again! No weed cookies, brownies, or gummy bears for me, thanks.

That episode aside, I was so happy for Big Pun when his album went platinum and when he and Fat Joe showed the industry that there was much more to come from Latin hip-hop artists. New voices were coming into their own from other corners, and overall the players in the game were a more diverse cast of characters than ever. In 1998 OutKast's *Aquemini* put a spotlight on hip-hop coming out of the South. It was a big time for super crews like The Fugees, Murder Inc., Ruff Ryders, and Shady/Aftermath.

As Y2K came into view, it was a done deal just how wrong the people were who had said that hip-hop was only a phase and wouldn't last. This was not a bad time to be in the middle of it all as I swung into a higher gear on my show in the afternoons, pulling out all the stops. The pace was crazier than ever.

On top of that, I was single and caught up even more in the fast life, hosting parties, hosting mixtapes, hanging out and having fun but always working and always running. After the split with Tip, I'd moved to a new apartment on Prospect Avenue in Hackensack, New Jersey—which was one of those neighborhoods where you would run into rappers at the supermarket. Lots of music-industry new-money folks living in high-rise luxury buildings, that was us. Mike Kyser from Def Jam lived up the block, and either I or someone else would host a night of playing spades or extremely intense Monopoly games with people like Irv Gotti and Ja

Rule joining in. When my girlfriend Liane got engaged, her bachelorette party was at my crib. And since hosting was my thing, I started to have taco nights on the regular. I mean, that apartment brought me so much fun. Well, that is until . . .

Yup! It happened again. Eviction notice on the door. Padlock on the doorknob. Me standing there in horror. Again.

*What is wrong with me?! I didn't think my rent was* that *late?*

Now, in addition to the shock and embarrassment that I felt the last time this had happened, I was also so *mad* at myself. At this point I'm twenty-seven years old and this shit is not cute.

Nikki was in between apartments and had been staying with me at the time. So now, not only was I homeless, but I had made my best friend homeless, too! All because my dumb ass wants to live check to check, drive Benzes, and pay my bills whenever I got around to it . . . just dumb irresponsible shit.

That first night Nikki and I stayed at Margarita's house. Then we went to a hotel. At that point, I thought hard about what it was going to take to get back into the crib and never let anything like this happen ever, ever again.

The immediate goal was to figure out how to pay the six thousand dollars in back rent and get back into the apartment. The problem was I didn't have it! I was only able to scrape together three of the six.

Nikki shrugged. "Why don't you call Tip?"

Of course I knew he would say yes and bail me out. But I couldn't. My pride wouldn't let me. Instead I called my friend Mary.

Mary J. Blige. God, there are no words for how I love that woman! She is one of the most authentic people I know. Mary is all heart. Not an easy thing to be, by the way. It is the reason she is able to make the music she has made and touch the lives she has touched.

"Come get me now; I'm in the studio," were the first words out of her mouth when I told her what had happened.

"Are you sure?"

"Girl, bring your ass over here." She was going to lend me the money.

When we arrived at the studio it was almost midnight. Mary ran downstairs and hopped in the back of Nikki's '94 Honda Accord as we drove off to find an open check-cashing spot. I have no idea why Mary happened to have an uncashed check in her purse at that moment, but she did. We tried a few places, but they were all closed.

At that point I'm sitting in the passenger seat as Nikki drives and I look back to see a serious expression on Mary's face as she says, "Nikki, pull over. We gotta pray on this."

I don't remember the exact prayer, but I do remember Mary intensely rebuking the situation and asking God to spare me from these type of problems. Right after that we found a twenty-four-hour check-cashing place in Midtown. With no concern about any of the people who recognized her in there, Mary got the cash, handed me the three thousand dollars, no questions asked.

We got back into the apartment the next day. And I don't know if it was Mary's prayer session in the back of the Accord or my vow to never, ever let this happen again, but after that I started to get my shit together. It wasn't overnight, but I got serious about how I chose to support the lifestyle of being a grown-up in my late twenties. Sometimes you go through the fire of an embarrassing eviction, like I had the first time, and you just don't get the lesson. Or you do learn it, but you get so caught up in other demands that it loses its staying power. So you have to get through it again. And even though nothing disastrous happened in the end, twice was enough to give me a crash course in keeping a better eye on how I earned, spent, and saved money.

And thank God I did start to do that, because after all that talk about me recording an album of my own, Sylvia Rhone at Elektra Records actually made me an offer. The deal was for more than a hundred thousand dollars to go into the studio and record an album. Yep! A fucking hundred-thousand-dollar-advance check for me as an artist in my own right. And, as icing on the cake, Warner Bros. gave me a publishing deal—for even more than that!

Now, remember, at that point I had done eight bars on the "Ladies Night Remix" and had written a couple of verses for Doo Wop and Tony Touch mixtapes. Nothing more than trying it out, trying to learn, putting my toe in the water. But that was it. I had absolutely *no* clue how to even begin to make an album. But again, here I was with an opportunity that I sure as hell was going to embrace—as I would encourage anybody in my position to do. You show up, and you go for it all the way. And then you sink or swim.

# CHAPTER NINE

# UP CLOSE AND PERSONAL

My career as a solo recording artist got off to a rocky start. There was a lot more sinking than swimming from the get-go.

I booked a few sessions and paid a few producers to come in and sit with me and try out a few things. That did *not* go well. Then the label sent me to Virginia to work with the Neptunes.

The Neptunes were a production team made up Chad Hugo and Pharrell Williams. Yes, that Pharrell. The future singer of "Happy," judge on *The Voice*, and BBC mogul. And they were on fire at the time, producing everybody from Mystikal (with hits coming like "Shake Ya Azz" and "Danger") to Jay Z on "The City Is Mine" from earlier and "I Just Wanna Luv U" around this period. They'd produced hits for artists like the Lox and had a slate of new stuff coming up with Lil' Kim and Shyne. The list went on and on. What was I doing here? My self-doubts kicked in as soon as I got to Virginia Beach and tried to settle in at some damp hotel that felt dark and lonely. Maybe it wasn't really that bad, but I was so out of my element. And I was nervous as shit.

Since the Neptunes were so in demand, they had several projects going at once and I was told to just stay put until they were ready for me. Time passed way too slowly until finally, the label rep called to say, "Hey, your car is going to pick you up and bring you to the studio around ten p.m. The Neptunes are there finishing up with Kelis . . . Then they will start with you."

Sure enough, the car came and got me to the studio. As I walked in, music was *blasting*, playing a beat that sounded dope as shit! Pharrell stood there over the boards, bopping his head, while everyone in the room did the same. He looked up and saw me and came right over and gave me a hug.

"Yo, that's dope, right???" It turned out to be Ray J's "Wait a Minute." Then he gestured to the other room, saying, "C'mon, let's go talk in there."

I'd met Pharrell a few times and he had been a guest on my show. But the two of us had never really hung out, and I wasn't certain why he'd even agreed to work with me. As we sat down, he was super flattering, explaining that he was a fan of me on the radio and was totally open to hearing my ideas.

The problem was . . . I had no ideas!!! Like, none!

"Okay, no worries. Let's just vibe and see what happens."

For the next two days I was a guest in the Neptunes' creative genius world. I watched them make beats and do their wizardry, tweaking other people's songs. They played me raw audio of an Ol' Dirty Bastard session, where he spit like a thousand bars of bizarre drug-induced brilliance. At one point that second day, when we all got hungry, Pharrell and I ventured out on a Fuddruckers run to get some food. On the way, we listened to everything from some unreleased Kelis to Steely Dan. He put me on to this song called "Three Roses" by the seventies folk-rock group America that I love to this day. He pointed out how ill the guitar change in that song was and played it like five times in a row to ensure that I fully understood.

I love people who love what they do. How could you not be inspired by that?

Back to the studio. I was fed, we vibed, I was inspired, and then Pharrell uttered the five words I had been dreading for two days: "You ready to get started???"

Welp, here goes nothin'. "Let's do it."

"I was thinking something like this," he said, and plays me a beat called "Dem Things."

"You got somethin for this???" he asked.

"Nah, not yet, but it's dope," I said. That was my best attempt at playing it cool. He told me to take it to the other room and sit with it for a little while, so I did. For four hours! Annnnd . . . nothing. I mean nothing. Not a verse, a hook, a bar. Nothing.

I was in a full-tilt panic. I couldn't handle that much pressure, and now I was cracking in front of everyone. Pharrell, God bless his soul, was cool about it. He offered to have Pusha T and Malice from his new group Clipse help me. But as dope as they were, they were rappin' about drug life, and as desperate as I was for help, "pushing weight from state to state" was just not gonna fly. I asked Pharrell if I could take the beat home with me to New York and spend some time with it on my own. He agreed.

So I went back to New York, feeling defeated and with a full understanding that I was in way over my head. That's when I went looking for Salaam.

"Salaam, I can't do this."

"Sure you can, Billy." (Salaam and I call each other Billy—no clue why or when it started, but it's our thing.) "Get all the stuff you've done so far and meet me at my studio," he said. "We will figure it out."

Whatever had caused me to freeze up started to thaw. Salaam and I talked about some of the things I wanted to say, and he asked me what was going on in my life. Then he suggested we go outside and jump in my car so he could hear what I had in my CD changer.

The answer was waiting there all the time, the minute we hit play and heard, *"Suavemente, besame, Que quiero sentir tus labios . . . Besandome otra vez."* Of course. *"Suavemente"* by Elvis Crespo was my shiiiit!!

Salaam said, "Okay, so we will do a hip-hop version of this . . . Let's call Clef."

Now that Wyclef and the Fugees were bona fide superstars—and Salaam had been an instrumental part of that—getting Clef on the phone was easy.

That was the magic moment. From there I reached out to others who were artists and friends to help as well. At this point in my career, my relationships were solid, so when I asked the artists to come, they just all showed up. It really was humbling. Not to mention that ultimately I'm a fan, so to have the opportunity to be in the studio with most of them was like a kid getting to toss the ball around with his favorite baseball player. Pretty fuckin' cool!

It was everyone from Snoop Dogg, Jay Z, Mary J. Blige, Jadakiss, Busta Rhymes, Styles P, and La India to Q-Tip, Kool G Rap, Lil' Mo, Beanie Sigel, and, of course, Fat Joe, Cuban Link, and the rest of the Terror Squad. Well, most of the Terror Squad.

Sadly, in early 2000, a few months before I even started recording my album, Big Pun had passed after suffering a massive heart attack. He was so talented, so funny and irreverent, and had that larger-than-life persona. Even though he was a big guy, he seemed like he could just weather anything. Or maybe it was just that he was so young, only twenty-eight at the time, that it felt so incomprehensible.

One of my favorite radio drops ever was made by Pun: "Angiiie, come downstairs—the pump is open. . . ." I included it on the album. He was definitely with us in spirit.

My schedule was pretty insane. I would do my radio show from three to seven p.m. and then be at Salaam's studio till the morning. As all-consuming as it was, I knew that if nothing else, this experience would make me a better radio personality. From that point on, whenever an artist came to my show with their new album, I would have a much more developed understanding of what it took to make that album.

Granted, that still put me in the position of knowing that there were people out there sharpening their knives, ready to put me on the chopping block of extreme criticism. And I was probably my own toughest critic. Oh my God. I would write a verse and in my head it sounded good. Then I would get in the booth and hate the fact that I was not seasoned enough to execute it the way I'd heard it in my head. I would do it a hundred times over and over and over. "I want to do it again. I want to do it again. I want to do it again."

*Why is this so fucking hard?*

God bless the poor sound engineer, Gary, who would sit there with me all night, redoing every verse.

All that pressure aside, however, getting to do the album led to some truly great times, man . . . lots of weed, take-out food from the Jamaican spot, jokes for days, and an opportunity to make music with my friends. The lesson to be learned was that rather than being so hard on myself, I should have let that moment be what it was. Sometimes you have to get past the fears and insecurities that may actually hold you back from being great or from truly experiencing something the way it was meant to be experienced. Since then I have tried to do that more just by being in the moment—maybe as my imaginary mentor, Oprah, could have told me.

In any case, I finished! I made a muthafucking album. When the decision was made to hold the album release party at Jimmy's Bronx Café, I was psyched! After years of attending and hosting countless album release parties for other people, I was actually having my own, and I couldn't think of anywhere that would be more perfect than the birth place of hip-hop, the Bronx. When I pulled up that night, I saw a billboard with my picture and album cover on the side of this big building, so you could see it from the highway that runs by.

But the night was far from perfect. Before the party started, I'd gotten wind that Cuban Link had asked Fat Joe to be released from his Terror Squad contract. Apparently, Cuban was unhappy that his own solo album release had been delayed. The truth was that with Big Pun gone, the Terror Squad had been falling apart.

The last thing I expected was to have that tension spill out at my party—where Joe and Cuban and everyone else were there to show me love—but that's exactly what happened. What wasn't clear was who exactly started the fight. The only clarity I had was that I was downstairs feeling *pisssed offff* that they were upstairs fighting. *C'mon,* I felt like telling them, *if you want to fight, go somewhere else and fight!*

There were different versions of what happened next. I don't know what happened, but all I know is the fight ended with Cuban Link getting his faced sliced open by a blade.

The night went down as one of those reminders that there was a dark side to this journey I was on. Behind the mic, on the radio or in the studio, there was lots of drama, yet it was more contained. But the ride wasn't only about those highlights. There were also some lowlights—people fighting, getting stabbed, and shot. The violence and dysfunction.

Although the release party hadn't gone as planned, when we released the album, it debuted at #7 on Billboard's Top R&B/Hip-Hop album rankings—buoyed by lots of play for the three singles, "Mi Amor," "Dem Thangz" and "Coast 2 Coast (Suavemente)."

Now that I had to build from there and needed a manager, I turned to my friend Shawn Pecas. We called him Pecas because he had a face full of freckles, and *"pecas"* means freckles in Spanish. By this point Pec and I had known each other for years. He did rap promotions at G Street Records back in the day, helped break Peter Gunz and Lord Tariq, and was now working at Arista. I had no reason to think Pec would be a good manager, but I trusted him. I felt connected to him, and I liked the way he carried himself and treated people. That was good enough for me. He agreed. He then hired Yvette Davila to be my road manager. The three of us quickly became a family. Pecas and I would fight like brother and sister and Yvette would have to intervene. Pec and Yvette would bump heads and I'd have to jump in and tell them to knock it off.

All that said, we trusted each other and I knew they had my back. And I needed it. I had never in my life worked so hard. My radio show was in full gear and now, somehow, I was going to have to hit the road to promote this album.

. . .

Traveling across the country was eye-opening. Whether I was doing in-store signings or club appearances in major markets or small towns, the first thing that really struck me was the separation of blacks and Latinos. In New York, we all grew up together in the same neighborhoods. We liked the same hip-hop. There was no disconnect.

Out on the road, not every town was like that. I'd hear questions like, "What are you, Mexican?" Somebody asked me once if I was related to Lisa Lisa. I quickly realized that being a young Latin girl at a hip-hop club wasn't as common everywhere else. That was one more reason to feel lucky to grow up in a city where we weren't so separate.

Now in 2016, being a Latin girl at a hip-hop radio station is pretty common. If you'd let Salaam Remi tell it, he says every one of those stations tried to put an Angie on-air and that's why it's the norm now. When I need an ego boost I let him tell it.

But I will say, while touring for the album I did meet all these different radio personalities around the country, who would tell me, "Wow, I listen to your show." "I tape your show." "I got into radio because of you." It was super flattering and a surprise to get that type of love.

So while the album itself met with mixed reviews, it was a big win in terms of strengthening my career as a radio personality. Everywhere I went, I got the message that my voice mattered to other people in the radio world. Amazing.

At Hot 97, Tracy Cloherty—who was in charge at the time—made it possible for me to work only four days a week so I could tour with the album. That was unbelievable. Most radio stations don't support their talent that way; it's unheard of. I'd be on the radio Monday through Thursday and then I'd fly out Thursday night to do shows on Friday, Saturday, and Sunday. And no matter where we were in the world, we had to get on a plane Monday morning so I could be back on the air by three p.m. This was a new type of grind . . . even for me.

But whatever. The last thing I was going to do was complain. Or slow down. This was my time to shine, right? So I just kept grinding.

That is, until this one really late night in June when I was getting ready to head home after hosting a party at a club and suddenly I felt like something was wrong.

Two days ago I had begun shooting my video for "Dem Thangz." The label had only given us a budget for a one-day shoot, but trying to get the most out of it . . . we were going to squeeze two days' worth of video into a one-day shoot. That meant four wardrobe changes, three different locations, and twenty-four hours of nonstop shooting. After a day like that, the smart thing would have been to go home and collapse. Instead, after a Red Bull and a quick shower, I went straight to the Puerto Rican Day Parade. And that is not an event where you can just call it in. The parade goes from Forty-Second to Eighty-Second Streets, and on every block there is a new group of people, so you have to show each of them the love—screaming on the mic, waving the flag, performing and engaging the crowd.

And this is June, and it's hot. But feeding off the energy of the people along the parade route, I'm running on adrenaline. So I keep going for hours.

Everything culminated at four, and then we went and grabbed something to eat—me, Pecas, Yvette, DJ Enuff, Monse, and a few other guys from the station. Only, I wasn't really eating because I was taking some over-the-counter diet pills—to keep my energy up and my appetite down. After that, around seven o'clock, we headed to Carbon, where I was hosting the after-party. When we showed up, I felt myself fading fast, and I said to Pecas, "Could you get me an apple martini?" hoping it would put me in a more festive mood.

Two hours later, after just that one drink, we hopped in the SUV and started home. I began to feel queasy in the backseat, like I'd had too much to drink.

"Pecas, pull the car over."

"Huh? You didn't even drink that much."

"Pec, just pull the fuckin' car over."

As he did, I opened the door and stuck my head out of the door as if I were going to vomit. That's the last thing I remember.

When I opened my eyes, I was staring at a paramedic as I lay on a stretcher on the corner of Fifty-Seventh Street and Tenth Avenue. He kept talking to me and asking me questions. I could hear him, but I couldn't muster the energy to speak back. He kept repeating, "Can you hear me? Did you take anything?"

All I could remember were the stupid diet pills. But I can't form the word "Xenadrine." I could only say, "It starts with an X." As the words were slurring out of my mouth, I realized how this was going to be misunderstood; someone was going to think I'd taken ecstasy but I didn't have it in me to explain. And so I went back to sleep.

When I woke up, I was in the emergency room with an IV pumping me full of fluids. Along with Pecas, the girls were all there—Nikki, Tracey, Liane, and my mom.

It took me half a day to convince my mother that I wasn't doing drugs. The doctors reassured her that there was nothing in my blood. I had just pushed my body to the absolute limit. To this day my mother likes to remind me of that night whenever she sees me pushing myself too hard.

Apparently, I was not invincible. Not that I believed in limiting myself, but clearly there was only so far you could push your body without putting something in the tank. Or, as I started to say at the time— and still do—you have to respect the temple. Even if I'd wanted to keep up the pace, I knew that this had been a warning and had to decide what was really important to me. Being an artist and performer was something I really loved doing, and I wanted to do it more and grow. And, in fact, pretty soon after that incident a second album would be in the works.

But the real question that I started to have was whether I had the same hunger to be famous that I saw in others who were. The truth is that deep down I had this small fear of being too famous. Of course, I could appreciate the perks that come with fame. But there was a part of me that liked having my own normal life. A lot of people close to me by then had lived with fame 24-7 and they did not have normal lives.

Around the same time, during that summer of 2001, when I was really trying to pull back and find more balance, everybody else in the hip-hop world was having a crazy year. Shyne had been sentenced to ten years in prison for a shooting at Club New York involving Puffy and J. Lo. At Summer Jam, Jay Z debuted "Takeover" and dissed Prodigy by projecting a photo on the big screen of P as a kid in dance class. At the same time he set off his beef with Nas: "Ask Nas, he don't want it with Hov, no!"

In fact, even before that Jay had stopped by the station to play me *The Blueprint* album and get feedback before it dropped. There was no denying that this was Jay's best work to date. As much as I loved his first album, *Reasonable Doubt*, this album was more mature on every level. Lyrically, creatively, and from a production standpoint. It was just Jay at his finest. And then he played me "Takeover." He saved it for last. For dramatic effect, I'm sure. Not that it needed it. And with no warning he pressed play: *Had a spark when you started, but now you're just garbage / Fell from top ten to not mentioned at all . . .*

"Are you talking about Nas?!"

He smirked.

And then the most disrespectful line of all—*'Cause you know who did you know what with you know who* . . . Was he saying that he had sex with Nas's girl??? It sounded like it. Wow!!! Could Nas recover from this?

On-air and in the streets, all summer long, I was getting an earful as all sorts of shit was brewing. And then all of a sudden, everything stopped.

# CHAPTER TEN

# HEART OF THE CITY

Ask anyone about the day before in New York and they'll usually talk about how normal everything was. That Monday night my mother had stayed at my apartment in Hackensack, as she had just traveled back from Paris. That next morning, September 11, we woke up and saw on TV that one of the two World Trade Center towers had been hit. Like everyone else watching that morning, we thought it was a terrible accident—that a plane had crashed into one of the towers.

Then a short time later, when the second tower was hit as we all watched in horror, it was beyond terrifying. What was happening? Immediately, I tried to call Nikki, who worked down there in the Financial District, but I couldn't get her on the phone.

*Oh my God, oh my God. Why doesn't she answer? Why can't I find Nikki?*

Many hours later I would learn that Nikki was one of the people who had to walk over the Brooklyn Bridge to get out of there. But in the early hours of not knowing where she was and listening to the news coverage, I went into a full-blown panic attack.

The terror that everyone felt watching it happen in real time was that you didn't know how far this was going to go. You didn't know if your building—the one you were sitting in, watching TV—was next, that all of a sudden the explosion was going to come through your window. You didn't know if we were going to be in a nuclear war. And then they said the Pentagon had got hit, and I just remember sitting there thinking, *This could be it for all of us.*

So many years later you hear all of these different stories, and everybody talks about the loss and the sadness and the devastation. Or they talk about how the city came together afterward. There are so many different perspectives about that tragic day, but we don't talk a lot about those moments of feeling like, *This could be it for everybody.* I remember sitting there with my mother, thinking, *This could be it.*

Early that day Q-Tip had called. We had been broken up for almost two years by now and our friendship was as strong as ever. Something was wrong with his TV and he couldn't see what was going on, so he asked if he could come over with the girl he was dating at the time. Of course it was okay. The four of us sat in front of my TV for hours, watching in horror.

Even if I'd wanted to go to work that day, I couldn't. Everything was shut down. You couldn't move. The station was on-air—Sunny Anderson had just started working with us and was at the station when it happened, and she just kind of stayed there. We also did a feed of the ABC News station as the emergency system started to kick in. So if you were a Hot 97 listener, and you turned Hot 97 on, it sounded unfamiliar. Because either you would hear Sunny, who was an unfamiliar voice, or you would hear the feed of the news.

Nothing made any sense. We were numb, we were scared, and we were all glued to the media—phones, e-mail, TV, radio—as we tried to account for friends and relatives. Each time you breathed a sigh of relief that someone was okay and at home, you'd hear of someone else who had a loved one who was missing.

I woke up on September twelfth and thought, *I can't go anywhere.* I'd heard that you couldn't get into the city, especially downtown. The station was no longer in the Garment District but had moved to a fancier building on Hudson Street, about fifteen blocks away from Ground Zero. It was impossible to get there.

That may have been true, but Tracy Cloherty had other thoughts when she called and said, "You have to come to work today."

"I can't even get in the area."

"Angie, you have to figure it out. You have to get here. People need to hear you. Everybody is freaking out. Your listeners need to hear you. They can't turn on the radio and have it sound foreign. Everything is already foreign. They need to hear your voice today."

And something about what she said hit me in my core. *Got it.* "Oh my God, you're so right. I'm on my way."

The least I could do was make the effort to be there. I didn't know how to handle anything like this. What do you say on the air? What are the guidelines? What's the protocol? I didn't know. But I knew that you just fucking show up. And so I did. Monse—the little brother of a friend of a friend I'd helped get hired at the station and had mentored—met me at Thirty-Fourth Street because every street below that was closed down. Monse was one of a handful of assistants I called my "sons"—in the loving sense of the word, not patronizing. He was always right there with me in the studio all night if that's what I needed. He always had my back and he had a bright future in radio. He gave me a hug and the two of us got going, but we were stopped right away by cops on Thirty-Fourth and Fifth Avenue.

"Look," the officer informed us, "nobody can get in from here."

An emotional Monse spoke right up. "Yo, that's Angie Martinez," he told the cops. "She's gotta talk to the people. We gotta be on the radio." So then we showed them our IDs and they let us through, and we started the long walk from Thirty-Fourth Street toward Houston Street.

Walking downtown, we passed through throngs of people, and everybody was just looking up. Those Learjets would pass overhead but way too low, and each time, all of us just stopped and stared. Everybody was jumpy and scared. It was a terrifying sight you never wanted to see, you never wanted to experience. The soot, the smell, the smoke, and the horror. Everybody's face had fear on it. And you could see it. Everybody was walking around in shock.

You had to show your ID not only to get past Thirty-Fourth but also to get past Fourteenth. Law enforcement had to be told where you were going and why you had to get down there. In fact, we had to show FCC validation so that I could get down there. And they let us go. And the closer we walked, the closer we got to downtown—Houston Street—the stronger the smell. It was something you never forget—the smell of dead bodies.

Inside the station the mood was somber, and I went straight to the studio and got on the air. I opened the mic and took calls all day—people talking, people crying, and people asking other listeners to help find their loved ones. I let anybody get on that wanted to get on. I was glad this was something I could do and glad to just be there. Other than relay emergency info, there was nothing I could do to help anyone really. But if being there made anyone at least feel a little bit normal, a little less alone, then that's what I would do.

All of the other parts of life and career pale in moments of crisis when you're faced with a challenge you have no clue how you're supposed to handle. Unless you're trained for that, there is no right or wrong thing to do. You just have to show up, face the moment head-on, in a way that is real, and let the moment dictate what happens. There were other crises that I'd have to face, and all I could do was show up.

To be able to have a platform and use my voice that week and for a while to come, that was a privilege for me. My job was not to know everything, only to share the mic and give others their voices, too. What is it? What are we doing? I'm here, guys. What do you want to talk about? How do you feel?

After I went off the air that day, instead of going home, I talked to Monse and my show producer, Paddy Duke. The three of us decided to walk farther downtown together—as far as we could go. We wanted to feel it. Walls of buildings and barricades were plastered with Miss-ing People posters. We stopped at the firehouse and looked at all the posters there. There was so much sadness. People's faces, and the smell, and the soot. And the loss.

The stories of that day are endless. It was as if the whole city had suffered a death in the family. Whether you knew someone who died that day or not, everyone felt the pain.

For months after that, driving down the West Side Highway on my way to work every day, it was amazing to see that day after day, people continued to line up on the sides of the streets, applauding every time a police car or fire truck passed by, heading down to the World Trade Center. Every day the good people of New York came out in any weather to stand there—cheering and holding signs that said "Thank You."

Thank you to the police, the firefighters, the EMTs. Thank you.

# PART THREE

# BEYOND RADIO

## 2001 TO 2014

# CHAPTER ELEVEN

# ETHER

When I think back to 2002 and everything that happened in culture and media, my head fills with competing voices. These were noisy times. Technology was dramatically changing the music business. Even though Napster was found guilty for illegal use of file-sharing technology, the possibility that consumers could get their music for free and online was out there. And the industry was starting to panic. On top of that, while Twitter and Instagram were nowhere in sight, this was the beginning of social media sites like BlackPlanet and MiGente, which let users connect and share information without needing the radio. They were the precursors to sites like Myspace, where emerging artists could showcase their music without radio or record labels. This was also the year that *American Idol* debuted—with Kelly Clarkson as the first winner. So now radio's job of breaking new artists was being shared with network television, and they had the power to engage *millions* of viewers to call in and vote.

Nobody knew where any of this was going, but those of us paying attention were very aware of the fact that we'd no longer be the only source for immediate information, no longer the only place you could hear your favorite hip-hop artist be interviewed. Now the artist would have a platform where they could speak directly to their audience, so neither would need us in same way they always had. The writing was on the wall. To stay afloat you'd have to make noise.

Entertainment in general had become noisy. Everything was epic. Like the big movies of the year Lord of the Rings, Harry Potter, *Star Wars*, and *Men in Black II*. The same was happening in hip-hop. Eminem, Missy, and Nelly all dropped huge albums that year. Eminem even went platinum in his first week, beating Snoop's record for albums sold by a solo artist in one week.

In that noisy, competitive atmosphere, a new battle was getting under way in my business, and few people really understood the implications. The moment happened on March 14, 2002, when Jammin' 105, the oldies station down the dial, changed formats. Power 105.1 was born. There was another hip-hop station in town, and the game was about to change. Up until that point, at Hot, we had always been able to do what we wanted. There had never been any competition. Since 1994, we'd been the only hip-hop station in the city. All of a sudden that would no longer be the case. What pissed me off about Power coming was not the threat of competition but the belief that its sole purpose was to split the hip-hop audience in two so that their sister station, the pop station Z100, could sit comfortably in the #1 slot. So the idea was not for Power to add to the vitality of hip-hop radio. Far from it. And we were prepared to fight.

We were not completely blindsided when the announcement was made. A couple of months before, an internal e-mail from Clear Channel had mistakenly ended up in the hands of Judy Ellis, our general manager. The e-mail had outlined their plans to launch Power, and although we couldn't stop it, Judy sure as hell wasn't going to make it easy for them. She quickly bought the main URL addresses that listed Power 105.1 and linked them to Hot 97. Judy was such a G. Even today if you go to www.power105.com or www.power105.1.com, you will be greeted with the front page of the Hot 97 website. *Pretty good!*

I wasn't necessarily afraid of competition, but Clear Channel's strategy infuriated me. The very notion that they valued their pop station more than their hip-hop station should have pissed people off, but no one seemed to care or notice. In my soul I knew this was going to ruin hip-hop radio. We could no longer take the chances we used to. We could no longer break records from new hip-hop artists because the competition would be down the dial playing a hit. We had to play smarter. For a long time we were able to keep them at bay because Power 105.1 had no history with the audience. They had no real hip-hop credibility. But then, that summer of '02, they found their opening as the Jay Z–Nas battle began to take on epic proportions.

Let me recap how this all happened. First, when I say "battle" or others say "beef," those words don't even begin to capture one of the most highly publicized wars of words in hip-hop history. It had been brewing for a while. As soon as "Takeover" started circulating, everyone was wondering if Nas was going to respond. At first he didn't. Well, not for a few months.

Nas's career had been kind of quiet at the time, and there were definitely people that had at this point begun to write him off. It had been two years since his *Nastradamus* had come out, and the reception for that was mixed. Perhaps "Takeover" had finished him? Nope! The truth was, it did the opposite . . . It reignited him. The consensus was that it woke a sleeping giant. On December 4, 2001, Flex debuted Nas's single "Ether"—which Nas dropped strategically on Jay's birthday. He answered

"Takeover" directly, and people went crazy. This was arguably one of the best dis records we'd ever heard. "You a fan, a phony, a fake, a pussy, a Stan. I still whip your ass. You thirty-six in a karate class . . ."

Feeling the pressure, I'm sure, Jay responded almost within the week with "Super Ugly." It wasn't "Ether." It wasn't even "Takeover." It felt slapped together, and people felt Jay crossed a line when he referenced having sex with the mother of Nas's daughter: *I came in ya Bentley back-seat / Skeeted in ya Jeep / Left condoms in the baby seat . . .*

The war of words became painful to hear. Jay and I, without a doubt, had become friends over the years. But I was also a Nas fan. *Illmatic* was one of my favorite albums of all time. And through the years we had developed a great relationship. But now there was this war and everybody wanted blood.

When Flex debuted "Super Ugly" on the radio, he played it and "Ether" all night back-to-back over and over. The phone lines were going crazy; people were eating it up. Not only in New York, but we were getting calls from all over the country.

At this point Flex wanted to make sure that we made the most of this moment and that, as a station, we owned it: "We're gonna bring Battle of the Beats back, Ang!!!! We're gonna let the city decide who wins this!!! And we're gonna do it on your show tomorrow!!"

My show? Why?! Flex said my voice was one of authority, and the contest could start at night with his show and could go into the day and end with me in the afternoons when I would announce the winner. The thought made me uncomfortable, but Flex convinced me that with Power looking to capture our audience it was important to remind people that if it happens in hip-hop, it happens here. And he reminded me if we didn't do it, someone else would. So I agreed. Although I didn't know how the vote was going to go, you could feel the Nas wave building.

In all this, Nas was being portrayed as the real MC, the underdog.

What I've noticed in our culture is that everybody roots for the underdog, myself included. The only thing about the underdog theory that bothers me is for some reason we feel the need to knock somebody down to build someone else up. In general, this is something that has always irritated the shit out of me. It's such a terrible, dysfunctional way to treat anyone successful who comes from where we come from. I have always made it a point not to subscribe to that mentality. We should celebrate success and be inspired by it, even while we're championing someone new. But nobody wants to hear that shit when you're in the middle of a battle.

We sat there and hand-counted the votes until the winner was clear—sixty percent of our listeners chose "Ether" over "Super Ugly." As much as it irritated me to hear the venom toward Jay, I agreed that "Ether" was the better of the two records. I'm literally getting ready to announce the winner when I look into the hallway of the station and see Jay Z walking into my studio. "And the winner is 'Ether.'" I had to deliver Jay that blow while he was standing right there.

To say he was uncomfortable is an understatement. I couldn't really figure out why he'd agreed to be interviewed in this moment. But evidently he had been under pressure. Like I said, a lot of people felt he had gone too far. Even his mother felt that way. She was the one who suggested that he apologize for getting a woman and a child involved by even mentioning them.

I can see him sitting there like it was yesterday—defeated. I had never seen him like that before. He's somebody who's always so big and confident. And I hated to see him down. This is a friend, and I was part of the machinery that brought him to this point.

After the interview, we walked outside the studio to talk alone. "Yo," I said. "Are we okay?"

"Of course. I don't blame you for this," he said. "This was just something that you kind of got sucked into. I'm clear. It's cool."

I wasn't sure if it really was, but I hoped so.

The hype of that lasted for some time, and Jay took a much-needed vacation. By the time he came back, he was ready to talk again. He walked into the studio and announced, "Hovi's home!" We had one of our most fun interviews that day. He had shaken if off. He was back.

That was not the end of the drama, however. The competition between radio stations was about to kick into another gear. Power 105.1 began to get a little traction by going commercial free for what seemed like months. They had the massive war chest of Clear Channel to fund their launch. But they still hadn't gained any real hip-hop credibility. In 2002 they finally found an opportunity. Nas was slated to perform at Hot 97's Summer Jam and had something planned for Jay, still fueled by winning the battle. He was planning to hang a Jay Z look-alike doll from a noose onstage while he performed. Our program director was like, "No fucking way. We're not hanging anyone in effigy on our stage." She didn't say he couldn't dis Jay, but she just didn't want a noose on the Summer Jam stage. Nas got pissed and didn't show up to perform. We were all there waiting for him to close the show when people started calling us to say he's on Power 105.1 instead, talking shit about everybody at Hot, me included.

It was supposed to be Hot 97's biggest night of the year. But all you could hear in the Summer Jam parking lot was everyone in their cars listening to Nas on Power 105.1. This was not good. That same night I must have been on the phone with Flex for, like, three hours. What the fuck was this guy thinking? "This is after the battle, after you played the shit out of his record and I did everything I could to be fair. Nas won the fucking battle!!! What is his problem?" Apparently, Nas felt like the station in general was loyal to Jay and didn't allow him to express himself the way he deemed to be appropriate. Hanging a noose around Jay Z's neck in front of sixty thousand people was the expression in question.

Not only did Nas go after Hot 97, but the Power interviewer was a disgruntled ex-employee of ours, egging him on. And Nas willingly took the bait:

"I'm letting my people know why I'm not at the Summer Jam. I've been bamboozled, hoodwinked, and the whole nine. I was told and begged to do the Summer Jam. I was begged to come to Hot 97, 'cause I had a hot new record that nobody wanted to support except for the streets. I was told to come there and save Angie Martinez's job. I was told to come there and help the ratings at Hot 97 by Flex and the rest of the crew over there. I'm here to let my people know, all my hip-hop community people know that I was dissed this morning by Hot 97 and told what I couldn't do on the show. It's really outrageous and really shows that the wrong people are in power. This hip-hop thing comes from the streets. We need our freedom . . ."

It went on. I never actually listened to the whole interview. But I heard enough to know that he was mocking the music I was making, questioning my credibility, and accusing me of being unfair. At the same time, Nas also gave validity to this competitive radio station. It was a one-two punch.

Like I said, these were noisy times. That's something that's been a constant in my career, my life—that I've always had to be aware of, that noise is just noise, good or bad. I just had to know that this was one of those times and it would pass. In these moments, I always try to get quiet and stay focused on whatever matters most in the long run. If I have a great interview and everybody's telling me, "Wow, that's amazing; you're the shit," I try to hold that middle line—"That's really nice. Thank you." But really, it's just noise. They're just excited about this one moment. It doesn't mean I'm straight in five years. It means I had a moment that's noisy in a good way. And when it's bad, that doesn't mean you don't feel the sting. But you feel it and then move through it.

It's a tough lesson but a powerful one.

And fortunately for me, I was able to tune things out and be gracious about it, because I knew ultimately that Flex was going to get on the radio and handle this as only he could, and he did. Not that I agreed with everything he said all the time, but when Flex went to war on the radio, it gave me the opportunity to take the high road, to not have to defend shit. It's like having a big brother who will do it for you. That's what Flex was for me.

Getting quiet and falling back was not my way of not having any feelings at all. No, I hated that Nas did that. I was disappointed that he had made it personal. I would have thought we were cool enough that, if he had a problem, he would come to me first, as opposed to getting on the radio and talking shit about me.

*I would never do that to you. Why the fuck would you do that to me?*

Yeah, even as I detached, I was annoyed for some time. Then I got calls from magazines like *XXL* and *The Source*. My statement was simple. "Listen, I wish the best for Nas. But, you know, I wish he would have come to me."

There was still blood in the water. People had taken sides across the industry—record reps, artists, managers, everyone. None of that really bothered me. But what did hurt was that Salaam was standing so close to Nas. He had produced songs on *Stillmatic*, the album "Ether" was on, and through the whole ordeal, he had never reached out to me to see if I was okay. Nas tried to shut my lights out, and to not hear from Salaam was like being left for dead. We'd reconnect in the future, but for the time being, I was disappointed.

Finally, Tracy Cloherty, holding the reins as program director, and

Steve Stoute, who was managing Nas then, came to an agreement that, "Okay, we're going to get him on the radio. Nas is going to come to Hot 97 so that we can squash this publicly." Stoute told Tracy, "Nas is going to come up and apologize."

So Tracy calls me into her office and says, "Listen, we're going to have Nas come up to be on your show."

"Fuck Nas."

"No, he's going to apologize."

"Well, he better apologize," I say.

Well, when Nas got there, I could tell he wasn't informed about the "apologize" memo. So now we're on the radio, and we're like two little mad kids with their arms crossed. I'm cocky with my arms folded like, "Well?" And he's like, "Well?" Because in his mind, he clearly felt something along the lines of, *Shit, I don't got nothin' to apologize for.*

Somehow we got through that interview. Nas admitted he had read one of my statements and thought, "Yeah, you were right. I could have just come to you." I asked that moving forward he would. He agreed.

Toward the end, we both lightened up. I think we were both aware that since we had agreed to be there, that neither one of us wanted to be in a bad place with each other. He was like, "All right already, Ang." And we just laughed it off and the topic slid off the table.

The following time I saw him, I mentioned it again.

"Are you ever going to let it go?" Nas asked.

"All right, fine, I'll let it go."

We've had amazing conversations since then. On and off the air. I don't think he's ever officially apologized. And I sure as fuck haven't. But just the fact that we were able to laugh at it after is enough for me. I probably did things, in his eyes, that I should have apologized for, too. But we both had enough respect for each other to just keep it pushing. And yes, it's true, my relationship with Nas was not my relationship with

Jay. But it doesn't take away from the fact that I adore Nas and, more important, I respect Nas.

And the good news was that we all pushed past it.

. . .

The P.S. part of the story is that just as the smoke was clearing, Power 105.1 was getting legs. Nas's rant gave them a credibility they'd never had before, and now Hot became what Jay was in that battle we just ended. Now we're the ones to dethrone. And the hate begins. Now we have to work harder.

That was the beginning. Much as I hate to say it as a current radio personality, it really hurt New York radio for good. Before we had this hip-hop radio station that was free to do what we wanted to do, and that was the beauty of it. But as we had feared, the other station made it such that the goals changed. We now operated in a different way. It was the only way to survive.

I remember the reality hitting me and wondering, *Don't people see it? Don't they realize that station is going to kill everything?* The new rules would have to become, *Oh, my interview has to be two minutes long, because if we go too long, they're going to change the dial and we're going to lose the ratings.* So the interviews were shortened.

This is what happens. It changes everything. It becomes about business.

I mourned. But this was the world we lived in. And to have longevity I had to relearn radio. *Oh, you want my breaks to be thirty seconds long? What? I used to talk for eight minutes. How do I do that?* At the same time, other changes required getting aggressive with social media because now people had other ways to get their info and music.

My way of making it work was to see this as an opportunity to engage my listeners in a different way, trying to focus my energy into forward motion as opposed to being stuck in what was gone. Yes, you can mourn things when they're gone, but also, you ultimately have to embrace change. Keep trying to use the things that you learned and implement them in new ways.

Maybe the bottom line is that you have to be honest about the times. In moments when I was nervous or insecure or uncertain, Flex was always confident, always reassuring me, "We got this. Don't worry, Ang. We're going to figure this out." Flex always wanted to win, even before I knew it was important. He always had that thing. So as things changed, he was ready for it.

"We're going to win," he'd assure me.

"Okay," I said, and tried my best to believe him.

# CHAPTER TWELVE

# FAMILY AFFAIR

B esides everything that had happened on radio in 2002, I had been pushing hard as an artist while promoting my second album, *Animal House*. The first single "If I Could Go" (featuring Sacario and Lil' Mo) was a legitimate hit! Not only was it top ten on urban radio, but it flew up the pop charts, too. The album debuted at #11 on the Billboard Chart. After that I scored a more modest hit with "Take You Home" (featuring Kelis).

When it came time to take stock of how far I could go or wanted to go as an artist beyond the radio mic, I had to face some complicated feelings. I'd worked really hard to create these two albums, which gave me a whole new respect for the artists who are great at what they do. And not just because they work hard to master their art but because they have to put themselves out there to be judged by everybody and anybody. The criticism I got was to be expected on the one hand, but still people were *really* critical. If a song didn't do well, then it was "keep your day job." When some of the releases did really well, I got hammered for being too commercial. The truth is, as hard as people were on me, I was even harder on myself. I wasn't confident enough to know if I'd ever deliver to my own standards.

In hindsight I wish I'd done a better job of not letting the outside negativity affect my goals as a recording artist. I wish I could have given myself the same encouragement I'd offer to anyone else in my shoes. Even if I wasn't that great yet, maybe I could have grown and gotten better if I had kept at it. But at that particular crossroads, I didn't believe I could ever rise to the level of what I could accomplish on-air.

So while I was considering my future as an artist, I didn't want to miss any opportunities to build my career. That's what I'd been saying to Pecas, pressuring him to step it up on my behalf. I thought he should be doing more, so I kept on him—*What are you bringing in? What's next?*

So I'm sure he was happy when *American Idol* called to meet with me. The show had debuted the year before and it was a huge ratings hit. After that I had a couple of meetings with FOX, and eventually they offered me the job as the fourth judge—joining the panel with Simon Cowell, Paula Abdul, and Randy Jackson. The craziest part of this was that I had never seen the show. Promoting the album that year, I'd been traveling so much, who had time to watch TV? It happened so fast. It was all in about two meetings, and then they waved me on in—*Okay, come on!*

We began with the first rounds of auditions on the road. I believe the first cities were Detroit and Chicago. I was excited that our next stop was going to be New York! The production spared no expense flying us out and putting us up, so I was feeling pretty good about everything as I arrived at the convention space where auditions were held. I saw the other judges, Paula, Simon, and Randy, with their big entourages of hair stylists, makeup artists, and assistants. Then I go into hair and makeup to find that they have no one assigned to me. *Excuse me?* This is a network television show and there's a hair person who doesn't even have a blow dryer or a flat iron. It's a girl with a comb!

*So clearly I'm the stepchild.*

Nobody ever sat me down and told me what the audition or even filming process would be, or how I could contribute. They just threw me in. All of a sudden I'm taking on this coveted role and not feeling the love and definitely not feeling cute. From the beginning, the energy was weird. Later it became apparent that the network had wanted to hire me but the production company did not want another judge. So I somehow got tossed in the middle of all of that.

There was another reason I felt not up to par that had nothing to do with not having a hair and makeup person. The truth was that I had just figured out I was pregnant and hadn't told anyone about it yet. Like nobody.

I had just started dating someone new and literally found myself pregnant three months into the relationship. Nauseous and emotional, I was starting to put on weight and couldn't do much but put on a velour Juicy sweat suit and try to cover it up.

I called Dame Dash, who had a clothing line with his then girlfriend Rachel Roy—and of course Rocawear, the clothing line he started with partner Jay Z—and he sent four big boxes of clothes right away.

Since the days of him and Jay pushing records out of the back of their Benz, Dame had always been supportive of me in my career. He's a polarizing guy; either you love him or hate him. But there's no question that he's a visionary who had great ideas and took on the execution of projects in his own unique way. He did all these Roc-A-Fella movies that would later become classics, and he put me in a bunch, like *Paper Soldiers*, *Paid in Full*, and *State Property 2*. The experience opened my eyes to the possibility of acting and trying things beyond radio. So at this point I valued his opinion. He was always somebody I felt was looking out for me.

And now, in this moment of utter uncertainty on the set of *American Idol*, I soaked up his advice about how to handle the situation. Dame reminded me how to stay sane and not get lost in the big Hollywood setting.

"Keep your real friends around," he said, "'cause your life is gonna change fast, and if you are surrounded by a bunch of new people . . . corny people . . . Hollywood types . . . that's how people lose themselves. Stay sane. Keep your crew around. Find jobs for them if you need to."

I kept that in mind as I sat there surrounded by new people, trying to be fair in my role as a fourth judge—the weirdness of what I was doing there, Dame's advice, my raging prenatal emotions, my empathy for the artists putting their dreams on the chopping block. It was a lot to process. I tried to focus on the talent. I gave enthusiastic feedback, but that was not at all what was demanded. In fact, the show's producer, Nigel Lythgoe, kept running over to me at the judges' table and scolding me. "You can't like everybody!" He kept pushing me to be harder, be harsher. I felt the pressure.

As I was assessing the process, it bothered me to watch the production people send in mediocre or bad singers on purpose. Outside the doors, the team would fill them up with hope about how great they were, only to send them in for us to crush them. And being crushed seemed funny on TV, but when you watched it right in front of you from twelve feet away, not so much.

I'll especially never forget this Dominican girl from New York who sang Whitney Houston's "I Will Always Love You." She did miss a couple of notes, but for the most part she was great. It could have been nerves that made her miss those notes, but after being told that I couldn't always like everybody, when it came time for me to give her a yea or a nay, I said no to sending her to Hollywood. That was hard enough, but before she left the room, as she stood there looking so crushed, she looked right at me and said, "You know, Angie, out of everybody, I thought you would have been the one to support me."

It broke my heart.

That was the moment when I had to face what had just happened. Wow, I did something that was against who I was. I let the powers that be make me treat someone in a way I didn't want to treat her. I wanted to support her. I wanted to help her. I wanted to encourage her. She was good! And I let this TV exec make me go there. I hated it. Maybe I was more emotional than usual because of the pregnancy, but the notion did occur to me—*What if one of these kids gives up their dream?* Or even worse, even darker, I thought, *What if one of these kids kills themselves?* When you're being asked to shit on people over and over, humiliating them for entertainment, this moment of paranoia doesn't seem that far-fetched.

On my fourth day of being on the road with the show, I'm in my dressing room, and Nigel comes in and very carefully, in his proper British accent, says, well, he doesn't know if this—me—is working.

"It's not," I say. "It's not working." I don't know if he's about to fire me or not, but I am honest enough to say, "It's not working."

"You hate it," he says.

"Yes, I hate it."

In the moment I knew I had to leave and the best thing for everybody concerned was to just bow out. Nigel looked relieved. Obviously he could now go to the network and say, "Well, she doesn't want to do it anymore." And then they would win.

Without any reservation I quit. The next couple of weeks were a publicity frenzy. After all, we had *just* made the big announcement that I was on the show and now it was over and time to explain. The thing was, I wasn't sure what had happened. I hadn't had a chance to process it, let alone put it into words. Besides being swollen and nauseous, I was also sort of foggy about everything. But this was a big deal and the news did what the news does, like the MTV News piece on October 31, 2002, that said, *A week after signing on to be a judge on the second season of* American Idol, *New York DJ/hip-hop artist Angie Martinez has bailed on the show, citing her discomfort with squashing the hopes of would-be Kelly Clarksons.*

After that Diane Sawyer interviewed me on *Good Morning America,* and just before we went on-air she told me that Charlie Gibson thought I was a hero. Evidently, he wasn't a fan of how some of the kids were being treated either.

Diane added, "I think it shows great character."

In that moment of vulnerability, her gesture of support and understanding made me feel so much more comfortable and confident in my decision. Sitting across from her, I felt like I was exactly where I was supposed to be.

After that interview, I really put the episode to bed.

Ultimately the opportunity of *American Idol* just wasn't for me. And it's funny, because later I would watch Jennifer Lopez do it, and she's so good at it. Plus, she was able to be kind yet also real. But Jennifer is somebody who has walked that walk. She has done those auditions; she knows. That wasn't my background at all. So I felt like a fraud sitting there looking at those kids and thinking, *How can I tell you what note you should be hitting when I haven't hit a note in my damn life?*

Actually, the highlight of the entire experience came at the very end, right after deciding that I wasn't going to continue with the show. Instead of going back to my apartment, I went back to my suite at the Four Seasons in Manhattan. That was one thing about *American Idol* that I would miss. They fly you first class, and they put you in suites at the Four

Seasons, with VIP perks everywhere you go. What now? I didn't know who to call or what to do with myself, so I just called the girls—Nikki, Liane, and Tracey—and they came over. They're always there for me when I need them most. We ordered room service on *American Idol*. Tracey was like, "Screw it, they paying right? We need to order some shit." We did—they ordered mimosas, mad drinks and so much food. We analyzed what the next few days would be like and together put some strategies in place and toasted to true friendship.

. . .

Like a blip that dissolved in time, the four days on *Idol* were soon behind me. My new job was trying to get used to being pregnant—which I never quite figured out. My whole pregnancy was horrible. Oh, it was horrible. People say they have morning sickness? I had all-day sickness for six months. I would be on the radio, do a talk break, and run to the bathroom to throw up. I had to go to the doctor because I started coughing up blood; I was throwing up so much that I started getting tears in the lining of my throat. Yeah, it was bad. Around month six the nausea tapered off a little bit. You would think with all the nausea, I would have lost weight—but all I craved and all I ate were carbs, so it was biscuits for breakfast and mashed potatoes for lunch—by the end of my pregnancy I'd gained nearly seventy pounds. My ankles looked like my thighs. Literally. Like two tree trunks. For the last three months, I could barely walk!

On the last day of work before my maternity leave, Mariah Carey surprised me with a baby shower on the radio. Mariah is a New Yorker and hip-hop fan, so over the years she'd become friendly with a bunch of us the station. And no one is more festive than Mariah! Oh my God, it was so sweet! The whole staff was there; there was cake, balloons, champagne, a huge poster of a baby that everyone signed, all sorts of gifts like a rosary from Jacob the Jeweler, a car seat from Mister Cee, Burberry baby robes! To this day, people I meet in the streets always say, "I remember you had your baby shower on the radio!" It was so personal, which I don't usually do. My mom called in to the show and put into words exactly what I was feeling when she said, "My heart is getting ready to explode."

Shortly after finding out that I was pregnant, I'd moved in with Tamir, the father of the baby I was about to have, in his house in New Jersey, which I'd decided to spend my album money fixing up. The nesting had begun. A lot of complicated issues came up the closer I got to my due date. Of course, I wanted my child to grow up with the benefit of two parents being there, something I'd never had. But this guy and I barely knew each other before conceiving a baby. Plus, I hadn't grown up with an example of what a good father or husband was. I honestly didn't know if this was the man I was meant to be with forever. But when I saw what a committed father he was to Jordan, his three-year-old son from a former relationship, I had faith that he would be a good dad to our child. That was the one thing I wanted to get right. The only thing I did know, because I just knew this was a blessing from God, was that I would try to do all I could to create that family setting.

June came around, and this was the first Summer Jam that I was ever going to miss. The station sent a camera crew to my house so I could welcome the crowd on the big screen. In the video, I look like four of me! When you're pregnant, you're supposed to have a belly. I was like a full house. You know I wasn't in my right mind if I agreed to let them film me like that. But I hated not being there and kept getting everyone to give me reports. Paddy Duke told me DJ Mister Cee was overwhelmed by the enormity of the show and said, "I wish Ang was here to see how far we have come." Mister Cee had been in hip-hop for a long time, DJing

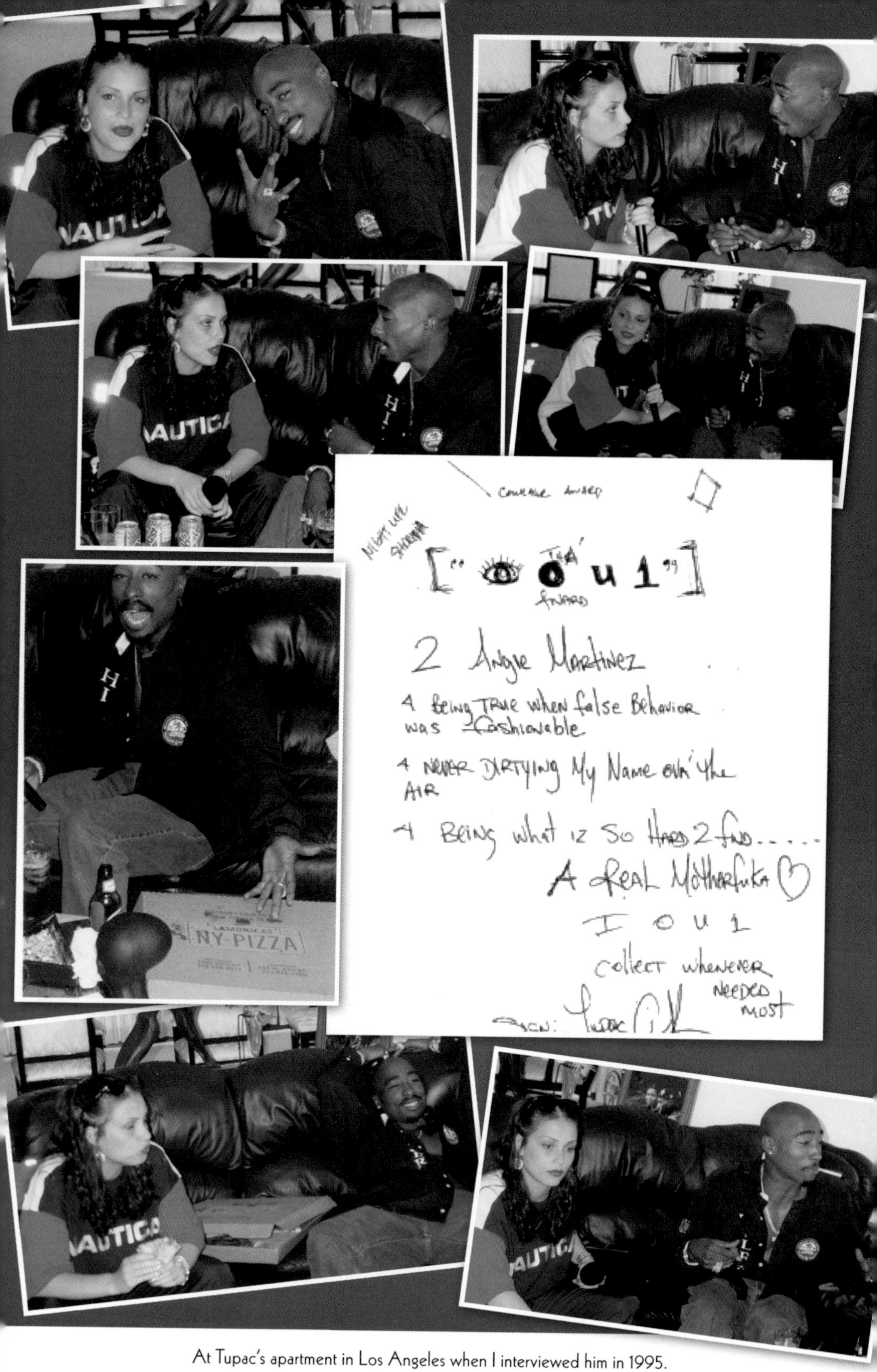

The handwritten note reads:

COUTURE AWARD

[" 👁 O'U 1 "] ЙGHT LIFE SPREAD TEA AWARD

2 Angie Martinez

4 being TRUE when false Behavior was Cashionable

4 NEVER DIRTYING My Name oN 'the AIR

4 BEING what iz SO HARD 2 FiND.....

A REAL Motherfuka ♡

I O U 1

collect whenever NEEDED most

SIGN: Tupac

At Tupac's apartment in Los Angeles when I interviewed him in 1995.

L to R: 1. Mariah Carey hanging out in the studio in 1998. 2. With Jay Z and Dame Dash, hosting an album release party for *The Dynasty* album in October 2000. 3. DJ Enuff and Nas at Summer Jam. 4. The Puerto Rican Day Parade with my original show producer, Speedy, and Frankie Cutlass 5. Doing what I love. 6. The Captain, Derek Jeter. 7. With Lisa "Left Eye" Lopes. 8. The Hot 97 team at Flex's birthday party. 9. Summer Jam, with the Lox, Swizz Beats, and Fabolous.

L to R: 1. DMX showing love. 2. Me and my "little sis," Adrienne Bailon, at a charity baseball game in Newark, New Jersey. 3. With Simon Cowell during my brief stint as a judge on *American Idol* in 2002. 4. That time I asked Pecas to fix my hair for me. 5. With my girl Lorena at a club in New York. 6. The MTV Video Music Awards in 1997. The one and only time that we all performed "Ladies Night" together. 7. Miss Info, Cipha Sounds, Tracy Cloherty and me. 8. Monse, Paddy Duke, Cipha Sounds, and DJ Bobby Trends.

L to R: 1. My sweet boy. Niko must be a few months old here. 2. My boys, Niko and Jordan, trying to stay up on election night. 3. Niko's sixth birthday party at the Chelsea Piers bowling alley. DJ Enuff's son, EJ, celebrated with us. 4. Niko with his godparents, Pecas and Nikki. 5. Visiting Shyne at Rikers Island Correctional Facility. 6. Celebrating Fabolous's birthday party, which almost cost me my life. 7. The legendary Rakim and A$AP Rocky.

L to R:  1&2. The Puerto Rican Day Parade.  3. Queen Latifah's Queen Collection campaign for Cover Girl. 4. Backstage at the Blueprint 3 tour in Miami in 2010 (left to right): Young Jeezy, Shawn Pecas, Bridget Kelly, Trey Songz, Chaka Pilgrim, Beyoncé, Jay, and me.  5. At Dawn Baxter's birthday party at the Hudson River Café in Harlem, with Idris Elba.  6. With MMG (left to right): Wale, Rick Ross, Meek Mill, Omarion, French Montana.  7. Ebro, Miss Info, and me!

L to R: 1. This just in! The day after my big announcement, Oronde brought this home. 2. After an amazing interview with J. Cole at Power 105. 3. Welcome to iHeartMedia! With John Sykes, Ryan Seacrest, and Tom Poleman. 4. At the 2014 New York City Marathon before the race with Amber Sabathia, Alexis Stoudemire, Tiki and Traci Barber, and Teri Hatcher. 5. Oronde at the finish line.

to R: 1. Cohosting *The View* for two days in July 2015. 2. In the Bronx interviewing the amazing Jennifer Lopez for *Extra*. 3. Sharing the stage at the White House with the President of the United States, Barack Obama, after I moderated a panel on criminal justice reform. 4. At the White House with Senator Cory Booker. We've been friendly since he was the mayor of Newark. It was nice to see a familiar face in Washington.

L to R:  1. With Nikki, Tracey, and Liane.  2. My boys: Niko, Jordan, Christian, Brandon, Cayden, and Mason.
3. Celebrating my birthday with my favorite people: Oronde, Nikki, and my mom.  4. My loves.

for Big Daddy Kane in the eighties, discovering B.I.G. in the nineties, and was now like our own personal mayor at Hot 97. He cared about the culture and the station as much as any of us and was moved by the massive number of people in attendance.

This was the year that Summer Jam moved from Nassau Coliseum on Long Island to the Giants Stadium football arena, with sixty thousand in attendance. It was bigger than ever! Eminem stole the show that year, dissing *The Source* and smashing onstage the Lyricist of the Year trophy the magazine had awarded him.

In the meantime, back at the station, Sunny Anderson had been filling my time slot. I'm sure Sunny wondered if I was ever going to come back. As it happened, my time off was more than a maternity leave. Actually, they never paid me for my maternity leave. Technically my contract was up and I was in no rush to sign another one. My explanation was that I needed time to figure things out. Not only was I moving into a new house and having a baby, but I hadn't taken a break since I was eighteen years old and desperately needed one.

Other than becoming a mother, I didn't have the bandwidth to consider what the next phase of my life or career would be. For the first time, in a long, long time, I wasn't going to just keep pushing to the next opportunity. I was going to experience this rite of passage to a different life and all that it entailed.

As motherhood inched closer, my ob-gyn kept waving off my insistence that I knew my own body. Throughout the pregnancy I'd been telling her, "Listen, all the women in my family have C-sections." I don't know if it's a curse. We don't dilate. My mother had one, my grandmother, my aunts. "Just schedule me as a C-section," I said.

"No, you have to try natural labor," she encouraged. "You'll heal so much faster."

*Okay, lady.*

During the last month of my pregnancy, they did a test and told me that if I didn't get the baby out soon, it would be ten pounds. Dr. Marks decided, "We're going to induce you on June eleventh."

On June 11, 2003, I arrived at the hospital at four a.m. or six a.m. or some ungodly hour and went through twenty-six hours of labor. SO TERRIBLE. Three epidurals! Why? Because the first two didn't work. I have a huge needle in my back and it isn't working. I'm screaming, "Try again! Put it in again!" I needed them to keep trying because the contractions felt like they were going to kill me. Finally, the third epidural kicks in. A few hours later, they tell me that I'm not dilating enough and that I am going to have to have a C-section.

*All of that labor for no reason!!!*

Then I go to have a C-section and they give me morphine for the pain. Well, it turns out that I have some sort of allergy to morphine. So I break out in hives. I'm scratching everywhere. Could it get any worse? No, instead everything becomes perfect because in that next moment, I'm holding my son for the first time and he is amazing and worth every moment and more. Niko Tamir Ruffin. Eight pounds, nine ounces, a hefty baby.

I was so high from the morphine, the first thing I'm told I said to my son was: "You're not gonna bring home any dirty girls to Mommy's house, right?"

By choice, that wouldn't have been the first thing I should have said to him. As part of a larger conversation, maybe.

At this moment, I just wanted a healthy baby. That's really all that mattered. Then I held him in my arms and fell in love and I realized my life was changed forever.

The thing that people rarely tell you is that having a baby is a big fucking deal. Sure, people do it all the time, so the attitude tends to be,

*Oh, it's just a baby*. No. It's a big deal. The media makes it look like, *She bounced back in two weeks and she's a size zero! She's back at work three days after having a baby!* You see all these new moms out brunching. Those women are aliens. I always tell my friends who are new moms, "Don't compare yourself to the aliens." God bless them; they inspire me. But for most women, it does not work like that. And for me it didn't. Reality is that you feel like shit. Your body is different. Your life is different. It's amazing and phenomenal and overwhelming and emotional, but it is a legitimate change and by no means a small one.

I had a baby and everything stopped. I felt all types of shit that nobody had prepared me for. When Niko was a newborn, at least four times a night I would go to his crib and put my hand over his chest to make sure it was moving. *Is he okay?* I rested my face gently next to him to make sure he was still breathing. I was paranoid. I was terrified. There was this constant worry.

One evening when Niko was about a month old, I was in the kitchen making a whole wheat English muffin with a piece of turkey bacon. That was my diet as I started trying to lose my baby weight. I was sleep deprived, completely exhausted from being up all night breastfeeding. Suddenly, I stopped breathing for a couple of seconds. I had this feeling like, *Okay, when is this part going to be over? When am I going to stop being worried?* And then I had this moment. *Holy shit*, I realized. *Never.* Anger swelled inside. *Well, why the fuck did nobody ever tell me that?* Nobody tells you that. Nobody prepares you. A terrifying feeling sank in. As a mother, *now I have to worry about somebody forever, for the rest of my life*. I didn't even think about that ahead of time.

My son's nursery was my version of what I thought a Pottery Barn pamphlet should look like. I bought all the things you're supposed to buy—the crib, the mobile, the changing table that I never used because I always changed him on the bed. And then he wound up sleeping in the little bassinet next to my bed. Since I was breastfeeding him every two or three hours, a lot of times he would be lying in the bed with me even though they say that's not safe. I was always half awake anyway, so he was fine.

But after being sleep deprived for three months, it started making me nuts. I thought I was going to die. Two hours of sleep here. One hour here. Two hours tonight. Three hours tomorrow. It was making me nuts.

I'm living in this secluded cul-de-sac in Westwood, New Jersey. It's beautiful, but I'm in this big house in this neighborhood that I don't know and I just had a baby with somebody that I barely know. I haven't even known him for a year. It was a weird time.

There I am, sitting in the living room in my chair facing the TV. The TV is on, but I am not watching it. I'm going through the Rolodex in my brain to think if I can remember ever hearing about anybody who died from exhaustion.

This was a serious thought; I wasn't being funny. The notion taunted me—*Wait . . . can people die from this? Have I known anyone who has passed away from sleep deprivation??? Am I going to die?* In the moment, I was really trying to figure this out. Could I die from being so tired?

My son's father almost didn't factor in, in such a weird way. At one point I began to wonder, *Is this guy going to do more? How does this work? Is he supposed to share more of this worry and responsibility?*

"You don't want them to do more because they're never going to do it right or the way you want it done," my girlfriend Yvette advised me. "So you should just do it yourself."

"You are so right," I agreed. It was such great advice. Let me just handle this.

This is not to say that Tamir didn't do anything, but in my own little world, he just didn't really play in. I mean, he was there. But the mother—the breast-feeder—you are *the one*. The guy will be sleeping and you are up at two in the morning, three in the morning, five in the morning, seven in the morning. At this point I was doing what I had to for Niko by myself.

My son was three months old when I started getting calls from management at Hot, asking, "Hey, are you coming back to work?"

*Work???! I'm still trying to motivate myself to change out of these gray sweats and brush my hair.*

I was more tired than ever, trying to adjust to being a mother, to living with somebody in a new place. In every way I felt disconnected from myself. While I could relate to those women who would say, "I couldn't wait to get back to work," a part of me was not pressed to go back to that set of demands. But I was still trying to clear my mommy brain and needed something to snap me out of it. It wasn't like I was financially set to not work. At some point I had to go back. But in that period I wasn't ready, so I ignored all the calls from the station.

It was Flex who drove out to my house to bring me back to work. I don't know if the station sent him or if it was his idea. He hid his shock at finding me in this hole, deep in Jersey, removed from everything. My roots were to my earlobes (this was way before ombré was cool) as I sat there in my gray sweats every day.

"You gotta come back, Ang," Flex said, trying to convince me. "There's a new general manager there." Judy Ellis had resigned and Barry Mayo had been brought in to replace her. Flex said, "You should go in and tell Barry how you feel about being underpaid. I think, at this point, they'd be willing to make a change there."

He hit a nerve. On a primal level, I knew that I still loved my job. But I was stuck. I had to get past the exhaustion before I could restart the engines. I had been working so hard for so long. Sometimes you've got to shut down.

"I just need a minute," I explained.

. . .

Niko was almost four months old when I got a call about being a guest host on *The View*. I was still in that cloudy state, in a daze. I still had my baby weight and felt swollen and gross. I didn't think it was the right fit for me, but it was an opportunity to be on a really successful show. That was some of the old me coming back to life, telling myself, *No matter how you're feeling, you get up and you show up. Of course you have to go.*

I arrived at *The View* studio on the west side of Midtown Manhattan and was shocked! I looked around like, *Oh, the world is still happening? People are still doing this? Everybody is still working?*

It was the *Twilight Zone*. During the show, I barely said anything. I didn't feel connected to anything that they were talking about. I mean, I'm okay with going outside of my comfort zone. I'm just not into putting a square peg into a round hole. The cast at the time was Barbara Walters, Joy Behar, Meredith Vieira, Elisabeth Hasselbeck, Star Jones, and that group. Those women, they talk fast. You have to be aggressive, get in there, get your points out. They don't wait for you to say your opinion. It was intense and did not feel particularly inviting or warm.

In my oversized black jacket, trying to cover my post-baby weight, I sat there feeling bloated and just wanted to get home to my kid. Ironically, *The View* appearance did plant seeds in my mind for one day having a TV show of my own that was more like the vibe I liked to have with guests on the radio. It wasn't a total loss as far as opportunities go, and I've actually been back on several times since then and the experience was much better. That was a lesson I was just starting to understand—

how everything leads to something and that even the losses can become material to grow from later.

Still, at that point in time I had this feeling of navigating with an outdated map. This whole period felt weird and foggy. Wasn't I doing what women were supposed to do? That was the map—*I am supposed to meet somebody. We are going to have a baby. We are going to get a big house.* I redid the house. I was cooking all the time. All of a sudden I was transforming into this domestic person because I thought that was what my life was supposed to be now. And it was uncomfortable for me. Reality check—*okay, well, what's real here? What's happening?* I started contemplating. *What is inspiring me?* Then I realized: *Oh, nothing.*

Not that I don't like to cook or that I don't like to be around my family. I do. But I was doing it in a way that was not authentic or organic.

The wheels started to turn. What map had I been using for my career? It was probably the one that said even if I wasn't making what I should have—and I was way, way underpaid for quite some time—I was still just grateful to be there. I loved what I did. I liked making money, but I wasn't pressed to make more. Maybe I felt like I didn't deserve it. My mother once told me that everybody is replaceable. She told me about radio personalities who were the hot shit and then if they left someone else replaced them. I always felt replaceable. So I never wanted to make too much money because I always thought that would mean I would be the first person that would be looked at like, "Well, is she worth it?" I still think that to an extent; I do know my value, but I try never to get too comfortable or to take anything at all for granted.

Then again, after all those years when I never really pushed for a raise, that began to change once I became a mother. Now I had a kid. I had a house. Maybe it was time to say, *Okay, I think I paid my dues already. It's time to pay me what I am worth.* I knew I wanted more.

As Flex had suggested, I finally set up a meeting with Barry, the new general manager at the station. When I arrived, bypassing all the familiar faces, I took a deep breath and walked into Barry's office. For the first time I just asked for it—what I thought I was worth. It was much easier asking him than it would have been if Judy were still in that chair. I had so much loyalty to Judy and felt so indebted to her for giving me my career that a conversation about what I was worth would have had to come from a more humble place. Barry and I had no history—which in this case was good.

"You're right. You deserve more," Barry said. I think he was probably surprised at how little I was making. Bottom line, they wanted me back.

And they doubled my salary.

. . .

Cut to: Friday, October 29, 2004, the parking garage of Madison Square Garden, where I'm waiting in a long line to get my car after seeing one of the most amazing and bizarre concerts of my life. Just then I get a call from Mike Kyser of Def Jam.

"Yo, where you at?" Mike asks.

"Just left the building," I say. It's late and I have to get on the road. But Mike has an interview that needs to happen right away.

It had been about a month since I'd been back on the air, but I still wasn't feeling completely like myself. But the moment when I first took my seat at the Garden that Friday night for the first of three nights that were part of the Best of Both Worlds Tour with Jay Z and R. Kelly, I became a fan all over again and got swept up in the anticipation of an amazing performance from both of them. And when they came out together to open the show, both of them dressed in all white, the Garden went bananas. They then started taking turns doing solo sets, first Jay, then R. Kelly, and then Jay. I was on my feet, singing or rapping along, rockin' out with everybody in the audience.

Then, all of a sudden, when it was time for R. Kelly to take his next turn, instead of performing, he stood there onstage and talked to everyone about something that had just happened backstage and why he couldn't continue with the concert. He had said that two people had come at him, waving guns. He was genuinely freaked out and was holding back tears. "I can't do no show like that . . ." and then he told everyone it was over as he dropped the mic and left the stage.

Everyone in the house was saying and thinking the same thing: *What the fuck? What guns? What people?*

We all sat there in shock and rising anger until Jay decided to take over and do the show "old-school" on his own, improvising with planned and surprise guests and whoever was in the house. Mary was there and was a showstopper. Pecas—who was working at Arista at the time—was sitting with Usher, who was signed to the label then, and suddenly heard from Jay that they wanted Usher to come up and do some songs. Pecas wound up DJing for Usher. No, Pecas is not a DJ, but somehow he pulled it off. All of these moments were improvised and spontaneous. It was amazing to see everyone do their best to have Jay's back. T.I. was there and performed. There was Memphis Bleek, Foxy Brown, Freeway and the Young Gunz. Ja Rule came out and did "Can I Get A . . ." with Jay, and it just blew the roof off.

I couldn't begin to say what my favorite song was, but when Jay asked, "New York, y'all got me?" and then did "Where I'm From" and "Heart of the City," I felt that shit! In that moment, I started to feel connected again. I was a hip-hop fan, on my feet along with everyone in that building.

Whatever had really happened to R. Kelly backstage was clearly a story yet to be told, but I'd never seen anything like this. For all the love that New York showed to Hov that night and he gave back, there were some die-hard R. Kelly fans who were *pissed!* People were threatening to sue for their money back and burn all their R. Kelly CDs.

As I was about to hear, in addition to the two people with guns, R. Kelly would claim that Ty Ty (Jay's longtime friend) had pepper-sprayed him and members of his entourage backstage. He couldn't perform at that point because he had to be taken to the hospital.

But none of this was known when I went to get my car at the parking garage and got the call from Mike Kyser. Before I could say anything, Kyser explained, "Jay Z wants to come see you. Tonight. He wants to go on the radio now."

"This isn't even my time slot."

"Ang, he doesn't want to talk to anybody but you."

"Okay. Let me call my Tracy."

Walking along, I've got the station on the phone as I begin to spread the word to some of my fellow concertgoers who are ahead of me in line, explaining why I have to get my car fast and drive to the station. When the people ahead of me flash dirty looks as I jump ahead of them, I say, "I'm really sorry to cut in line, but Jay Z wants to come up to the radio."

Everyone is instantly caught up in the excitement and drama: "Whaaaat?? Oh shit!! Go! Let her go to the front of the line!" "Yo, let Angie go! She's about to interview Jay!!"

As the crowd parted, I got the car and rushed to the station, bumping the on-air host, and am in position when Jay comes up. He's telling me the whole story of the tour and about how frustrated he is. Jay's not somebody who just talks to talk. He's not going to overexplain anything or overshare unnecessarily. But that late night/early morning, whoa, he has some shit to say.

**JAY Z:** First of all, Angie, you know, I'm not a catty dude. I'm not here to be catty.

**ANGIE:** Right.

**JAY Z:** You know what I'm saying? But—you know, you can't put me out there like that. You know what I'm saying? Like, there's people that had their tickets a month, two months. And—you know what I'm saying? And they—they're ready to see a show. They don't see a show. You know what I'm saying? So. We having problems on tour. I'm holding this kid down. Like—you know, he's (saying he's) having problems with life. He's not having problems with life. He's having a problem with—with the reaction that people give me. The love that people give me is really—it's hurting this guy's heart. He's insecure with himself.

**ANGIE:** Wow.

**JAY Z:** You know what I'm saying? So.

**ANGIE:** This is not the first time this happened, right?

**JAY Z:** No, this is the fifth time.

Maybe because I have a relationship with him, I believed everything he told me about what happened that night. But there's always two sides to the story, though, right?

In the middle of talking with Jay, my program director, Tracy, called. "Is everything okay up there? Is he on?"

"Yeah, everything's good. Don't worry."

"Well, I just got word from R. Kelly's people that he wants to come up, too." *Unbelievable!*

On-air, I told Jay, "Just so you know, R. Kelly wants to come by."

"All right, cool. Well, we almost done, anyway," he said.

We continued:

**ANGIE:** Obviously you don't want to talk to R. Kelly right now.

**JAY Z:** You could talk to him and I'll leave the building. Y'all could have a great conversation.

**ANGIE:** Okay.

**JAY Z:** You know, when he wants to talk to me, tell him, man, look me in my face and talk to me.

**ANGIE:** Okay... The likeliness of the tour continuing is very—[LAUGHTER]. It's—I'm sure, not good.

**JAY Z:** I'm going. You can do whatever you want to do. It's your radio station again. Thanks a lot, New York. I love you, I swear.

Jay left, and twenty minutes later R. Kelly came walking in. It must have been about two thirty a.m., and I was on the radio with R. Kelly, whose eyes were still red from pepper spray. He had glasses on, but you could tell something had happened.

R. Kelly, I'd only met him a couple times and I didn't know him well. But, as always, everybody that comes in the door, it's clean. I'm going to give you your side now. I pride myself on trying to be fair, always.

When I asked if he had a problem with jealousy or ego when it came to Jay, R. Kelly shrugged it off, saying, "I love performing. I'm very secure with who I am. I have no motive, no reason to be jealous of Jay Z. I'm a fan of Jay. I'm gonna always be a fan of Jay. Tonight had nothing to do with Jay getting the better response. I'm fifteen years deep in this game. I know what Jay is at home. I expected Jay to rip down the Garden."

So the deal with the guns, he said, was that he had received a threatening phone call prior to arriving at the Garden, and he said that during his first joint set with Jay, a man a few rows from the stage gave him a threatening gesture.

"Dude opened up his coat—I can't say dude had a gun; I don't know what I saw." But a little later he saw somebody else making a gesture like he was holding a gun. And because his family was backstage, R. Kelly said he became so upset that he panicked. At that point he was not going to continue because, "I wasn't going to take any chances when I saw what I saw. I'm not crazy."

Well, then, he went on to say, one of the promoters sent out more security and convinced him to get back out onstage, and that was when he and members of his entourage were pepper-sprayed. Then he went to the hospital to be treated.

I asked him to talk about the claims that he was having delays and cancellations on the tour and what the problem was with the lighting, and he said, "When you are a perfectionist and like to put one hundred percent in the show and you put a million and a half on the stage, you want your million and a half worth."

R. Kelly was adamant that he would be back at the Garden the next night and wanted to finish the tour. With that I thanked him for coming in and he left.

After the interviews, my phone was on fire! Everybody was listening. I had such a high from being the person to deliver this moment in the middle of the night on the radio. I felt like I asked all the right questions. And for the first time in a long time, I felt like myself again. *This is my shit! This is what I'm supposed to be doing. This is what I do!* I was excited. I was relieved. I was happy.

When I got home my son's father was sitting in the living room.

"Were you listening?! Did you hear?!" I asked him, super-excited. "It was crazy! Jay came to the station, and then R. Kelly came. And he had the pepper spray in his eye!"

"Yeah. You know what's crazy?" he said.

"What?" I asked as I noticed the sour expression on his face.

"I've never seen you so happy. You seem like you like being there more than you like being here," he said. "I see you moping around and then I hear you on the radio and you sound so happy."

"So you're upset that I had a good work night? How could you not be happy along with me, or even for me?" I wondered aloud as a sinking feeling set in. "Like how could you be on the other side of this moment?"

I went to bed. Numb again.

. . .

My turning point began over dinner with Mary at Nobu. It wasn't a hit-you-over-the-head turning point revelation, but it was like she came up with the key to the locked place that had me so stuck. The last time I'd seen her was at the Garden about a month earlier, and I was so happy to catch up with her over spicy lobster salad, yellowtail sashimi with jalapeño, and a good bottle of wine.

There was nothing profound in our conversation at first.

"So, how are things?" Mary asked.

"Cool," I said. It was all I could muster.

"Cool?"

"Yeah."

I was tired, exhausted actually. Both Tamir's father and sister were staying with us at the time and his son, Jordan, now six, was often there as well. Of course I had taken on the responsibility that comes with caring for people in your home: working, driving back and forth to Westwood every day, cooking, shopping, cleaning. By the time I did all of this and checked in with everyone in the house, it was late, nearly midnight. And the next day would be the same thing all over again. Part of me liked it because I had never had a family structure like this, but a big part of me was still numb and just going through the motions.

"How's your relationship?" How did she know? She knew me, that's how.

"I don't really feel anything about it," I admitted.

"That's not good," she said. Mary calls it as she sees it. "You can't be in a relationship and feeling nothing. You're either going to be angry, you're going to be sad, or you're going to be happy. But you have to feel something."

"I know. In theory I know that, but I'm fine." I was just like dead. Flat.

"Yo, you know that's not okay. Right?" Mary was the first person to say that out loud to me.

*It's not okay.*

Whenever you're making a dramatic change in your life, when it's a big deal, it happens in stages. First you have to acknowledge that whatever is happening is not working. I was in that stage. *This is not it.* And then you have to acknowledge that you're going to do something about it. Well, I wasn't there yet. There were too many people that counted on me.

But I was at least starting to articulate what I was feeling or not feeling.

When I mentioned the conversation to Liane a few days later, she offered, "I know somebody that you should go see," suggesting a life coach in Manhattan. That's the thing about having good friends. They can help you get there. I knew I had to do something. I just didn't know what or how.

Well, what did I have to lose?

"I feel indifferent about everything," I told the life coach during our first session. "I don't feel bad. I don't feel good. I don't feel anything about anything—except my son, of course." She listened, and when I came back the second time she shared her insight.

"I was thinking about what you were saying last time we met," she said. "I'm thinking, 'Wow, I've never met someone so indifferent about their life.' Then I realized that you're not indifferent. You are so worried about how you making a change will affect other people that you are not being honest with yourself. Let me ask you this: Who is worried about you and your well-being? Why do you feel like it's not as important to worry about yourself as it is everybody else? Where do you put yourself in that equation?"

*Holy shit.* Sparks were going off in my head as I was taking in what she was saying. I know it sounds cliché. It sounds like something the Almighty Mother Oprah would say. But that was the first time it resonated with me. And not only did it resonate, but it made me angry. *Holy shit.*

"Okay, so this person might fall apart if you leave them," she continued. "You're worried about this one. You're worried about that one. Well, where are you on that list? Why do you not value yourself as much as you value everyone else? Is one of those other people valuing you on a level where you or your happiness is coming first?"

When she said that, it was like a fucking lightbulb went off. *None of them are,* I realized. *None of them give a shit that I'm not happy here. They're just trying to hold on to me for dear life.*

*Holy shit!* Why do I not value myself enough to take care of myself the same way I did everyone else? The same care I give my child, the same care I give my man, the same care I give my career—I need to give myself that same amount of care. Everybody says, "You've got to put yourself first." I'm happy enough if I can just put myself on the same level. I don't know why I hadn't seen that before. But it's like, God, once I got that, I saw how I was living. If you don't know that, you set yourself up for failure. You set yourself up to be less than happy, less than worthy, less than anything. And you're teaching everybody else how to treat you.

It was my *holy shit* moment. Oprah has *Aha moments!* I have *Holy shit!* The floodgates opened and I started seeing everything. I could see how I was being treated. I could see that when I voiced that I was unhappy, it was more of a concern about me leaving than about my happiness.

I could see. And then that was it. I knew what I would do.

. . .

The idea was we were going to take a break, but I knew that I was never coming back. My son's father was out of town, so Nikki and I started packing up as much stuff as we could with just the two of us. Trying to fit all my shit into my convertible BMW and Nikki's Honda Accord, we realized we needed a truck. I called Pecas, but he said he was in label meetings all day and could not leave. So we continued to box my things. My thoughts and emotions were erratic, all over the place.

*I don't wanna be here when he gets back. Where am I gonna go? How the hell is everything going to fit in my car?!* My anxiety level was off the charts.

And just as I could feel myself cracking, I looked up and saw Pecas's black Escalade driving down the cul-de-sac road. Whaaaat? *How did he get here so fast? What about his meetings?? How did he know??* I dropped the box and I just started crying. He hugged me and said, "I'm here. I got you. What do you need me to do?"

That was him to a tee. "I got you" from a friend like him and from someone who is always in the trenches with me like Nikki was exactly what I needed to stop worrying.

And so Pecas and Nikki packed me up out of that house, and then that was it. I got the fuck outta Westwood.

For a brief and minor chapter that followed, I rebounded with a relationship that was exactly what I needed at the time. He was charming. He knew all the hot spots and brought me back outside again. He was driven like me and he championed my ambition. I knew what type of guy he was, but my intention from the beginning was just to have some much-needed fun. The thing with dating a bad boy is that even though it's fun and sexy, they are not to be taken seriously. But for a quick moment I forgot that rule and chose to ignore the signs. It started to get complicated, and all my guy friends warned me that this was going to end badly.

The person who really got through to me was Ebro—he was a radio programmer from the Bay Area who had just been promoted to program director at Hot 97 after Tracy Cloherty left Hot 97 for a TV gig. Ebro, a big guy with a deep voice and a big scruffy beard who could be intimidating and aggressive to some, had become one of my closest friends. He was a member of my extended family. We did poker nights on Sundays and spent holidays together, and he even used to take Niko to football games with the guys. We had this unique relationship because we shared the same commitment to the station and he always was a great sounding board. I trusted him and his judgment and often confided in him.

Every day I'd go into Ebro's office and we'd talk shit about the girl of the week he was seeing. He was charming and good-looking, so he had his share.

Although Ebro didn't want to break any guy code and I'm sure he knew a lot more than he was letting on about the guy I was seeing, he felt the need to say something. They ran in the same circles and probably dated some of the same girls. Through his discomfort, Ebro sat me down and went about it in his own way.

Ebro shared a story about his childhood friend who wound up being with the wrong guy and having three kids with him. He was abusive and she wound up taking him back and got pregnant again. Then she found out he had a whole other relationship with a whole other woman and another baby. So she divorced him, but at that point she already had four kids.

As Ebro's telling the story, I'm like, *Yeah, so what? Dumb girl.*

"Ang," Ebro said, cutting into my thoughts. "I just want you to know she was supersmart. You're probably thinking she's some bird who didn't know better or whatever. She was ambitious and had shit going for her. She just made a bad choice in who her partner was. And now she's struggling. Her career is off track and she's taking care of those kids on her own. I just look at you and I would hate to see you make bad choices."

It resonated.

I beat myself up for a few months after that. *How could I have gotten so far in with somebody I knew was incapable?* It was my fault for lying to myself and his fault for lying to me. By the way, I know we've all been there. But I thought that normally happens in your twenties. This happened to me in my thirties, which was why I was so mad at myself.

At least I was smart enough to jump off that fucking train. There was no warning. I stopped answering his calls. I just stopped.

If there is a moral to the story, it's that. Friend by friend who had my back, every single one who, like Pecas, told me in one way or another, "I got you," set me on a path with a new map that put me back in charge. I found my way back to owning my life, to using my voice to put good into the world, to valuing the right relationships, and to being the kind of mother to Niko that gave purpose and meaning to everything.

I was back.

# CHAPTER THIRTEEN

# MY PRESIDENT IS BLACK

Michael Moore's *Fahrenheit 9/11*—which came out in June 2004—had a profound impact on me. Without knowing it at the time, this political documentary influenced how I saw my role on radio and opened my eyes to issues in the hip-hop culture that I could use my voice to amplify. Up until seeing the movie about how the Bush administration had used the post-9/11 fear and the media to build a case for the wars in Iraq and Afghanistan, I didn't want anything to do with politics. Whenever I tried to pay attention to what was going on, most of it was confusing and there was too much lying and bullshit to try to cut through that it always turned me off. Maybe politics scared me.

But for some reason Moore's ability to tell the story with facts and audacity made me want to investigate and not ignore these bigger political issues that were affecting us all. Obviously, his was one perspective and there were others, but I was inspired to start asking more questions and to do my own research. It was time to widen the conversation, not just with points of view that resonated with mine—and what is probably ninety percent of my audience who I thought would be interested in the movie, too—but also with that ten percent that would most likely hate the movie.

That's when I got the idea to do something that I'd never done before with my listeners, which was to take a bunch of them to go see *Fahrenheit 9/11* with me. I'd come back from seeing it and had been just moved by it. As a piece of filmmaking, I had never seen a delivery like that in a documentary. And because it was so interesting and so powerful and thought provoking on so many levels, I wanted to bring it up on-air as something current to recommend. My first idea, as I proposed it to my boss, was to give some tickets away on the radio, and I got the green light—"Sure, whatever you want."

From there I called the movie theater, bought enough tickets to buy out the place, and then gave the tickets away on-air so that we all went to see the film together. It was an amazing experience to see my listeners in person and watch the movie and then have something to talk about later on-air.

A short time later I had the opportunity to interview Michael Moore on the show. When he called in, I realized that he didn't know about the ticket giveaway and how we'd gone out to see the movie together. He was blown away. The one thing he did know, he said, was that my audience and I had helped him get his "street cred."

*Fahrenheit 9/11* catalyzed my listeners, and I think it affected many younger voters who had been apathetic in the past. This was at a time when Rock the Vote, which partnered with MTV, had been around for a while, but it started to make inroads around the time of the 2004 campaign season. That growing consciousness for younger voters wasn't as evident then as it would be four years later. But you could feel a shift as people who weren't as informed before as they might have been started to become more politically involved. The Rock the Vote approach was powerful; encouraging people to vote was an easy way to inspire everyone who had voices to use them. It was also nonpartisan, so getting younger voters engaged was another method to get people to say something positive, get them involved in an easy, noncommittal way. They didn't have to pick a side. They didn't have to choose a party. They didn't have to voice their political view. For celebrities, who may not feel comfortable taking a stance, something like Rock the Vote was a brilliant way to let them get out there and promote activism without being partisan.

This period opened the door to have more conversations with politicians. Back when Hillary Clinton was first running to represent New York in the US Senate, her campaign staff reached out and set up a phone interview. It was a great, quick conversation, and I did appreciate the fact that she thought it was important to speak to my audience. That's what her staffer said, "She wants to talk to your audience."

During the interview, when she talked about her desire to hold elected office, even after having been the first lady, I was impressed by her commitment to public service. I was impressed by her knowledge and her confidence. And in wrapping up the interview, I jokingly said, "Well, good luck! And if my listeners help you win the Senate seat, don't forget to call back and thank them!"

She laughed and promised she would. And, sure enough, she did.

Both interviews were memorable, and I was left thinking it was pretty cool and pretty smart of her to reach out to an audience that a lot of others would have overlooked. It was either cool and smart of her to think of it—or to listen to people on her team who helped make the connection.

By this point, having politicians on my show was not that uncommon. Former President Bill Clinton called in when he opened his office in Harlem. Ted Kennedy called in to talk about immigration reform. And Cory Booker, who was the mayor of Newark at the time, was on air often and would become a friend to the show. He even allowed me to tag along a couple of times to watch the great work he was doing in the community. During the holidays, he introduced me to the mayor of Jersey City, where we served Thanksgiving Dinner at a local shelter. I joined Cory, Queen Latifah and Wyclef on a bus tour of Newark in 2009, going door-to-door to inform residents about the government assistance available to avoid foreclosure at a time when people really needed it.

About a month after the Michael Moore interview, I found myself watching the Democratic Convention—the first time I had ever watched a nominating convention in my life. Again, politics had never been my thing, even to the point of feeling over my head. But then, after *Fahrenheit 9/11*, I had decided to start paying greater attention, so I chose to tune in to the convention. And I'll never forget watching the keynote speech by Barack Obama, a candidate running for the Illinois US Senate and how he looked like such a star to me. All I could think was—*why don't I know who this man is*? *Why doesn't everybody know who he is*? His ideas resonated for me and I believed in him from that moment. I bought and read his book, *Dreams from My Father,* and I bought it for friends and guests of the show. Long before it was even a topic of conversation, I started telling people, "Barack Obama could be president one day."

For the longest time, all the way to the election, in fact, I'd get into arguments with a lot of people who were adamant, "There's no way we would ever have a black president."

"No, this is the guy. I'm telling you this is the guy."

From that '04 convention on, I felt invested and raised my level of wanting to be informed about policy and decisions that affect us domestically and globally. Not that I think of myself even today as politically savvy, but as a citizen and a parent, I choose to look at a bigger picture—not just at the headlines or the stories that the news deems important for ratings. The lesson learned is that once you begin to get your information from multiple sources and use your own judgment, you can never go back. I can never just not care or not be informed or not pay attention. Before, when I was younger, I thought, "How does it affect me? Why does it matter? There's no difference in my life from day to day." Now I know better.

• • •

've never been afraid of controversy on the air. Not much could top the Tupac interview, so my feeling was that as long as I maintained honesty and fairness, something authentic and provocative could happen on-air and be worth it. In November of 2005, I had an interesting and controversial situation on the show that I didn't see coming. But when it did, I know Puffy wasn't happy about it.

For the past six years or so, I had not felt good about what happened with Shyne, then a twenty-one-year-old rapper with so much potential who had been signed to Bad Boy. I first met Shyne when he was a teenager delivering packages to Hot 97. He would always promise that he was going to be on my show one day. So when Shyne actually started making some noise as an artist, I couldn't help but to root for him. I never knew what had gone on in Puffy's mind or why he'd handled things the way he did, but after the nightclub shooting that led to Shyne being convicted, I always felt like he had been left for dead.

And so I would visit him periodically while he was in prison in Rikers and Clinton Correctional Facility, and we wound up becoming much better friends while he was in jail than when I knew him outside.

The fact is that when you go visit somebody in jail, you're forced to really talk. Sitting across from someone for hours at a time, you try to say things that are real and that matter. In the process, my feelings for Puff were not good. Granted, this was from Shyne's perspective of how Puff treated him while he was going through this. But it had actually started when Shyne first got sentenced. Suge Knight came to my show and basically said on the radio that Puffy dry-snitched on Shyne because Puffy had to put somebody on the stand to defend and help himself, but it hurt Shyne. I didn't say anything at that point, although I knew that Shyne felt the same way. I was just quiet.

Puff took great offense to that and went to Flex's show that night and went after me, saying something to the effect of, "You know, everybody talking this gossip, talking rumors. This Wendy Williams shit, this Angie Martinez shit—" Basically by doing that publicly, all he did was give me reason to draw my line in the sand.

*You know what? I don't like you anyway. Now you gave me a reason to not fuck with you.*

I didn't say a word, but a month later I saw Puff backstage at a concert and he came very close into my personal space, saying, "What's up, Ang? We have a problem? Do we have issues?" He was not asking but telling, leaning over me, or leaning into me.

"I need you to back up," I told him. "You are too close to me."

It was very hostile. And mutual. We both just were not feeling each other. And I was okay with that. Because I would rather that than have to fake it. So I barely spoke to Puff for the next few years. And I did not have him on my show once.

It was in that time in '05, when we weren't good, that this conversation happened about questionable practices at Bad Boy. On my show that day, I had Jadakiss, Sheek Louch, and Styles P from the Lox. I love the Lox, and Styles P, in particular, is one of my favorite people in the whole rap game. As a person, I think he is as authentic as they come and we always clicked. Anyway, when they came to the show, they decided that they were going to put their relationship with Puffy on blast. They outed him for taking advantage of them when they were young and accused him of stealing their publishing money when they had first signed to Bad Boy.

The wanted their money and they wanted *out* of their Bad Boy contract.

So the Lox are on my show, talking about how Puffy sold them the old story—"We're family. We take care of you. Family for life. Bad Boy for life." And when the Lox started to voice their gripes, Puffy's defense was something along the lines of, "Well, it's just business."

This problem happened in the music business a lot. Didn't make it right. They were kids—you're taking them out of the hood, acting like you're their family, and then defending questionable practices with "just business." That's a confusing message.

And aspects of all that came up on-air. All the members of the Lox were going in on Puff, talking crazy stuff like pushing a refrigerator off a building onto him.

There was nothing I could say. Again, I did not jump to Puff's defense because ultimately I didn't think I should.

My boss, Tracy, came into the studio and took me aside. "Look, Puff called. He wants to call in to the show."

"What?!"

"Yeah, he wants to talk to the Lox."

I let the Lox know it was totally up to them. They welcomed it.

*Fine.*

The minute Puffy calls in and gets on the air, he immediately tries to turn the tables as the wronged and yet reasonable party, talking to the Lox like misbehaving kids.

**PUFFY:** I'm at my office now. I'm always accessible, and y'all ain't gotta get on the radio and do certain things to holla at me. I told Jadakiss, I'm accessible. I said if somebody standing in the way of you expressing yourself, y'all can come get at me directly, know what I'm saying? A refrigerator ain't gone kill nobody. We businessmen. We mature adults. All that right there? I'm at my office right now and y'all can sit there and interview with her and talk as long as you wanna talk. Or you can take the invitation I gave you before. But it's not even getting there because of your getting on the radio. Because I ain't your enemy.

**JADAKISS/STYLES P:** Dog! Dog! Just yesterday we got a note from your office saying you don't know nothing of this. None of it! We just saw you at the concert, at the Hova, and you said you'd find out what it was . . .

**PUFFY:** . . . Don't sit here and portray that Puff took something from y'all . . . !

**JADAKISS:** What is it? What is it, then? What do you call it? What do you call it? And don't say we can come to your office or none of that 'cause we can't do that. We can't handle it no other way than with lawyers and you know that . . . so don't get on the radio and act like a tough guy. You actin' tough.

**PUFFY:** You know how we can settle this? At the office. So why don't we stop talking on the radio.

**JADAKISS:** You just wanna stop talking 'cause you don't want to know the truth!

**STYLES P**: We made one record with you, *Money, Power & Respect*. It's ten years later and you still got half of our publishing. And it's no way you can make it justifiable that you deserve half of our publishing.

**PUFFY**: You didn't say that to my face. . . .

**VOICES FROM THE LOX**: You a coward! You a thief!

**PUFFY**: Come to the office so we can straighten it out.

**STYLES P**: You had a bunch of artists whose careers never went right with you. Be for real, dog. Look at the list . . . 112 not happy with you, gone. Faith not happy with you, gone. We not happy with you, gone. Mase not happy with you, gone.

**JADAKISS**: B.I.G. dead. Shyne in jail.

**ANGIE (after silence on the other end)**: Wow, wow, wow. He's gone . . .

The next day the whole city was talking about it, and when Puff wanted to come up to the show on his own, I advised that he wait a few days for things to simmer down. But he pushed. "Nah, I want to come up there today."

Ugh. "Okay."

His first matter of business was to come for me, insinuating that I was pitting artists against each other in interviews. But I didn't back down. And you could hear the hostility, too, like he's not fucking with me and I'm not fucking with him. Ultimately, I let him have his say—*and* the Lox got their publishing back. And that to me felt like I'd done my part in resolving their issues.

By that point in my career, I had developed my voice and built a platform. And I realized that day that sometimes the right thing to do is to pick a side. Because ultimately, if you can use your voice to make a difference in someone else's life, that is what you leave behind.

I didn't want to let being impartial get in the way of doing right in the culture. Yes, as a radio host I try to be fair to everybody, but I also care about the people and I care about what's right. The Lox getting their publishing back was right. It's not just about The Lox specifically. It also sends a message to the industry and up-and-coming rappers to be mindful of their business practices. And I was proud to be part of that conversation.

Eventually everything smoothed out between Puff and The Lox. And years later things would get smoothed out between me and Puff. I've gotten less judgmental as I've gotten older and, being fair, the reality is that I don't know why he handled things like he did. And I have *no* idea how I would have handled things if put in similar circumstances.

• • •

The year 2007 was about to go down as the worst year in the music industry. CD sales dropped. Labels were consolidating, jobs were cut. iTunes was putting music retail stores out of business. And small artists were struggling to stay alive. Kanye West and 50 Cent were the exception to that when each sold nearly one million copies on their first week out. From that position, 50 Cent came on my show criticizing indie label Koch, calling it the graveyard for artists. He managed to offend a lot of people, including Cam'ron and Styles P from The Lox. Both called into the show that day and got a little heated. Off-air, 50 and I argued about whether or not he was a bully.

When I say "argue," I use that word loosely. There's something about sparring with smart people that I enjoy, even if our perspectives are different. I've gotten that from all those years of trying to get to the point during interviews.

I like to get to the point quickly. I hate small talk. It makes me want to punch myself in the face, repeatedly. Radio has only magnified that impatience. As Ebro and I used to say, "In radio there's no foreplay. You gotta get right to the fucking."

The problem for me was that for all my growth in this period, I had become more impatient than ever. Just ask any of my assistants and members of my teams who I mentored. "Don't write a three-paragraph e-mail to me when it should only take one sentence . . ." It makes me crazy! On the upside, because I was tough and exacting, those who could handle it have gone on to thrive—like Monse and then TJ, my friend Tracey's little cousin who started as my assistant as a kid and would go on to be an engineer for Beats Radio, and my producer Drewski—all who would have my back throughout these later years at Hot. I used to call these guys my other sons. Because as tough and impatient as I could be, there was nothing I wouldn't do for anyone on my team and they all knew it.

As I evolved I began to feel less guilty about running a tight ship. It was necessary. As much fun as we were having, this was a job. We needed to be efficient and productive and at the top of our game. So almost daily I would be kicking someone out of the studio who didn't belong there. I tried to teach everyone who worked with me about boundaries. My friend Adrienne Bailon says that's one of the most important things she's learned from me, that people will take advantage of you if you don't set boundaries. I met Adrienne when she was thirteen and in a group called 3LW. She has so much personality and I just felt a connection with her immediately. She's somebody I wanted to look after, and I always have. To this day she calls me her big sister.

I began to see that I had some life experiences worth sharing with others and I found confidence in that. I was now seasoned. I had been in the game a long time. I'd seen a lot, and I had great relationships that

I valued. I tried to show up for people whenever I could. I never wanted to disappoint anyone, and I often found myself saying yes to too much. I probably needed some boundaries my damn self in this area.

There were appearances and social events that were part of doing what I do, and sometimes, even if I was tired or had too much on my plate, there were certain people I made sure I showed up for.

Like the time that Fabolous was having his thirtieth birthday party. Fab and I had known each other for years and he often showed up for me. He was having a great year with his new album *From Nothin' to Somethin'*, and the party was packed with so many people I knew that every time I tried to leave, somebody else pulled me over.

As the night got later, I could feel almost a dizzying exhaustion starting to set in, along with my impatience to get home. For the last time, I announced to whoever, "I gotta fuckin go!" and walked out with Pecas making sure I got to my Range Rover. I climbed in and started on the twenty-minute drive home to my apartment.

About a block away from pulling into my complex, I start to fall asleep at the wheel, and in that split second, I jolt myself back and slam on the brakes. Only instead of hitting the brakes, I slam the gas so hard that it slaps me into a parked car. I crash so hard into the parked car that as it flies up and over the curb—whoosh!—my Range Rover skids into a massive metal gate as everything is literally crushed around me. It's like I've woken up in a metal coffin with a car caved in everywhere around me, except for my little space where I'm sitting.

For a second I think *This is it; this is the end*. Death. Then I black out again, and when I come back, I see spinning police lights and hear sirens and I'm standing barefoot in the street with glass all around me. Just standing there. *How?* I'm in this tiny little gold lamé dress that barely covers my ass. *Where are my shoes?* Somehow in the crash, I must have lost my shoes.

My focus is going in and out. First, I'm sitting back in my car, seeing myself standing there barefoot in the street. Then I'm turning to see two cops walking toward me, one of them saying, "Stay where you are. Don't move." When I blink, I'm looking at the two officers putting me in their car. In the next moment I'm seated in the backseat and looking back at me in my crashed car.

None of it connected. At one point one of the cops said, "Stop moving." The other asked, "Are you okay?"

"I am," I told them. Which was ridiculous. I was not. They asked if I'd been drinking, and though I'd had one drink earlier in the night, I explained it had been a long day and I was exhausted and had fallen asleep.

"Are you sure you're okay?" the cop asked.

"Yeah," I said, pointing across the street. "I live right there."

"I don't know," one of them questioned. "You're really okay?"

"I'm fine."

They did not give me a Breathalyzer test. They did not take me to the hospital to check me for a concussion or brain trauma. They just assessed that the Range Rover was totaled, so they insisted on driving me across the street to my house.

As I recalled it the next day, my out-of-body experience continued as they ran my license and had me sit in the car. That was when I was again somewhere else looking down on me. I'm sitting in the cop car and I suddenly can see myself in the car with the cops.

As soon as I got into my place, sent the sitter home, checked in on my sleeping child, and stumbled into my bedroom, I collapsed and went to sleep. Thank God I woke up! And I realized I wasn't fine at all; I was in bad shape. *Holy shit!* Right after the accident, I hadn't been able to process what happened. I thought I had just crashed and that was it. I didn't realize until the next day, *Wait a minute. I crashed and then the cops were there already. How could that have happened?* I had passed out, totally unconscious, and didn't even know it. *Wait. That doesn't make sense—for the cops to fucking let me go home?*

My mind was all scrambled and my leg was fucked up. I went to the hospital and got cleared—thank God again—but then I had to hobble to the Hair & Beauty Expo later that day. Still not totally sure what all had happened, I sent Fab a picture of the crashed car with a text: *Yo, this happened on the way home.*

*Are you okay?*

*Yeah.*

*Really, Fab? Well, that's how you know it was a hell of a party!*

Yeah, a hell of a party. He almost killed me.

Not exactly, but over the next few days, as all the pieces came together, I had that full-on feeling of, *Wow, that was almost it.* That was the closest I ever felt to death. It wasn't like the fire, when I could have died. Or other close calls where I could have died. I was actually out the door and there. But somehow I got pulled back. For some reason I was spared.

This was the time when I felt death and valued the warning—don't forget this moment. The part of almost dying that terrified me most was

the thought of not being on this earth for my son. After that night I resolved never again to drive tired. If it's been a long day, I'll stay at a friend's rather than drive home. And if I hit the road and start to get tired, I'll find somewhere safe and pull over to close my eyes.

Just being more careful may have also helped me to develop more patience in general. Or maybe not.

• • •

The last highlight of 2007 that I can't forget to mention was getting to interview Senator Barack Obama. Earlier in the year, in the midst of Uelo's funeral, I received the announcement that Obama was going to run for president. I wanted to jump for joy, literally. I was overwhelmed with excitement, and I screamed out to my mom from across the funeral parlor, "He's running!" She was thrilled and whispered back, "That's great, honey."

Then came his call to the station as the primary season took off, and I was out of my mind with excitement. This was crazy. *Is this happening? Am I for real chopping it up with Barack Obama?* He was so gracious, so generous, telling me how cool it was to be on the air with the Voice of New York. And he was just himself and down to earth, admitting to me, "I'm old-school and generally I'm more of a jazz guy. But having said that, I'm current enough that on my iPod I got a little bit of Jay Z, a little bit of Beyoncé."

In the months that followed, slowly but surely there was a change of heart for a lot of friends and family who had said that Americans would never elect a black president. People got past their fears, and even the most skeptical became supporters. The hip-hop community soon came out strong to support him. A turning point was Will.I.Am's "Yes We Can" video. Again, it was music connecting to the moment, bringing in so many voices we hadn't heard together before.

There were so many exciting moments that led up to the day of the election in November 2008. The momentum was real and powerful. I'll never forget the morning of election day, when I was driving in to work and I turned on the radio to Power 105.1, where Ed Lover was now on the air in the afternoons starting an hour before my show. People had been pitting us against each other, although, as I like to remind Ed, I was killing him in the ratings. Still, I would routinely listen to his show as I drove in to work, just to check out the competition. That day I tuned in to hear him say, "Oh my gosh, you're never going to believe who I've got in the building." There was a beat before he said who it was. And then to my complete and utter horror, he says—OPRAH WINFREY! *Holy shit, fuck, my life is ruined! I no longer want to live!* My ultimate dream interview of life and she was on Ed's show, in the same time slot, talking about this historic election and how much she cared about it. She was so good and so gracious and funny, but of course she was—it's *her*, the Almighty Mother Oprah.

I could barely breathe. How did this happen? How had Ed gotten this interview? Everybody who knew me understood that this was not an easy loss for me.

During my breaks, all I could do was tune in to Ed's show and listen. Even though I had my own show to do, I couldn't focus. Besides, the whole city was listening to Ed that day. Oprah had recently received a lot of criticism from the hip-hop community after being super critical about it and distancing herself from the culture, something I had been dying to interview her about. I'd had the conversation so many times already in my head. But there she was, having the conversation with my competition.

As much as I wanted to criticize him and hate on him, the truth was he did a great job. I hated the negative feelings I was having—jealousy, disappointment, embarrassment—and I knew I needed to get them out. So all I could do was release them in the most positive way possible. The second his interview was over, I sent Ed a text: *If somebody had to steal my dream interview, I'm glad it was you. You did an amazing job!*

Ed sent me back a gracious text, telling me I couldn't know how much that meant to him. And as quick as that, I felt better. The negative feelings were gone, and I learned something that day: to be aware of my own negative energy and the power of finding a way to release it in a positive way. The truth is that I could have held on to that jealousy for a long time. Instead I felt empowered. Oprah would be proud.

It was a big day for me, and it was a big day for our country. Knowing that Niko was old enough to witness history and that he, too, could be president one day made me so proud. I took him into the voting booth with me, and I let him cast my ballot with his little five-year-old finger.

Young Jeezy said it on the trap song, and now we could all say it, too. "My president is black."

# CHAPTER FOURTEEN

# THREE-CARD MONTE

The Hot 97 where I grew up was different from the place where I found myself working in the years between 2009 and 2014. Before I ever really thought of going anywhere else, there were certain moments of awareness that took place and made me start to think about life beyond the only radio home I'd ever known.

Some of these had nothing to do with Hot and everything to do with me—and my own fears that I couldn't make it anywhere else. It was true that my identity just seemed synonymous with the station and that my relationships were intertwined. Without Hot 97, who was I? Was it enough just to be me, Angie Martinez? Did I have enough equity in my own personal brand to survive outside of this mega platform that I had helped build? I knew my relationship with my audience was real, but how would I connect to them if I were to leave? Would it matter to them, or would it be on to the next? I wondered the same thing about people in the industry even though I knew my relationships were strong.

In fact, there were plenty of times over the years that I'd feel humbled when people extended themselves and showed real love outside of my day job.

One of the most over-the-top gestures happened one year on my birthday and I got a call from a label rep saying, "Lil Wayne has something he wants to send you for your birthday and wants to know if I can pass along your number to him."

It was not strange that an artist would send me flowers or a fruit basket or something for my birthday. I didn't know Wayne. He'd been on my show once, maybe twice, and he'd never really been super talkative. So the fact that he would even call me for my birthday was so weird to me. I gave the rep my number but was still puzzled—*Okay, Wayne.*

That phone rang right after that. "Hey, it's Weezy. I heard on the radio that it was your birthday, and I just want to wish you a happy birthday."

"Oh, thanks so much," I said.

"I have something I want to send you," Wayne said. "Can I have my man get your address so I can get it to you?"

"You really didn't have to. Thank you. Sure, have him call me."

In five minutes I got a call from some guy that worked for Wayne, saying, "I need your address. I'm coming for Wayne. I'm going to jump on a flight from Miami now."

"Wait a minute. You're flying here to bring it to me?"

Yeah, that's what the man said.

*This guy is coming from Miami to give me a present?! Okay, maybe he's coming here anyway . . . Who knows!?* (Clearly this is not a bottle of champagne or an Edible Arrangement.)

The guy shows up in front of my building at ten p.m. that night. Out of a taxi comes a Wayne look-alike. I mean the guy looks just like Lil Wayne, but it's not him. It's clearly somebody from his crew.

"Hello, Ms. Angie," he says. "Here you go." He gives me this little box. As I start to open the gift, I ask, "Did you just get in from the airport?"

"Yeah. I came to bring this to you."

"You're not staying in town?"

"No. The taxi is going to take me right back to the airport."

"Are you kidding me? Is Wayne crazy?"

"Kinda," he said. "'Hold on. I've gotta call him. I was supposed to let him know once you have it."

As he's calling Wayne, I'm opening the box, and it's a diamond tennis bracelet! An outrageous, brilliant, flawless diamond tennis bracelet. I'm just staring at it. *Why would he do this? What is this?! Is this real? Is this, like, rhinestones? This can't be diamonds! This has got to be a forty-thousand-dollar bracelet! Is he crazy? No fucking way is this for me. I don't even know this man. What is happening?!*

"Yeah, I'm here with her right now," Wayne's boy says into the phone. "She got it." He then looks at me and asks, "Do you like it?"

"Uh, yeah!"

He tells Wayne, "Yeah, she likes it," and then hands me the phone.

"Hello?"

"Hey, Miss Angie." In his laid-back New Orleans accent.

"Wayne, why would you do that? Are you crazy?"

"Well, you know, I heard it was your birthday, and I started thinking about that time I came to your show and I had a really bad migraine that day and you told me that you took Imitrex when yours got really bad. And I was just watching you. You was in your bag for five, ten minutes, like emptying out your whole bag, trying to find me one. And you gave it to me, and it was the first time I had any relief from my migraine. I've been taking them ever since, and it showed me that you was just a nice person, and I wanted to say thank you and wish you a happy birthday."

*Wow.* Normally, I don't accept gifts like that. But it was so kind and so sweet that I just wanted to keep it. I almost felt like he would be offended if I didn't.

"Thank you so much, man," I said. "I don't even know what to say."

"You don't have to say nothing."

"Well, you have my number now, so keep in touch."

"All right, you have mine, too. Enjoy. Have a happy birthday."

And I haven't heard from him since. Isn't that amazing? He never wanted anything. He never asked me for anything. After we hung up I debated whether I should keep the bracelet or not because it was so expensive and I felt weird about it. But fate made the decision for me. A short time later I was on a flight to Miami and noticed the clasp was a little loose. I made a mental note to have it tightened when I got back to New York. Unfortunately, somewhere in transit, it must have fallen off my wrist. The universe took it from me before I could return it.

Though I lost the bracelet, I still have the memory of him doing that and the realization of how thoughtful and dope he is. Also, his very generous gesture reminded me that all the professional relationships I had built would endure no matter what changes were to come. And that was no small thing.

. . .

I'm always asked what my favorite interview was and I can never answer that. I've had bad interviews. Maybe the artist wasn't into it. Maybe I didn't ask the right questions. My goals as an interviewer are for me to learn something new about that person and to learn something in general; I want to be entertained. I want to have a good vibe. If I get that, I know my audience will, too. The main thing is that I want to feel something, and so I always shoot for that.

I love to be surprised. When Dave Chappelle came on my show, we laughed a lot, but more than the laughter, I was enthralled by how interesting and smart he is. It was such a pleasure to talk to him that once the interview was over and we went off the air, we sat in the studio for another hour or two and hung out, talking some more.

Derek Jeter was another guest who would surprise me. I'm a huge Yankees fan and a huge Derek Jeter fan, and he just represented all that could be good about an athlete. Even now to this day, for me, with a son who likes sports, there's no role model better than Derek Jeter, and he was just the king of the Yankees in his heyday when he used to come to the show—as a fan of the station and as a fan of hip-hop.

He would call in after winning the World Series or come in and do a full interview. He didn't have to do that. He didn't have to do anything; he's Derek Jeter. He really just came because he knew what it would mean to us and to our listeners, and it was surprising and humbling.

Sometimes I like surprising my guests. One of my favorite interviews was the second time that I had A$AP Rocky on the show. He's great and he's young and all swaggy, and during our first interview I found out that his real name is Rakim—named by his mother after Rakim the rapper, one of my favorites of all time.

"That is so dope," I said. "Have you ever met him—your namesake?"

"No," he said, but talked about how much he'd love to one day.

So the next time I had A$AP Rocky on the show, I'm in the middle of the interview when I mention, "Oh, remember last time when you said you always wanted to meet Rakim?"

And A$AP kind of shrugs, being cool, a typical rapper, all laid-back attitude, and at just that moment—as planned—the original Rakim walks into the room, and A$AP Rocky transforms into a little kid seeing the real Santa Claus. *What?!!* He came over and gave me a big hug; he couldn't even help himself.

The two looked like they were having a long-lost reunion and A$AP asked Rakim, "Can you call my mom?" It was the cutest. A$AP was giddy. The surprise brought out the authentic, sweet side of him. Rakim was so gracious. It was a great, great moment.

For me it was an emotional high because A$AP Rocky is the epitome of the new-generation rapper right now. Rakim is arguably one of the greatest rappers of all time and represents earlier hip-hop, when I was coming of age. So being able to create a moment that was so multigenerational but so hip-hop helped me to define my space in the culture.

The ability to do that and make it happen was just a perfect moment.

I have had other interviews where I felt that I could create a safe space, a little like therapy for artists who needed it right then. Busta Rhymes was someone who was always animated and always happy who came up to the show when he was physically and emotionally just exhausted. And, man, haven't we all been there? He was at the peak of his career, but when he came that day and was willing to let loose about the challenges, it was brave and moving. Another time I had DMX on where he was in full tears—exhausted and battling with his demons—and he wanted to talk more, but at that moment I wanted to protect him and had to cut the mic off a couple of times.

I think it became known over the years that I tried to do right by people, and with that, I earned their trust. And in those instances when it became something of a therapy session, as it did sometimes between Mary J. Blige and me, our friendship was there on the air as much as off of it.

One of the times that stands out was when she signed on to do a Burger King commercial about crispy fried chicken and she got so much flak about it. The reaction really was over-the-top about her singing about chicken. In her mind, she was just trying to make an iconic commercial—like the "Two all-beef patties" McDonald's campaign—but the execution of the spot wasn't what she had hoped. As much as that saddened her, nothing disturbed her more than how the public responded. I mean, the

Internet went bananas, calling her names for portraying a racist stereotype and for being a sellout. For somebody as beloved as Mary, it's shocking to see how one questionable move could make people flip on you. I hate that about our culture.

Mary really didn't react in public initially, and the first time she talked about it was on my show—how hurtful it had been not just to see the criticism but to think that fans wouldn't know her intent, that they wouldn't trust her integrity.

Probably the hardest interview I've ever done—and one I feel proudest of—was with Chris Brown in 2009. At that point I was seasoned and ready; I knew who I was. It was such a sensitive moment and it had not been broached on radio. It was raw—the first lengthy interview he had done after the horrible incident with Rihanna, where the whole world saw what he did to her: her bruised, bloody face. Yes, he had gone on Larry King and that was awful for him. That was all the public had heard from him, and people were angry—rightfully so—but my goal was to be fair and hopefully have him confront the truth of it.

I had known Chris from the time he was fifteen years old. So we had a relationship that made me feel I could be direct and he could handle it. When he arrived with his whole team trying to be super hands-on, I just wasn't having it. I took Chris out of the room before we started.

"Listen, there are going to be points where I'm gonna go hard on you because I have to. I have to be honest in that," I said. "But also, I'm gonna give you a chance to be heard. And I care about you, so my intention is not to hurt you. But we have to be honest and I have to tell you how I really feel."

"No, I totally get it," he said.

In wanting to be fair, I thought about how you'd treat a member of your family who'd done something awful. Even in your disappointment, you don't leave them for dead and you don't disown them. You want to know what happened and you want to know why. I wanted to talk about it so that Chris could own it—to give him the space to do that. At the same time, I didn't want my audience to think that what happened was okay. I didn't want any young girl listening to think that this is okay. Not okay.

As horrified as I was and as concerned as I was about Rihanna, I also was concerned for Chris. When I asked him if he was okay, he reacted like somebody who had never been asked that question before. For a moment I thought to myself, if one day my son made a horrible mistake I would hope that someone would give him the opportunity to make it right.

Chris was this young kid who had done a profoundly wrong thing and he was going to pay, probably for the rest of his life. If I felt like he was getting away scot-free, I may have felt differently. But the repercussions of his actions were inevitable, and I chose to hope that through those consequences he'd learn something that he could later teach.

**ANGIE:** I definitely want to talk about how you can redeem yourself. Do you have a plan?

**CHRIS BROWN:** I just feel like whatever God has in store for me. One mistake, I can change. I can turn a bad into a positive. And take the situation that was in my life and kind of change it and make it into a positive, making people aware of situations.

**ANGIE:** I want to be careful. [Rihanna] clearly was the victim in this. But I've got to imagine that this has been awful for you.

**CHRIS BROWN:** Yeah.

**ANGIE:** I see you on Larry King and I am torn. Like I don't want to let you off the hook. Because it's not poor Chris, right? But just as someone who knows you, this has to be one of the most awful experiences of your life.

**CHRIS BROWN:** People don't realize I am human. I hurt. I cry. I feel pain, I feel embarrassment, I feel ashamed. . . .

**ANGIE:** You were such a role model for the kids. And then everybody was just, like, in shock.

**CHRIS BROWN:** Yeah. I mean, and that was one of the most embarrassing things for me, too. Because of my image and who I was as a young role model to a lot of kids, and how people look up to me. Even parents and stuff like that. It was hard for me, because I let a lot of people down. And I felt that it was like turning my back on a lot of my fans, and turning my back on a lot of people, even the people I love, you know what I'm saying?

It was like walking on a tightrope. He fucked up and he was going to pay for it. We all knew that. He needed to. But also, he's a human being. And I chose to focus on that while most of the media, even my Oprah, had chosen to ignore the possibility that Chris could be redeemed, that he could learn from this and look at how abuse had played a role in his upbringing, and focus his energy on never letting something like that happen again. From my perspective he deserved a fair hearing, even if he had a lot of work to do as he picked up the pieces of his shattered persona.

That was an empowering moment to take a stand that was against the grain and to handle a tough interview and to do it well. Owning that also let me appreciate my position within the culture and my unique perspective. I don't know if anyone else could have had that same conversation.

I was proud of how far I'd come. At the same time, in this newfound confidence, deep down I was starting to get restless.

. . .

Things were starting to feel different at Hot 97. There was this new regime, and they were making decisions that seemed weird and off brand. They were adding all these pop records and coming up with all this corny digital content. In the past, when upper management had these bright ideas, they would always consult with all of us in programming because they valued our knowledge of our station and our listeners; we'd fight to keep the integrity of the brand intact. But more and more we weren't even being asked—by management that had no connection to the culture and our audience whatsoever. It started to feel that we were losing control of the place, like we were losing our voice. I was showing up and I was doing the job, but I began to feel removed. I had never felt this way before—like the station was losing its heart.

Everything was changing. Our morning show—with deejays Cipha Sounds and Peter Rosenberg—was struggling against Power 105.1's *Breakfast Club*. Cipha, who was funny and dry, had been at the station for a really long time and was loved by everyone. Rosenberg, newer to the scene, was smart, championed underground hip-hop, and like Ciph was dry and witty. The two were getting their rhythm, but it was hard to compete with what *The Breakfast Club* was doing in the market. Angela Yee, formerly of Sirius Radio, DJ Envy, formerly of Hot 97, and Charlamagne tha God, former sidekick of Wendy Williams, were a force. They were seasoned, they were digitally savvy, and they were provocative. To respond, Ebro, still programming director, would step in occasionally with some edge and help round out Ciph and Rosenberg.

Ebro was good. So good that corporate eventually asked him to do it on a permanent basis—with the stipulation that he had to give up his job as program director. When Ebro asked my opinion about whether he should make the change, I encouraged him. "If being on-air is what you want to do and that's what will make you happy, then absolutely."

However, I couldn't see the future and how this would affect all of us. The problem was, it was going to take a good amount of time before they found a new program director, and Ebro was still sitting in that chair but he wasn't protecting us the way our program director had in the past.

In this vulnerable position, the fucking TV-show thing happened with VH1. For months there had been rumors of a reality show about the station. But nothing had been said until the day Ebro sat me down in his office.

"You know, Mona Scott wants us to do this TV show," he says. "But, of course, we would need you to be all in so you can help position how we would be portrayed and all that."

"I'm on the fence about it. It's risky." Mona was behind *Love and Hip Hop* and reality shows that weren't the same type of tone as what I viewed Hot 97 as a brand to be. I said to Ebro, "That's like fast-food TV. Ratchet TV." Hot 97 was always a little smarter than that. Not to say Mona wasn't capable—she was hugely successful—but I had questions.

Ebro assured me that nothing would move forward without my approval and that he would suggest I be a producer in order to protect the station's integrity.

Months passed and I hadn't heard anything. Then, all of a sudden, I get wind that they're negotiating a TV deal with VH1 and Mona Scott. But nobody's talking to me. Nobody's talking to Flex. Nobody's even talking to Ebro at this point. Upper management is negotiating a show on behalf of us without even talking to us. We don't hear about it again till it's already to the point where they're sending us contracts to sign. We get the paperwork. *What the fuck is this?!* These were like the contracts you give to the cast members on *Love and Hip Hop,* who are virtually unknown and just happy to be on TV. *What the fuck?! Who negoti-ated this?*

The way the deal went down revealed that the people in power now didn't care about protecting the Hot 97 brand anymore. They weren't consulting with us and they weren't paying us shit. We launched a revolt.

I marched into our general manager Alex's office. "You cannot do this. This is not okay," I said. "Number one, I'm not signing this, and number two, what you're saying to your staff is that you don't value them. You don't even discuss this with them?"

In her defense, she was just trying to get it done fast. She didn't want to lose the deal. And I'm guessing she thought that the big bosses in Indianapolis would be impressed with all the extra free marketing from this TV show. So in Alex's mind she was doing the right thing—making deals based on numbers. And from what I understood, the numbers were in trouble. Our ratings were fine, but our small company going up against a monster corporation like Clear Channel had other challenges. Like a corner-store bodega going up against Walmart, we didn't have anywhere near the same leverage when it came to generating advertising sales—which is the name of the game. And clearly for management a VH1 reality show could make a difference.

A lot of the younger staff wanted to do the show because they were looking to get as much opportunity and promotion as they could. And I couldn't be mad at them. I understood that. But for some of us who were a little more seasoned—me, Flex, Cipha—it was a different story. Our stance was—*You have to pay us, and we have to have some creative control, which this contract is not giving us.* We fought and fought and management started pointing fingers at us as if we were holding the station back from this "amazing opportunity." Meanwhile, Ebro wasn't doing *anything* about it; nobody was protecting us. And now top management was telling us we had to do this stupid show for fucking peanuts!

Flex and I go right into Ebro's office and we take turns. I say, "Yo, this is the stupidest thing ever. These people are talking to everybody crazy!" Flex says, "What are you doing about it? We know you're leaving to go be on-air, but you're still sitting here." Or words to that effect.

And Ebro kind of just puts his hands up, as if to say, "Well, that's what they want to do. I'm staying out of it."

*Staying out of it????* I took that as a statement that he would stand by and watch this bullshit happen. I couldn't believe it. Ebro had always fought for the station and the brand and the staff, and in that moment I realized how different things had become. His agenda had changed. And I no longer felt protected. And the fact that the station had the nerve to slide me this bullshit contract to sign proved it.

These contracts, by the way, pretty much want to own you. That's how those television contracts are. You can't do anything! You've got to get approval from VH1 if you want to do any other television show, make any appearances, or a whole bunch of other shit that was not gonna happen. I didn't work all these years on my career to have VH1 and Mona Scott control what I do with the rest of my life! Worse, this was what the people at Hot 97 were trying to do to me. They were going to let that happen to me. In fact, they were setting me up for it. I felt betrayed by that. I also felt extremely protective of the talent that didn't have the tenure I had and who had less leverage to fight for themselves. Now, not only was I fighting for myself, but I was fighting for the Ciphas and Miss Infos and Laura Stylezes of the team. Ultimately, however, everyone wanted to do it, and the majority of the team felt like this was an opportunity they didn't want to miss out on.

My solution was to let them do it without me, but I was informed that they would not do the show if I wasn't a part of it. Great. If I don't sign on, I ruin the opportunity for the rest of the team. So I fixed a few things in the contract that were really disgusting and I got my money up a little bit and reluctantly agreed.

**VH1 Announces New Reality Show, *This Is HOT 97***
**BET**
**Posted: 03/06/2014**

TV station's latest program gives a behind-the-scenes look at New York radio.

From their nationally known deejays to their infamous yearly hip-hop festival, Summer Jam, HOT 97 has long been known by their catchphrase, "Where hip hop lives," and now they're inviting viewers behind the scenes via VH1's newest reality show, *This Is HOT 97*.

Then it's time to shoot the TV show. Now we have producers in there who give less fucks about the station than our management did. They're creating a show called *This Is Hot 97,* and now, in addition to putting the station's brand in jeopardy, we all have to put our own personal brands that we had worked so hard to build in the hands of people we didn't know or trust and who didn't know anything about us. It was such a sloppy and desperate move. But you know, the days I had to show up, I showed up.

I like to joke I'm not afraid to try some goofy shit. So I was game for some of it. And once I commit, I'll do it. *All right. You want me to fucking act like an idiot? Okay. When do we start? Fuck it.* Especially when you're with people that you love. I love Miss Info. She's one of my best friends. So if you put us in a scene together, I'm gonna have fun with her.

Right before they called "Action," I'd turn to her and say, "Kill me."

She'd laugh.

"No really, punch me in the face right now. That would be better than this."

Then we'd turn to the camera and have our fake watercooler talk. Like on *The Office* when actors broke the third wall and talked about their meetings.

I hated how we got here, but I tried to have as much fun as I could in the moments when I was actually shooting. It got harder and harder as time went by.

While I'm going through the motions and laughing at the ridiculousness, I start to realize how Ebro is being positioned on the show. He's the center of every fuckin' episode. He's doing the voice-overs. He's involved with creating the story lines. Me and Flex are looking at him like, *Oh shit. He just fuckin' went and let this show happen because he's about to be the star of this show!*

And I loved Ebro so much that I said it to him multiple times. Like, "Yo, fam, you look crazy. Not just to me, but how do you think that makes it look to these people that you have on the air for five, ten years? They're not even on the show." We had a midday guy, Big Dennis, who had been with Hot 97 since I have been—all these years—and they didn't even have him on the show! He'd been there way longer than Ebro. And then there were DJ Camilo, DJ Enuff, Mister Cee—all these solid personalities, the people that really are in the streets representing Hot 97— and they were not included, and you have Ebro as your fucking star.

It was fast becoming a mockery of the station. *How sad, for everything we've done, everything we've built—this corny TV show will be our legacy.*

Ultimately the problem wasn't the TV show. Had the opportunity come along when we were at our most stable as a station, it might have been different. But we weren't in the same place. For the first time I felt foreign in this home that I'd helped to build. Man, we loved that place.

We cared about that place. We went to war for that place. And now we're sitting there watching it fall apart.

I'll never forget this one day when I walked in to work and I realized that the lights were really dim. It felt so dark and gloomy. I'm sure the lights had always been like that—it just had never really bothered me before. Now it started to feel depressing. After all the years and the loyalty, I started to realize that the thing I was so loyal to no longer existed.

*Maybe it's time for me to move on?* I didn't know what that thought meant. Leave radio in general? *Maybe I could move to LA or Miami and open a bar, a restaurant. I don't know.* I had no clue what I would do. I just started to sense that I couldn't keep doing this.

The first step is realizing there is a problem, and this one was staring me in the face.

# CHAPTER FIFTEEN

# IT'S BEEN A LONG TIME

For everything that wasn't going so well at work, my love life was in a new and amazing place. In a roundabout way, the change started back in 2010 or so, when I had a general "hi, how are you" meeting with a lady from Telepictures. She'd had to cut it short because she had another meeting about to start.

On second thought, she offered, "My next meeting is here. If you want, though, you can stay and meet him. He's a matchmaker."

Hmmm. Single at the time, I was curious, and apparently this guy was good. Like a young Hitch, the lady told me. "So, do you want to meet him?"

"YESS! I do!"

They wound up letting me stay for their whole meeting because the conversation was so good. The meeting was with Paul Brunson, a good-looking, supersmart young man who had married his high school sweetheart. I had one of my "I feel connected to this person" moments.

The thought crossed my mind that this was maybe someone I could work with in some capacity one day. Intrigued, I started asking him a zillion questions about what he does, how he does it, and how does he know? Then he turned the conversation to me and asked why I was single.

"Because I haven't met anybody."

"Well, how much work have you put into it?" When I asked if you shouldn't just let it happen, he said, "No. It's the same way you work on your career. When you want something, you get it done. If you want to be in a relationship, you have to work for it."

*Work!?* That was different. And when we got into a whole discussion about who my type was, I had no idea.

"Well, let me offer you this. What are your three core values?" I had no idea what he meant. He pressed on. "Tell me what your three core values are. I want you to think about what your three core values are, and then I want you to look for those. Because you can get distracted with somebody who's funny or smart, somebody who entertains you, or somebody's swag—but none of that is real. None of that is the thing that is going to hold you together. So I want you to find out what your three core values are, and I want you to start looking for that in somebody else. Because if you don't know what they are, you can miss it. It could show up right in front of you and you could totally miss it."

And the three things that came to mind right away were (1) Family. Family and friendships were so important, and loyalty is right up there. (2) Honesty. It's at the core of who I am. And I know everybody says that, but it really is who I am. I like to be honest, even if it's not comfortable. I look for the truth in everything. (3) God. I'm private about my faith, but my spiritual connection to what's good in the world matters a lot.

Now what? And why did I have to work at it? Didn't I have enough on my plate as it was? Did I even have time for a relationship? Paul argued that with the right relationship, you can actually accomplish more.

In the meantime, Tiffany—one of my girlfriends I've known for years, and a much-loved wardrobe stylist—was tired of me not going out on Friday nights and said, "Look, he's not going to come knocking on your door. Maybe you need to change your circles. Meet some new people." As it happened, she was going to a listening party for Ne-Yo at Ink48 Hotel, where Idris Elba was going to be DJing. I had been trying to book him for my show and Tiffany offered to introduce us.

I didn't know if I would like him or not—but I knew girls went nuts over him and I knew he was a really dope actor and that I'd love to have him on the show. So I went with Tiffany and found myself in the middle of a private party up on a rooftop of a hotel with music blaring, a swimming pool, and lots of pretty people. When she started to drag me over to meet Idris, I could see that the booth was mobbed.

"Well, there's his manager, Oronde," Tiffany said. "Let's go say hi."

Tiff takes me over and introduces me to Oronde Garrett. He says, "Hey, Tiff," and gives her a big hug. Then, turning to me, there's an awkward clash as he goes to give me a hug and I go for the handshake.

There is so much noise and distraction, but there is something about Oronde that feels familiar. A tall, dark-skinned guy originally from Brooklyn before going to college in Maryland, Oronde looks at me with a big, genuine smile and asks, "Do you want to go meet Idris?"

"No. It's too crowded over there, but I'd love to have him on the show."

He thought it would be a great idea and then added, "But we gotta hang out."

Not sure what he meant, he gestured to me and Tiff and said, "What are you guys doing tomorrow night?"

"Oh, I can't do anything. I'm going to a fund-raiser for Mary J. Blige's charity."

Oronde said, "Oh? Well, then, we're going, too!"

*Is he trying to be cute???* "You're not going." I laughed.

"Why can't I be going to that?" He laughed, too.

The next night, when I arrived at Cipriani's for Mary's FFAWN Gala, yep, it turned out that Idris was in fact hosting the event. And Oronde was there. I noticed him sitting a couple of tables way, and just as I spotted him, he waved, as if to say, *Told ya.* I laughed and shook my head.

After the event I had plans to head uptown to Harlem for my friend Dawnie B's birthday party. Dawn worked for Nike and knew a lot of the same people I did. As I was leaving, Oronde asked, "Where you headed?" When I told him, he grinned and said, "Oh, yeah, we were invited to that, too."

This was fun. A bunch of us headed up to Dawn's party. At one point I thought my ex might be there, and it tickled me to think he'd see me all decked out, having a great time and sitting at a table toasting it up with Idris.

Then, right at the table, Oronde leaned over and quietly asked me, in the most direct way possible, "Are you into my friend?" Before I could answer, he explained, "Because I thought there was a connection with you and me, but now you're over kee-keeing with Idris in the corner. It's totally cool if you are . . . I just don't want to be barking up the wrong tree."

*Oh, my God! Honesty and directness! Thank you, Jesus!*

I took a breath and answered with equal honesty. "Well, actually, no, I'm not. At all. But, honestly, I think one of my exes is here, and I was just kinda being a dick."

Oronde got it and he got me. "Okay, I can deal with that."

"I'll stop now." Besides, at that point, he had my full attention.

We went out to a late dinner that same night and that was it. We've been together ever since.

· · ·

Billboard February 13, 2014—Emmis, Owner of NYC's Hot 97, Buys WBLS, WLIB for $130 Mil, Increases Urban Market Share

Emmis Communications, a radio and publishing company which owns WQHT (Hot 97) in New York along with a host of other stations across the country, has announced a deal with YMF Media to purchase two New York radio stations for $131 million in cash. The acquisition of the two stations, urban adult contemporary station WBLS 107.5 FM and WLIB 1190 AM (and the city's first station targeted at African-American listeners), will double Emmis' annual station operating income, the company said.

The company announces not just that they are buying WBLS but bringing in somebody to run both BLS and Hot 97 together. Our general manager, Alex, is out. This guy who's gonna run the place, Deon Levingston, comes from WBLS. That was *his* baby, his shining star. Now Hot 97 would become the stepchild.

People were getting fired left and right, good people who had worked for Hot for a really long time, and it was merging into an unfamiliar, strange stepfamily.

When WBLS came in, we were still shooting the TV show. So we're in the hallway shooting this buffoonery and these older BLS people are walking around like, *What the fuck are they doing?* Deon, the general manager, did not like the show, you could tell. Very weird energy. We're shooting this show that we all hate that Alex made us do. Alex doesn't even work here anymore! Ebro's the fucking star of the show. We don't have a program director in place. It's a circus.

I didn't even recognize the place anymore.

When the show aired that spring, I didn't tune in. I couldn't do it. My weird ability to ignore something as if it doesn't even exist kicked in and I was just so happy it was over. It was canceled after the first season. Everything was unraveling, and the whispers grew into shouts.

*What am I holding on to? I don't feel the same way about this place. I mean, I love being on the radio. And I love my friends here. But I don't love how this ship is being run anymore. Either I'm going to sit on this sinking ship or I am going to get off the fucking boat.*

At that point I still didn't know what that meant, but I knew it was time for me to move on. It was coming. It was getting close. My contract was up already. With all the changes in management, nobody seemed to notice or care. This new general manager barely had a conversation with me. Maybe once. Maybe he had too much on his plate.

So anything could happen to the station at that point. And it wasn't just us. This move was going to do the same demolition to the legendary KISS FM and put some of the most iconic names in radio off the air. The same could easily happen to HOT.

Almost everybody at the station was feeling uncomfortable, uneasy, hating the way shit was going down. I was walking into the studio one day and Enuff approached me in the hallway outside.

"Hey, you good?"

"Yeah," I said.

"I know shit is crazy," Enuff said. "Ang, I know you're frustrated."

"Yeah."

"Just let me know when it's time," he said. "Give me a heads-up."

I looked at him and I said, "I'm giving you a heads-up."

"You are?"

"Mm-hmm."

"Like right now?"

And I just nodded my head like right now. I went back into the studio and I still didn't know what I would do or when I would do it, but the feeling inside had gone from foggy to clear. This chapter of my life was ending.

. . .

*What am I gonna do? What's my next move?* Oronde knew everything I'd been going through and had witnessed my building frustration. He came home one night and told me that Chris Green, a record rep who also happens to be Tiffany's boyfriend, had said that Power 105.1 had been asking what was up with my contract.

"They've been asking that question for years," I told Oronde.

His point was, as bad as things were, "You should meet with them. What could it hurt?"

As much as working for Power was not an option for me, and I couldn't even fathom the thought, I *was* intrigued by Clear Channel, the parent company. They were doing some innovative things in the industry with their iHeart app and music festival. A lot of people were paying attention. *Maybe Oronde was right. What could a conversation hurt?* The first thing I did was call Pecas. Over the years Pecas had come to me a few times about Clear Channel wanting to work with me. "I'm not talking to them," I had insisted in the past. "Fuck them." I had always been fiercely loyal to Hot 97. Could I really work there? I wasn't sure, but I had to know my options.

"If I talked to Doc, do you think he could keep it confidential???" I asked Pecas. Doc was the head program director for all of the urban stations at Clear Channel, which is now iHeart.

"Yeah," Pec said, sounding slightly surprised yet totally unfazed.

Pecas, promising we would keep it confidential, set up a meeting for me with Doc. "He's at the London Hotel," he said. "He's gonna meet you by the bar."

"The London?" The London Hotel is a popular spot; it's not a discreet place. But I was so removed at this point, I really didn't even care; and it was an eleven a.m. meeting, so—*Ah, fuck it*. I just went.

Sitting down with Doc was so weird for me because of all of the history, all of the years that they had been the enemy. Now I'm actually sitting here having tea with him! I didn't even want to get a meal. I wasn't even committing to breaking bread. "I'll have a mint tea."

"Well, it's really nice to meet you," Doc said. "First, I just want to say how much I respect you and everything that you've done. I think you're amazing." He went on to talk about what he knew of my career. I'd heard that he was a really nice guy. We had a great conversation.

"So where are you in your career right now?" Doc asked.

"You know, I'm at a point where I want to know what my options are for my future. Not just for right now, but for five years from now," I said. "I want to have an understanding of what the landscape looks like in radio, and I thought you would be a good place to start."

"Well, is your contract up?"

"Yup."

"Really?" His eyeballs opened wide. "You know, it's so funny," he said. "I've been with the company for so many years. And every year we get these numbers about what radio personalities resonate in the market. Your name is always at the top of that list. So every year it comes up. The question is, 'What do we gotta do to get her?' Every year we have the same conversation. 'We can't get her. She's too loyal. She's never gonna come here.' That's always the conversation. But you know what's so crazy is it got to the point some years ago that nobody even asks anymore." He goes, "But this year we had somebody new to the company that hadn't had that conversation yet. So we get the numbers back just like always. You're at the top of the perceptual for the market. And the person says, 'Well, can we get her? Well, what do we got to do to get her?'" Doc had said, "It's never gonna happen. We've tried. She won't even talk to us." Two days later Pecas called him. Doc couldn't believe it. "She wants to talk?!"

It was funny and flattering.

"So what would you want to do? What would your ideal situation be?"

"Honestly, I don't know. I would want to be on in more cities than one. I want growth. I don't want to go somewhere and have the same exact thing. I want more."

He understood that. And to be honest, I don't even think I had wrapped my brain around the fact that I would have to be on Power 105.1. I was really looking at them as a big company—*maybe I could be on in LA, in Miami and Philly.* At that point I was still not mentally prepared to commit to the idea that I would go to the competition.

"Well, you know, we'd want to have you on in New York," he said just as I gulped my mint tea. *Oh God.*

Doc promised to poke around and offered to get back to me.

"Sure. Whatever," I said, telling myself to stay open yet feeling kinda crazy.

*Holy shit! I just met with Clear Channel! Oh my God.* Just even having tea with the man felt like such a big deal. I'm sneaking out of the London, hoping nobody sees me.

The next step was a meeting Doc wanted me to have with Thea, the vice president of programming for all the New York stations—Z100, Power, KTU. She's the program director of Power, and she oversees all the other ones, so she's the New York person. I knew meeting Thea was gonna include talking about me being on Power. I knew what that con-versation was.

So now Thea and I are meeting at the Dream Hotel. Even more fucking popular than the London! I'm going to meet them in their suite. At least we're not going to be in the main bar. So I pull up to the hotel and Thea sneaks out of the elevator, and we are walking really quietly, quickly to the elevator. We ordered sushi and wine up to the room for dinner. I love sushi and wine, and the fact that Thea wanted to order sushi and wine gave me some sense of comfort. *She's not the evil enemy. She's somebody in radio who likes wine and sushi just like me.* I know that sounds corny and crazy, but it took away that whole facade of her being this big bad enemy person. Both of us were a little guarded. A lot of radio personalities, they'll talk to the competition to get their money up and then go back to their station and go, "Well, Clear Channel said they're going to give me XYZ. What are you gonna do?"

So maybe she was skeptical. "Why now?" she asked. "Why would you meet with us now?"

"Honestly, Thea, I don't even know what I want to do or what my next step is." And I told her the truth, the same thing I told Doc. "I'm just curious to know what my options are. I'm evaluating my career and what I want the next few years to look like. And honestly, the station has changed a lot."

I didn't want to give her too much. I didn't want her to think I was unhappy and ready to go right now, but I wanted to be honest. After a little bit of wine and some sushi, we got a little bit more comfortable, but we still didn't say that much. 'Cause, you know, at this point, we're still competition sitting there together eating.

From there Thea and I started talking, texting, e-mailing. "I would love to make this work somehow," she said. "Let's start thinking about what it would take to do that." Thea and I are a lot alike in terms of that we say what we mean and we mean what we say. We're not gossipy people. It was a very direct conversation from the beginning, and we agreed about not letting word get out to the public or anyone, for that matter. *This conversation is safe here.* It needed to be.

After a few very honest talks, they sent me an offer that was good. Really good. And it wasn't just about the money. I was now going to have a more national profile with a show airing in multiple cities.

All this time, I hadn't thought about what my vision for growth even looked like. Suddenly, I realized that this was exactly what I needed—to take what I did to something bigger than being at one station. To a company where even further growth was possible. Clearly, as in all breakups, I had to face the truth that Hot was no longer the place I had fallen in love with. It was a really easy decision. That part was easy!

But then I'd stop myself and panic. *What about Enuff and Flex, Miss Info and Mister Cee? Am I not going to see these people anymore? How does this work? How is this gonna be perceived?*

First came the logical decision that I made clearly with no outside thoughts. Then came the understanding of all the noise that would come with it. *Do I not leave and take this great opportunity because I want to work with my friends forever?*

I talked it over with Oronde, who was wildly supportive throughout the whole process. He was able to look at everything from a more practical perspective because he didn't have the emotional connection to Hot that I did. All he cared about was what was in my best interest. These were some of the benefits of dating a talent manager, and I took full advantage. He helped me see that my fears were unfounded. The people who are my friends, they're still going to be my friends. Sure, it's fun to work with your friends, but when you have a family and you want to grow and evolve, then sometimes that means change.

Yet even with Oronde's counsel, I had to sit with all of this on my

own. That's me. Again, it's how I problem solve. I have to throw out all
the other opinions and get internal and figure it out for myself. In that
space, it became clear—I know that ultimately I have to deal with myself,
by myself. I'm going to have to go in and resign. I'm going to have to sit
in that chair a last time. I'm going to have to get on the radio and tell
everybody that I'm doing this. So ultimately I have to be okay with all
parts of that. So I got really quiet and figured it out.

Other than Oronde, I didn't even tell my lawyer until Thea and I
had already come to a bunch of agreements. As I was closing in toward
the end of the deal, I was at Don Coqui in City Island having dinner
with Pecas and my longtime friends Fat Joe and his wife, Lorena. The
three of them were there at dinner with me as I was at the table texting
with Thea, negotiating little details, the last points. She had me down
for three weeks of vacation.

*I need four weeks of vacation.*

*Fine, four weeks.*

*Oh my God, I feel like we're done.*

*It feels like we are.*

Right there at Don Coqui, it hits me—*Holy shit!*

"I think it's done," I tell Pecas privately. Mind you, I had kept him
out of the loop after he set up that first meeting with Doc. "I think I have
a deal."

Pecas was already a few drinks in and I'm not sure he believed me or
fully understood what I was trying to tell him. I didn't mention another
word to anyone and spent the rest of the night toasting to my big secret.

The next day the lawyers start going over the details. I'm in contract
mode, but I'm still going to work every day at Hot. I'm not telling anybody anything. We're promoting Summer Jam. I'm there and I'm still in
it, but I know that I'm not going to be for long. Being at Summer Jam
the last time was the weirdest and most surreal thing ever.

Standing on the stage, I took a picture of the audience. *The crowd is so big*, I marveled. I definitely had a moment there. My breath—it was like a gasp. *Wow, this will be the last time I'm here.* I felt the weight of it. For the past eighteen fucking years, this was who I was. It was the end of an era.

Staring out into the crowd, I wanted to be *fully* in the moment. I wanted to make sure not to miss it. Sometimes I ignore shit and keep it pushing, just to get to the next step, but I wanted to feel this. Be there. Appreciate it. And I didn't feel any sadness about it. That's how I knew I was so ready. There was nothing about this that I wasn't ready to walk away from. Yet I didn't feel a disconnect from the audience in any way. I didn't feel like I wasn't going to see them again—they were just going to see me somewhere else.

Nobody knew, so that whole day was just me, deep in my own head, in my own world. When the day was over, I went home, feeling full, complete, and ready for whatever was next to come.

• • •

I had my assistant TJ start backing up all my files at the station. I had multiple lockers full of cassettes, DATs, and CDs of interviews from the nineties and all my old archives. He was putting them on hard drives and taking boxes of tapes and CDs to my car two at a time. I don't think he realized why he was doing it, but TJ was a soldier and he was loyal, so even if he did suspect, he would never question or say anything. I didn't know how the station was going to take it when I left. Sometimes what happens in radio is that you leave to go to the competition and they take your key card, erase all your shit. You don't get anything and your past is your past.

Anxiety starts flooding my mind, thinking about all the things that could happen. *Is Flex gonna be mad at me? How is Enuff gonna take it?*

*Can I, at some point, bring Enuff with me? Would he even want to come?* In your contract, you're not allowed to take anybody with you for at least six months. It's called poaching. I was worried about what was going to happen to some of them.

In preparing myself for these conversations, I got the tragic news that Flex had lost his mother. This was awful. Flex was very close with his mom and he was taking it really hard. It broke my heart to watch him go through that. At the funeral, I stood in the back of the room, looking at him, hurting for him, and just praying for him to be okay. I went over to offer my condolences and saw him sitting in the chair, in so much pain. I bent down to kiss him on his forehead.

Even though I dreaded having to have the conversation with him about going to Power, it needed to happen soon. Still, *he just lost his mom. I don't want to tell him this.*

Thea and I had come up with a strategic plan. When are we gonna do this? Thea had to make some changes in her lineup and fire her mid-day girl, so she had to be able to tell her staff. I had to be able to resign and tell my staff. And neither one of us wanted to do it and let the other side find out in a bad way. We had to do it at the same time. I was honest with Thea about one exception. "Listen, I do have to tell Flex beforehand," I said.

"No, he's gonna—"

"Thea, this is not negotiable. I am telling you this out of respect because I don't want to be dishonest with you and say, 'No, we're not gonna tell anybody.' I'm gonna tell Flex. I promise you it will be okay. But I have to."

"Are you sure?"

"I promise you."

And so I called Flex the night before I planned to resign. I didn't know how to resign. A letter? Did I walk in there?

"Hey, Ang. What's up?" Flex was in his car, driving. I'd been check-ing in with him a lot since his mom passed.

"I need to talk to you."

"Uh-oh. What's wrong?" I guess he could hear in my tone that this was serious.

That's when I broke it to him that I had been having conversations with Clear Channel.

"Yeah?"

"Well . . ." I couldn't even get it out.

"Nooo—" His voice starts cracking. "Ang, nooo . . ." I remember him saying it in such a painful voice, my heart hurt. I wanted to start bawling.

"Flex, I have to." For a second it got really quiet. Silence on the phone.

"Hold on. Let me pull over," he said. So he pulls the car over and I told him everything they'd offered me.

"Okay," he said. "You're doing the right thing. I don't want you to feel like you're not. You are . . . So who have you told?"

"I haven't told anybody. I'm telling you first."

"Well, let's just wait . . . You didn't sign anything yet, right?" Flex asked, hoping this was still negotiable.

"No, Flex. I signed the contract. I'm resigning tomorrow."

"Tomorrow?????" There was a beat. "Well, you need to call Rick."

Rick Cummings was vice president of programming for all the Emmis radio stations. He wasn't based in New York, but he'd been with the company since I had.

Flex said it again. "You gotta go to Rick."

"You're absolutely right. I'm gonna call him tomorrow."

"No, Ang. You have to call him tonight. Don't do that to him. Don't blindside him in the morning. Give him the respect and call him tonight."

I had already told Thea that I was only gonna tell Flex. But Flex walked me through what was the right thing to do and who I should talk to first, second, and third. "You call Rick tonight. You show up at the station tomorrow and tell them in person. And then you get on that radio and you say goodbye."

"Do you think they're gonna let me do that?"

"Ang, you're gonna say goodbye. You're not gonna walk out of that building without saying goodbye—that's not gonna happen."

So I call Rick.

In the whole time I worked for that company, I maybe had called Rick two times ever before. Bizarrely, about a month before, in the middle of my negotiations with Thea, Rick asked me to dinner. At first I thought he had gotten wind of my news. Instead, he apparently wanted to pick my brain, as he seemed to sense that things weren't great at the station. The irony was that after all these years, this was the first time I had really spent with him, and as much as I was dying to help him put out a few of the fires, I had to remind myself that it was time to let go. Instead I ordered another round of sake. Finally, Rick and I had a chance to bond and now I had to make *this* call.

No answer. Just voice mail. I hang up, somewhat relieved, and call Flex back to tell him Rick didn't answer.

"I have another number," Flex says. "Call it."

*Fuck.* I call and leave a message. "Hey, Rick, it's Angie Martinez. Call me when you get a sec. I really need to talk to you." I hang up. *Fuck, I left the message. Now it's real.*

This was on a weeknight at around ten thirty p.m., and these are corporate guys in Indianapolis. The phone rings and I see this weird area code. *Shit. I know this is him.*

"Hey, Angie. It's Rick. What's going on?"

With my heart pumping and my voice cracking, I blurt out, "Well, I got an offer to go somewhere else."

"Ohh," he said.

"Yes. Clear Channel made me a really great offer to come there and give me multiple markets, and I want to take it."

"Wow. I'm assuming your contract must be up, right?"

"Yeah."

"Wow. We really messed up there, huh?"

I just kind of laughed.

"Well, look, Ang, you know I can't offer you that. I don't have that to offer you," Rick said. "If I could, I would. As much as you've done for this company, I can't think of anything else to say to you but thank you for everything you've done. And to wish you well."

It was so sweet. "That means so much. Thank you, Rick," I said. "I was really worried about having to tell you."

*Holy shit!* Every time I told someone, it became more real. Later that night, I'm texting Enuff. "I need to talk to you. Call me as soon as you can." He doesn't reply. Come to find out the next day that I was actually texting the wrong number 'cause I had like three numbers for him! I barely slept at all that night 'cause I was so worried about missing a beat. At two a.m. I was anxiously writing everything down—everybody I needed to tell, anything that could go wrong, plotting what I would do, drafting what I was gonna say on social media. I didn't know what the fuck was going to happen when the sun rose on a very different day for me.

If ever there was a "Holy Shit, this is *it*" moment in my life, it was that next morning. I was going in to work for the last time and would be letting everyone know. Thea was going to tell her staff at ten a.m. when *The Breakfast Club* got off the air, and I was going to tell my general manager at that same time. On my way to the station, I called Enuff, and he still didn't pick up. I texted him again, but of course it was the freaking wrong number, so he never got the text, which breaks my heart to this day. I called Miss Info. I trusted Enuff and Miss Info and knew they could hold off for a couple of hours and not tell anybody. Miss Info knew how bad it had gotten at the station. We'd spent many, many hours talking about it and trying to figure out how to fix it. And when I told her I was leaving, she didn't react as a coworker. She reacted as my friend.

"Wow!!! That's great!" Miss Info said. "That's what you should be doing. This makes so much sense." She was so positive and excited about it, and she made me feel better.

"Well, I'm on my way there now to tell everybody."

"Oh my God. Good luck," she said. "Let me know if you need me to do anything."

At ten a.m., I walk into the general manager's office. And he's not there. He's not even in town. It didn't even occur to me that this could happen.

"Is he coming back today?" I asked his assistant, Pat.

"No. He's in DC," she says.

"I really need to talk to him."

"Okay. I'll leave him a message."

"No, Pat. I need to talk to him, like, now."

So I wind up having to tell Deon on the phone, which was fine because I didn't really have a relationship with him anyway. Next, I call Ebro and tell him, and he says he's on his way back to the station. At this point, since I had said it a few times, it started to feel more comfortable hearing these words come out of my mouth. The brand-new interim program director, Jay Dixon, was really gracious about it. He said he was happy for me but bummed that he was going to miss out on the opportunity to work together, something he had been looking forward to. Jay and I are in his office talking when Ebro comes in, and Ebro is mad—like jaws visibly tight angry.

"Ebro, what's up?" Jay says, sitting in the office that used to be Ebro's.

"I mean, I'm already just thinking about seeing you next to that logo, seeing you next to that . . ." Ebro's saying this all in an aggressive way. He's already in war mode. "You're our sister. We wish you well, of course. That goes without saying. But I'm already thinking about how this is gonna play out, how they'll spin it, how they'll use it against us."

"Ebro, do you know that out of every person I've told so far, you're the only one to react this way?"

"I get it, Ang. I get it. I'm just being realistic about what we're going to have to face," he said. "So how do you want to do it?"

"Well, I would like to do my last show today so I can say goodbye."

"Okay," Jay said. He asked if Clear Channel might be willing to wait a week to make the announcement. I said probably not. He looked concerned. "Can you just give us a few minutes so we can figure out how we're gonna handle this?"

Now it's eleven a.m., and I'm supposed to be on the air at three p.m. At that moment I say, "Sure, I will give you guys a minute." I stand, leave his office, and walk out of the building, and I'm literally shaking. *Holy fuck, I just quit! This is crazy!*

As I'm walking to Sushi Samba to get lunch, I call Thea.

"Well, I did it," I said.

"How'd it go?"

"They're asking if we can wait a few days before the announcement."

"I don't know, Ang. Clear Channel wants to go. They wanna announce."

"Please, Thea. I want to be able to get on the radio and say goodbye. Can you please buy me at least a day?" If Clear Channel announced right away that I was gonna be on at Power, I knew I couldn't get on the radio at Hot for my final show.

She agreed.

I hang up the phone and I'm just frozen. I hit Nikki and told her I did it. She leaves her job immediately and hops in a cab to meet me. By the time I get to Sushi Samba, she is already there.

"I need a white wine," I said as soon as I sat down and started telling her everything.

"Well, you know I had to call for some backup," Nikki said. I look up and Tracey and Liane are walking into the restaurant. I just started bawling. Something about the three of them all being there, in the middle of this big moment, made me emotional for the first time during this whole situation. No matter what, my three girls were right there with me.

While Liane was proofreading the statement I had written for Instagram, I called Flex and told him what had just happened.

"So we're gonna go on at three, right?" he asked.

"Honestly, Flex, I don't know if they're gonna let me. They told me to give them some time to figure it out, and Ebro is angry."

"Nah, fuck that. We're going on the radio at three," he said. "I'm on my way."

After lunch I'm walking back to the station, and from across the street I see Enuff and Paddy Duke sitting in front of the building, looking like somebody died. *Oh my God, everybody knows.* I walked up and Enuff gave me a big hug. "I've been trying to reach you since last night," I said, and showed him my phone.

"Ang, that's the wrong number. I got this other number."

"I'm so sorry. I wanted to tell you."

"It's all right. You know I love you. I understand."

And that was everything that happened before the memo went out and I was confronted by everybody lined up in the hallway in tears. What I couldn't say in that moment was that I knew my leaving would be good for everyone, that the change wasn't just about me leaving but about creating opportunities for others that couldn't happen the way it had been going. Sometimes you have to shake shit up to get forward motion.

• • •

B y now you know most of the highlights that flashed in front of my eyes as I walked down the hall to the studio for my last installment of The Angie Martinez Show on Hot 97.

Right before we started, I had a conversation with Flex, Ebro, and Jay Dixon about how to approach the show. Jay felt we should still play music and be mindful of the length of our talk breaks.

Flex wasn't having it. "No. There's no rules for today," he insisted.

Even Ebro got on board, understanding that we needed to have the moment. "Nah, it's not that type of day, Jay," Ebro said. "You gotta just let the rules go. You have to let it happen."

**ANGIE:** Today will be my last day on Hot 97.

**DJ ENUFF:** Right. We gonna celebrate!

**ANGIE:** So today—I know. Everybody, let it sit in for a second. It's sad. But it's also exciting. And I—and I want to celebrate today. I want to celebrate you guys. I want to celebrate what we've built. I want to celebrate my time here. Flex is on his way in. Terrence J is even here. What are you doing here, Terrence?

**TERRENCE:** I came to support Angie. She supports me. I love you, sis.

**ANGIE:** I love you, too.

**DJ ENUFF:** That's what's up.

**ANGIE:** So, yeah. It's—you know, it's time. There have been things that I've wanted to do for quite some time. And—you know I love you guys. Oh God, I'm not gonna get emotional. We're on till seven tonight. I gotta hold it together. It's very emotional. Everybody's emotional here. You know, it's a family. So you get stuck sometimes and afraid to—

**EBRO:** To move on. Spread your wings.

**ANGIE:** Thank you, Ebro.

**DJ ENUFF:** But you got some great things coming up, Ang.

**ANGIE:** And it's time. You know, I have opportunities that I want to pursue. And it's time . . .

And we just took it from there.

It was an emotional, heartwarming, and phenomenal day. I was proud of how far I had come and what I had accomplished. And I was filled up by the outpouring of love. Although the magnitude of it hit all of us on-air by the end of the show, I reassured my listeners that, "Life moves on. You can't stay still. You have to grow."

And my listeners reassured me that if you respect them and stay honest with them, they'll ride with you for a long time.

I was no longer Angie Martinez from Hot 97. That was how I had introduced myself for years. It was how I thought of myself. Part of me was afraid to let that go. But I was more afraid to only ever be that. As much as Hot 97 had helped to make me who I was, I was ready to stand on my own.

. . .

A couple of days after announcing that I had resigned, I was having a drink with my friend Tiffany at the bar at Houston's in New Jersey. Two Latina girls in their thirties were sitting next to us. I could tell that they knew who I was because they kept kinda looking over but they were mostly minding their business.

Then, finally, one of the young women leaned over and said, "I'm sorry to interrupt, but I just had to say that I want to wish you luck. We were listening when you resigned."

"Thank you," I said. "That means a lot to me." It did, especially because of all the flak I'd been getting on social media, people calling me a traitor. And worse.

"No, I wanted to thank you," she explained. "I just left a job that I had for a really long time, so what you did and talked about inspired me to feel like I'm doing the right thing. Because I was so nervous."

We had such a real conversation. *This is so dope.* That was more important to me than any negative spin that anyone could put on my journey. I love that she said "inspired," because that feeling was what I wanted to take with me when I started the new job.

It was real.

My first day at Power was like the first day at a new school. I didn't know what to expect. I was walking into a station and going to work with people who had been considered our enemy at Hot 97 for so many years. Thea told me that everybody was excited, but I wasn't sure how people were going to treat me. My first introduction was as a guest on *The Breakfast Club*. Friends or foes, I had met most of them before and they were all radio pros.

**DJ ENVY:** Morning, everybody. It's DJ Envy, Angela Yee, Charlamagne tha God. We are *The Breakfast Club*! We got a special guest that's usually not on that side of the mic. She's usually on this side of the mic.

**CHARLAMAGNE:** Yes!

**ANGIE:** This is—I hate being on this side of the mic! It's the weirdest thing ever.

**CHARLAMAGNE:** A radio icon.

**DJ ENVY:** That's right.

**CHARLAMAGNE:** The legendary—

**DJ ENVY:** Yes.

CHARLAMAGNE: Miss Angie Martinez.

DJ ENVY: The Voice of New York!

ANGELA YEE: One of the only people that has ever made Charlamagne nervous. Because he used to say to me all the time, "I wonder if Angie Martinez hates me. You think she hates me? She doesn't like me?"

CHARLAMAGNE: No, no, no, no, no. What—what we—

ANGIE: Why would you think that? I mean, you've said dumb things in the past that bothered me.

CHARLAMAGNE: Nothing about you, though.

ANGIE: Have you?

CHARLAMAGNE: Never.

ANGIE: No. Maybe not. But I—

CHARLAMAGNE: Never. Never ever.

ANGIE: —never hated you. I respect what you do—I told you this.

CHARLAMAGNE: And that's how I felt when (I seen you at 40/40)—I was like, "Yeah, I just want to go up there and tell her I respect her"—but I was always too pussy to go do it . . .

DJ ENVY: . . . How does it feel? Everybody wants to know why. You know, you've been with the station for fifteen years.

CHARLAMAGNE: Let's get it out of the way.

ANGELA YEE: Yeah.

DJ ENVY: Why? Why, why?

ANGIE: I honestly—it was time for me to go. And this company offers so much opportunity for growth. I want to be on in different cities. I want to be able to grow. I want to be able to have new challenges— see new things. I want to learn this studio, how this studio works. And I just—it was time. You know, I feel like I—I'd done what I can do in that company. And I think my friendships remain.

Not bad for a first day. But I have to admit that I was definitely having some anxiety about my first show on the air. For starters, I worried that I'd say Hot 97 instead of Power 105.1—out of habit or whatever, or that I was going to give out the Hot 97 number by accident, just because it was such a part of my brain by now. In the new place, I had all kinds of worries, but the funny thing is that as soon as I hit that on-air button, it was like . . .

"Is this me? Is this the right button? What's up, New York! Tristate area! It's Power 105.1. I said it. It's Angie Martinez."

*I'm still me!*

That's all I needed to remember, that I had the experience and expertise to rise to the new challenges. And ultimately, I was as comfortable as ever on the air. Everyone was happy for me, too. A ton of friends and artists called in to wish me good luck on that first day, including Puffy, DJ Khaled, Alicia Keys, and Swizz Beatz. And right before I signed off Jay called. "Oh, you think you gonna do this without me?!" he joked. I didn't book any in-studio guests for my first show because I really wanted to talk to the listeners. And I did. That first day on-air, I felt like half the city called in. I talked to so many people who truly helped to put my fears to rest.

It was that simple, just pressing the on-air button that first time and thinking, *And we're off!*

That day and every day since, the show continuously has been #1. We've broken all types of ratings records, not only on-air, but digitally as well, with people watching our interviews online all over the world. And as much as that makes me happy, ultimately, what motivates me the most is that I still really love this shit.

I hear people complain all the time about how hip-hop has changed, and while I miss some of the elements of what it used to be, I'm still very much inspired by the notion that we are forever evolving—the music, the technology, and the way in which we exchange ideas and share new content. Even with the content itself changing, what we talk about, what we care about, what moves the needle. I'm constantly inspired by people within the culture who push the boundaries. There's always something new to learn.

In the past year alone, I've had the opportunity to sit across from Ice Cube talking about prejudices based on race and hip-hop culture in Hollywood, right after he broke records telling the groundbreaking story of icons NWA. And J. Cole sharing his perspective on capitalism, integrity and the power of hip-hop. And Nicki Minaj bravely and emotionally opening up about love.

These are the moments that matter most to me, when I can be part of a conversation that resonates and has the potential to spark something in someone else. These are the moments that keep me engaged and connected. These are the moments that remind me how powerful our voices can be.

# FIND THE INSPIRATION

'm not saying it's all been happily ever after since the big move. But I know that I'm where I'm supposed to be. My family is healthy and thriving, thank God, and I love our squad—as we call it—that Oronde and I have with his son, Christian, who I am so lucky to have as a second son, and, of course, with Niko, my beautiful, funny, good-hearted boy. I love seeing the brotherhood between Niko and Christian. Where Niko's more like me and can be more reserved and thoughtful, Christian is possibly the most fearless kid I've met in my whole life. The two balance each other very well.

We take our family seriously and enjoy each other. These boys, and Oronde, too, crack me up and make me laugh out loud every single day. Nothing is better than laughter. We have Sunday family meetings over crab legs to talk about the highs and lows of our weeks and let the boys bring up anything on their minds. Being with my family in those moments keeps me balanced and at my happiest.

We also have an amazing extended family, an unexpected blessing. In an effort to keep Niko close with his half brother, Jordan, his father Tamir's elder son, Jordan's mother, Margo, and I began to get the boys together regularly on our own when Niko was about three years old. In the process, Margo and I just clicked. Before long we started having family celebrations with her and her husband, Clayton, and with Jordan, as well as their three other boys. Over the years we've gotten so close, spending holidays together, cheering for each other's kids at basketball games, and going to Disney World multiple times as one big family. In fact, I'm now the godmother for all four of their children, Jordan included. So on a Saturday night it's not uncommon for me to have six boys lying around in my living room: Niko, now twelve; Christian, ten; Jordan, fifteen; Cayden, eight; Brandon, six; and Mason, five. Can you imagine breakfast?

And then there is my new family at my new home at Power 105.1—which has been an amazing place for me to challenge myself and learn new ways to do radio. As a company iHeart is growing in such unique ways; it's been incredible to watch that firsthand.

I'm also passionate about my production company, Media Noche, which I launched to tell different stories than I can on the radio. I'm excited to develop content for unique voices that don't currently exist in media—stories and platforms for voices like mine.

I'm intrigued by underserved voices, and I've had the opportunity to try to champion them in other ways, including recently being tapped by President Barack Obama to participate in a criminal justice reform panel at the White House. In fact, the morning of the panel, when I arrived in DC, I was told that Obama would be saying a few words and I was asked to introduce him. *Meee?!?!* To me it seemed crazy, but the people on his administration who put the panel together seemed to value my voice and my audience. So I stood up onstage as a representative of hip-hop culture, of Latin culture, and women, and introduced, "The president of the United States, Barack Obama." To say it was an honor would be an understatement. I still show the video of it to anyone who will watch, and the screensaver on my phone is a photo of me standing behind Obama like a nervous Olivia Pope. A few months later I was invited back to serve on another panel, this time representing women in hip-hop. I'm proud to have a role in these panels and to use my voice to represent my culture.

The response to my White House debut was overwhelming, as it was the year before, when I started at Power. I was feeling so much inspiration and energy from the support of my listeners, the hip-hop community, and my city. The beauty of inspiration is that it goes two ways. When people tell me that I've inspired them, it inspires me to want to do more, to push myself and make them proud. It was then that I thought, *Now is the moment I could do something great.* I was just looking for the right opportunity.

As it happened, I was at my son's baseball game one afternoon when my girlfriend Amber Sabathia—our kids play ball together and she's married to CC Sabathia, who plays for the Yankees—told me that she was running the New York City Marathon for CC's foundation, PitCCh, to raise money for kids in underserved communities. She was putting together a team and offered me a spot to run. It wasn't the challenge I'd envisioned, but I'd been watching the marathon since I was a kid and was always in awe of it.

The thing was that I hated to run and could never imagine doing that, which is exactly why running the New York City Marathon was on my bucket list. I thought, *If I could do that, I could do anything.* And in a moment of courage I told Amber, "Okay, I'm in."

It was only four months before the marathon and I hadn't been working out for some time. Did I mention I also *never* ran? Still, I signed up and made an announcement on the radio. Then there's a press release, a race date looming, and there's no turning back.

It's not pretty: I cannot run a mile. Not one fucking mile. I feel like a fraud every time someone congratulates me. *If I went outside right now and somebody asked me to run two miles, I would drop dead.* The New York City Marathon is 26.2 miles long!

Amber sent me a training schedule of how to go from nothing to the marathon in three and a half months. So I go outside the first day to start training. *Let's see how this goes . . .*

I wanted to cry. Not only because I realized I was in such terrible shape, but also because I realized how ridiculous it was that I'd committed to this. *Why would I do this to myself?!*

I got in touch with a trainer I'd worked with years before, Mark Jenkins, who also trained Puffy for the marathon. On our first day out, Mark teaches me how to dogtrot. It's like walking with a lift. He explained that when you want to stop, instead of stopping, just bring it down to this dogtrot. After having to cancel a few sessions because of my schedule, I knew Mark wasn't going to work out. So from there, I was on my own. *I know how to push myself. I need to be in tune with my body. I'm going to be out there by myself, so I need to figure this out by myself.*

According to the training schedule, I was supposed to be running four days a week, sometimes five, but I quickly started falling way behind the rest of the team. So for the most part, I ran alone.

*Find the inspiration*—that became my mantra while training for the marathon. There's inspiration everywhere, by the way—coming across another runner who's struggling to keep pace and never stops, the sunset over the Hudson River, the music blasting through my headphones. I'd put on a song that gave me a burst of inspiration. *Find the inspiration.* I listened to music all the time while I was training. Marc Anthony's "Aguanile," a Héctor Lavoe remake, made me feel like there was a holy ghost in that song that gave me extra energy when I needed it. *"Aguanileeee . . . Aguaaaaniiileeeee . . . Santo dios, Santo fuerte, Santo Inmortaaal . . ."* That was definitely high on my playlist. Along with J. Cole, Young Jeezy, Meek Mill. Anything that moved me or made me forget I was running.

To switch it up, I'd try different routes almost every time I trained—around my neighborhood, Central Park, the George Washington Bridge, Washington Heights. I would run over the George Washington Bridge and run past my old neighborhood in Washington Heights and feel inspired by how far I'd come.

A few times Niko would ride his bike alongside me. I loved those days. And before one long run, when I was feeling really down about my progress, Oronde offered to run with me. He's not a runner, but there he was alongside me in full support. When we got back to the house, he took two steps inside and lay down on the living room floor, still in his running clothes. That sixteen miles kicked his ass! He literally couldn't move and stayed there on the floor until the next day. At some point, I brought him a pillow for under his head. Marathon training was taking a toll on the whole family.

Something definitely started happening in that training. You start seeing the city in a different way and thinking about your life. It's almost like meditation because you're resting your brain. So that part of running I did learn to appreciate and actually enjoy.

The whole purpose of our team running the marathon was to raise money, and now we're starting to get support. I had a donation jar in the studio. Ne-Yo came and put a hundred dollars in there. Khaled dropped a hundred, as did most of my guests. Then Puffy called in and donated a thousand dollars for every mile that I ran. That's twenty-six thousand dollars! It was such a nice gesture. Especially considering our history. I appreciated it and was grateful for it. But it also added pressure, because now there's tens of thousands of dollars involved and I'm clearly not even close to ready.

*Holy shit. Everybody expects me to do this marathon . . .* The pressure built as the day drew closer. Every day I'd be limping into work because I was so hurt from my run the night before. I always had sneakers on. I couldn't even bear to do my hair anymore. It was all about training.

In the middle of my training, there was a half marathon at Central Park, so I signed up. I didn't tell anybody. I didn't want anybody to know I was there. I just wanted to see if I could do a half, knowing that in a month I had to go do a whole. I took an Uber to Central Park and sat there by myself, looking at all these people stretching. I felt like, if I could do this, and if it was kind of easy, then I would have a lot more confidence. Just the opposite happened. I was the second-to-last person to finish the whole thing. That includes the senior citizens and the handicapped people. I'm not even kidding.

I finally get to the damn finish line and they're already closing it down, cleaning up, and putting the boxes and bagels away. I'm pathetic, asking, "Can I get a bagel, please?" I grabbed my bagel and was looking at a bench not too far away. *Can I make it to the bench to sit down?* I could hardly walk. *Oh my God, that half marathon almost put me in my grave. How am I supposed to do a whole one in a month?!*

Three weeks before the marathon, Amber and the team decided to do an eighteen-mile run together—beyond anything I'd ever tried. I did it and I didn't die, but I hurt my right hip flexor. In a lot of pain, I hoped it would just be a couple of days. It wasn't. A week later I still couldn't walk. So I started going to physical therapy every day straight for two weeks. But for those three weeks before the marathon, I didn't run at all. I was in recovery, taking ice baths, trying to just walk normal, let alone run. I was absolutely in freak-out mode at this point, panicking.

The doctor gave me the okay to show up at the marathon, although he warned that it was going to hurt.

Crack of dawn on Sunday, November 2, 2014, I showed up, the same way I always fucking show up through my whole career, even though I'm not prepared. Yes, I'll show up. I'll run the marathon. I could barely run the half as it was, healthy. Now I've got to go do this whole, and I'm hurt.

I came up with this mantra that running the marathon was similar to having a baby. Giving birth hurts like hell, but no matter how bad the pain was, the baby still had to come out. There's no option. And I applied that thought to my race. *I know this is going to be really painful, but ultimately, like delivering a baby, I have to finish.* I took the option of quitting out altogether.

They put our team with the elite runners and the "celebrity group." It's the actress Teri Hatcher, who's an avid runner, Olympic gold medalist Billy Demong, tennis star Caroline Wozniacki. With one look around, I can tell I have no business in this tent. They have all kinds of gadgets, roll-on things, and tape things. Billy the Olympic gold medalist is telling me how he was training in the Himalayas and explaining how he'd stay hydrated. He didn't have an ounce of fat on his body and he was going to run this thing in an hour. I was still hobbling. *Fuck . . .*

It's freezing that day. The winds are abnormally strong. We get to the starting point, lined up by the Verrazano Bridge in Staten Island. As soon as we start, the whole group quickly sprints ahead of me. There goes Teri Hatcher; there go the fucking Olympians; there go the Kenyans. Everybody's passing me. My girls Amber and Alexis were in pretty good shape, so they were moving ahead, too. We were not even half a mile in and Amber, God bless her, turns around.

"Come on, Ang! We've got to get our pace."

"Amber, go!"

"No, it's too soon! I don't want to leave you—we just started!"

"Amber, just go!" I didn't want to have the pressure of trying to keep up. "I need to go super slow or I'm not going to finish this."

"Are you sure?"

"Go!"

So they all leave me. There's hundreds of us. Then there's tens of us. Then there's, like, five of us. Then there's me. By myself. On the Verrazano Bridge. I am literally the last person on the Verrazano Bridge. Not only am I the last, but I'm the *only* person on the Verrazano Bridge, by myself. *I could jump off the bridge; that could be a way I could get out of this . . .* It was so cold out there, so quiet. *But fuck it . . .* I run. I'm slow, but I get over the bridge, and I run off the bridge into Brooklyn. The streets are empty; it's still just me. Eventually other runners from behind me start catching up and I start feeling less like a loser and an outcast. Now I'm just part of the group.

Even though I was sore, I was so present the whole time, paying attention to the people in the cheering crowd, amazed at how many people were standing in the cold to support us. "Come on. You got this! You're just getting started! You're going to do this! Congratulations!" The whole way through the marathon, they're encouraging you. It was so touching and overwhelming that I did not put my music on, not one time. I was like fucking Rain Man out there. *I'm just gonna finish, just gonna finish, just gonna finish.*

Every time my brain went into *This is impossible,* I would find something else to distract or inspire me. Stopping was not an option. Everybody says, "Run your own race." You really do have to run your own race—in everything, in anything. It's a good lesson in life, not just in marathon running. At mile seven, I had the notion, *Holy shit, you're going to run the marathon. Yes, you're going to do it!*

And then there was the Queensboro Bridge. Mile fifteen. Everybody talks about that moment, and it's real. It's where you hit the wall. I'm already pacing slower than I had hoped. I was really trying to be in the six-hour range; that would be my goal on the perfect day. My right knee started to hurt really bad as soon as I got on the bridge. Even stepping on it was painful, and it was beginning to swell.

I was looking for something that I could tie around my knee, to put some sort of compression on the swelling. As people get hot, they start throwing their scarves, hats, gloves off. There are clothes everywhere on the bridge. I found a piece of material—it could have been from a head-band or a piece of ripped T-shirt or something—and tied it around my knee, trying to make some kind of MacGyver bandage.

*This is what I was afraid of. This is the pain. I want to stop right now.*

It was so windy that the flaps of my hood were clapping against my head, and I began praying: *Please, God, just get me through this. I'm going to need help here. Please, just carry me the rest of the way. Carry me the rest of the way.*

And then, when I most needed it, I would find the inspiration. I'd see a few other struggling women out there running, determined to make it. And I'd run alongside them for a few minutes and we'd give each other energy. I know it sounds kind of kooky, but there was really something powerful about looking around you and finding inspiration. It does push you.

And that's how I got through the marathon, literally. The people in the city, the crowds cheering and holding signs, and the marathon volunteers on the side giving out Gatorade. I really took energy from the people in the streets to get me through.

I make it through Queens and the Upper East Side, and then in the Bronx it was quieter. I was dragging my right leg at this point, like skipping, to try to get the pressure off that leg.

After that it got a little blurry for me. It was an out-of-body type of push toward the end. The next thing I remember was seeing my girlfriend Liane out there waiting for me on the sidelines as the route wound back into Manhattan.

"Liane!" I gasped. I was so happy to see her. She ran alongside me for a little bit, all the way up to the entrance of Central Park. Liane veered off and I was on my own again and in a lot of pain. As close as I was, I could stop.

*I know it's only a mile or so left. But it's still fucking one more mile, and I'm going to die right now. I'm not going to make it.*

As much as I wanted to keep going, I couldn't stop from visualizing my body caving in and falling to my knees, and then lying on the ground. I could feel my knees buckling and I could see it—knee, knee, elbow, elbow, on my stomach, on the ground, on the fucking side of Central Park. My body was pulling me down, as in, "Lie down, bitch." Like it was literally giving out and pulling me down.

The crowd is thinning out because now it's late, it's freezing, and it's getting dark. I remember that moment vividly because there was a lady on the sidelines. She was so sweet and so direct. She spoke right to me. "Don't do it, baby! I know it hurts, but you're almost there. I'm so proud of you. You almost got this."

That lady made me cry. It was like she could read me. She saw that I was close to the end but was ready to give up. And she gave me a little breath, a little energy. From there I pushed toward the finish line, lifted up by that lady and the grace of God and everyone else along the way.

People like that are amazing to me. Who was that woman? What was she doing there? Does she live in the neighborhood? Did she know that she was going to make a difference for somebody?

As I was coming toward the end, I heard some friends from work call out my name and I waved to them. Then I saw Niko a few feet before the finish line. I had to stop and give him a hug. My mom was with him, calling out, "I'm so proud of you!" And Nikki was there with flowers.

I saw the finish line; it was right there. As I approached, with whatever energy I had left, I raised my arms in the air in celebration and hobbled through the finish line. I was overwhelmed, exhausted, proud. I had done it.

Of course, the rest of the team had finished more than an hour and a half before me, but they waited. We did it! And we raised more than a hundred thousand dollars!

The point is, you never know what you can do until you really put yourself out there and try. Do it. Whatever it is. Challenge yourself. If you can't imagine the finish line, the first step is to just show up. And don't worry about what everyone else is doing. Run your own race.

I'm not saying it will always be easy. Things haven't always been easy for me, but I worked hard and I put myself out there. I've accomplished things that I never dreamed were possible. I've seen a lot and learned a lot, and I'm proud that I've been true to myself the whole way. In that, I found the power of my voice.

## ACKNOWLEDGMENTS

Nothing inspires me more than working with people who are great at what they do. This book was possible because of Ray Garcia, the publisher of Celebra. Your passion and vision helped me believe I could write this book. Jen Schuster . . . editor, writer, motivator, problem solver. You are my literary guardian angel! Thank you for caring so much. And thank you to Mim Rivas and Laura Checkoway for helping me to find the words.

Thank you to my team . . . Roc Nation for always having my back: Desiree Perez, Nelly Ortiz, Ayanna Wilks, Nadja Rangel, and Kelly Cornut. To the people who help me cross my "t's" and dot my "i's"—Margarita Sullivan, Chantal Felice, Honey German, Dan Shulman at Tavel & Shulman, Natasha Bolouki and Ryan Hayden at UTA, Ryan Robichaud and Evan Jehle at Focus Financial Partners, and Jo Mignano at Krupp Kommunications.

To Miss Info and Chaka Pilgrim, who I trusted enough to share this book with before the rest of the world, thank you for being so dope and for caring enough to help me get this right.

I would need an entire separate book to thank all of the amazing people who have supported and encouraged me along the way. My family and friends especially. Please just know that I take none of you for granted.

Mom, everything that I am is inspired by you. If you don't believe me, read the book but please skip Chapter 1 and portions of Chapter 8. Love you.

Oronde, my love, my partner, and my best friend. Thank you for having my back and believing in me the way you do. You make me a very happy girl. Christian, you've brought so much joy into my life and I love you with all my heart. Niko, I love you more than words and my proudest accomplishment in life is being your mom!!